THE PRESOCRATICS

THE PRESOCRATICS

The main fragments in Greek with introduction, commentary & appendix containing text & translation of Aristotle on the Presocratics

M.R. Wright

Bristol Classical Press

First published in 1985 by Bristol Classical Press
an imprint of
Gerald Duckworth & Co. Ltd
61 Frith Street
London W1D 3JL
e-mail: inquiries@duckworth-publishers.co.uk
Website: www.ducknet.co.uk

Reprinted 1995, 2001

A catalogue record for this book is available from the British Library

ISBN 0-86292-079-5

CONTENTS

PREFACE

The aims of this work are to provide a basic text for early Greek philosophy and to encourage those with an elementary knowledge of Greek to read for themselves the most important fragments of the Presocratics. The notes therefore concentrate on elucidating the language of the early thinkers, which can be obscure and is frequently ambiguous. An occasional firmness of interpretation should be accepted with the general understanding that there is controversy past and present over almost every sentence handed down from these first philosophers.

The most relevant lines from Xenophanes open the collection. The fragments of Parmenides, Melissus and Anaxagoras are given almost entire; there is major coverage of Heraclitus and a key selection from Empedocles. In the absence of the original wording, Zeno's four paradoxes and the statements on early atomism are taken from Aristotle; the main notices on the Presocratics from the first book of his *Metaphysics* are added in the Appendix. It is beyond the scope of the present work to enter into the doxographic tradition.

I would like to thank Fr. John Fitzgerald for reading the translation of Aristotle in the Appendix, and Christopher Rowe for his exact and most helpful editing throughout. I also wish to record the generous encouragement of Gwil Owen, who fostered my interest in the Presocratics, and discussed this project with me one pleasant winter afternoon.

M. R. Wright
Aberystwyth, 1984.

INTRODUCTION

The 'Presocratics' (or more fully the 'Presocratic philosophers') is a general term covering the Greek thinkers who lived before the time of Socrates (470-399 B.C.), and some of his near-contemporaries. They are characterised by their attempts, from different view-points, to find a rational and comprehensive explanation of the world which adapted or discounted theological tradition.

The first Presocratics, the pioneers of European philos-ophy, lived in the sixth century B.C., in the area of islands and coast of western Asia known as Ionia. There was then a swing to the opposite side of the Greek world, to the colonised towns of south Italy and Sicily, typi-fied in the Ionian settlement at Elea and the migration of Pythagoras from Samos to Croton. Athens emerged as the third and most enduring centre of philosophy in the time of Pericles, when intellectuals were attracted there from all over the Greek world. They included the Ionian Anaxagoras and Democritus from Abdera, as well as the sophists from the west and north who captivated the new generation. The pattern of migrating intellectuals continued into the fourth century, with Aristotle moving down from the north, and then Epicurus and the Stoic Zeno from the eastern islands of Samos and Cyprus. Of all the great names in Greek philosophy, only Socrates and Plato were native Athenians.

Why should a new way of thinking, which marks the begin-ning of European philosophy, emerge at that time (the early sixth century B.C.), and in that area (the Ionian coast)? The Greeks there were closest to influence from the Lydians, Babylonians, Hebrews, Phoenicians and

Egyptians, all of whom had long established cultures. Mutual exchanges then increased with trade expansion, Ionian colonisation and the inexorable westward encroachment of Persian power. Political movements in the Greek world generally, together with the emergence of city-state democracies, fostered independent argument, reflection and decision-making; and constitutions and laws were hammered out within the *polis*, not externally imposed. In these activities effective verbal expression was crucial, and the Greek language was proving a tool of precision - lucid, elegant and concise, inherently balanced and capable of fine nuances of meaning. Finally, with the adaptation of the Phoenician alphabet and the spread of literacy, what was said in this language could be written down. Laws and poems were then read at leisure, studied, promulgated and criticised. And the poems composed at the time were not the grand Homeric epics, describing the deeds of a past heroic generation, but lyrics, the intimate analyses of personal emotion, which fostered the awareness of the thinking and feeling 'self'.

When Aristotle, at the opening of his *Metaphysics*, mused on the origins of philosophy, he distinguished the expert by his ability to generalise, to abstract universal principles from individual instances, and to cope with difficulties beyond the comprehension of the average mind. He further contrasted the man of experience who knows facts with the man of wisdom who asks 'why?'. 'It is through curiosity that men now and in the beginning became philosophers, first asking the obvious questions, and then gradually worrying about more complex problems' (*Metaph.* 982b12). He goes on to suggest that there is an inborn craving for knowledge, not for practical purposes but for its own sake, and that in its pursuit a man finds the most satisfying life.

Aristotle perhaps idealises, but it is not difficult to imagine the curious and clever Ionian living in a bustling harbour town at a time of political and commercial excitement. He might view with interest the ancient civilisations of Egypt and the near East, and yet be impatient of their static learning, enshrined in centuries-old collections of data. He was ready to argue and wonder, and his own ideas, even if simplistic and disconnected, in their potential opened a new era.

The Milesians

The first thinkers to be named - Thales, Anaximander and Anaximenes - come from Miletus, the foremost Ionian city. Their interests and methods, which involved in particular a search for a unifying account of the origins and present diversity of the world, are known as Milesian or Ionian. Thales was on the list of the Seven Sages, and his attributed sayings formed part of the repository of received wisdom. He wrote nothing himself, but, as far as we can judge from the comments of Aristotle,[1] he sought to explain the earth's stability, as well as the source of life which continues to nourish and maintain an animate world, by the abiding presence of one 'stuff' - water. Aristotle admits that he is filling in gaps, and there is no way of knowing how far Thales' own arguments went, but three features are incontrovertible: a new confidence, the expectation that the complexities of the world can be readily explained, and the stimulus to others to discuss, adapt and improve on the first attempts at such an explanation.

---

[1] The main notices are from *Metaphysics A*, reproduced with translation in the Appendix.

Anaximander wrote down his thoughts, and he wrote in prose, the first recorded prose work in European literature. One quotation survives, and even there it is not certain where the original words begin or end:

> ἐξ ὧν δὲ ἡ γένεσίς ἐστι τοῖς οὖσι, καὶ τὴν φθορὰν εἰς ταῦτα γίνεσθαι 'κατὰ τὸ χρεών· διδόναι γὰρ αὐτὰ δίκην καὶ τίσιν ἀλλήλοις τῆς ἀδικίας κατὰ τὴν τοῦ χρόνου τάξιν', ποιητικωτέροις οὕτως ὀνόμασιν αὐτὰ λέγων.
>
> *From the source from which they arise, to that they return of necessity when they are destroyed, 'for they suffer punishment and make reparation to one another for their injustice according to the assessment of time', as he says in somewhat poetical terms.*
>
> Simplicius, *In Phys.* 24.29

The context indicates that the subject here is probably the opposites - hot and cold, wet and dry and perhaps others - viewed not as qualities but as 'things', acting and reacting on each other like quarrelsome neighbours. At some time or place one encroaches on its counterpart, and that in turn, at another time or place, makes good the loss and itself becomes the aggressor. Gains and losses balance out overall in a cosmic equilibrium or ἰσονομία, exemplified in the succession of bright days and dark nights, hot summers and cold winters.

In Anaximander's cosmology, according to the ancient sources, the whole system of balanced opposition began when something capable of producing hot and cold was separated from the ἄπειρον, the vast and characterless origin of all things. As a result of a rotation, this developed into a fiery sphere surrounding a mist-shrouded earth, and then the various features of the world as we know it emerged. Explanations were given for the appearance of the heavenly bodies at proportionate distances, and for eclipses, storms, earthquakes and the like. The earth was thought to be drum-shaped, with life possibly on the under-surface, and to stay where it is because there is no reason for it to move in one direction rather than another. (This argument was to have a long history as the 'principle of sufficient reason'.) The extended infancy of men and women implies that they would not have survived in the beginning in their present form, and so Anaximander suggested an origin for the human race from creatures in the more protected element of the sea.

These first moves in the study of nature, which were to develop into the different sciences of meteorology, geography and anthropology, were firm strides rather than faltering steps. It was thought that the world could be made intelligible in its own terms by audacious reasoning; and then this reasoning was made public and available for scrutiny.

Anaximander's views were immediately challenged by his fellow-townsman Anaximenes. Again, there was one work written in prose, of which one sentence is extant:

> οἷον ἡ ψυχὴ ἡ ἡμετέρα ἀὴρ οὖσα συγκρατεῖ ἡμᾶς,
> καὶ ὅλον τὸν κόσμον πνεῦμα καὶ ἀὴρ περιέχει.
>
> *As our soul, which is air, maintains us, so breath and air surround the whole world.*
>
> Aetius 1.3.4

The sentence is packed with meaning. First there is the new use of the word ψυχή. In the Homeric poems this had not been connected with the living, but said only of that which leaves the living at death, and continues as a flitting shade in the realm of the dead. Here it is the principle of life, which holds together, strengthens and controls the individual.[2] Then there is the connection

---

[2] συγκρατεῖ covers these three meanings. The verb has [cont.]

established between the relationship of ψυχή / ἀήρ to us and that of πνεῦμα / ἀήρ to the whole world order, so that it too is alive and controlled. The cosmos is like a large animate being and the individual man a miniature world or 'microcosm'.

Most significant is the role Anaximenes gives to ἀήρ. Anaximander's indeterminate ἄπειρον now has a character, that of the air we breathe - essential for life and an obvious candidate for the boundless source of that life. In itself air is invisible, but on thickening it becomes mist (the ἀήρ that hides a man is one of its senses in the Homeric poems). But Anaximenes went further, and derived all things from the one substance according to the differences of quantity. Condensed air is water, and when further condensed he thought it would become earth and then rock, and when thinned appear as fire. Temperature changes accompany the process, condensation bringing with it an increase of cold, and rarefaction of heat.

Air, the source of life which now encloses the world, was also the immeasurable vastness from which it first arose. Whether Anaximenes used the word or not, the concept of ἀρχή was grasped, the understanding of the functioning of a 'first principle' which explains and is responsible for the original emergence and subsequent maintenance of life. And, agreeing probably in this with Anaximander, he attributed deathlessness and therefore divinity to the limitless and all-controlling beginning of things.

---

been queried, but even if it is not the original Ionian, the sense would be much the same; cf. the metaphor of the pilot in Anaximander and Heraclitus (Diels/Kranz 12A and 22B41).

Like his predecessor, Anaximenes had a whole system of explanations for astronomical and meteorological phenomena. Despite the errors - he went back to a flat earth, for example, supposed to rest on air - his achievement is remarkable for the range of problems that could be tackled, once change was understood to be a *process* of quantitative alteration of one comprehensive substance.

Xenophanes of Colophon

In 546 B.C. the Persians defeated the Lydians and took control of the Ionian cities. With the loss of freedom many of the Greeks emigrated, among them Xenophanes of Colophon, who spent sixty-seven years of a long life wandering 'up and down the land of Hellas', including a considerable time among the western Greeks in Sicily. He composed a variey of poems in different metres, the larger part of which seems to have been a *mélange* of homespun wisdom, set in an agreeable background of leisured evenings. Some were *Silloi*, a form of satirical writing in hexameters, and it is the extant lines of these that are relevant here.

There is first an attack on the anthropomorphic attributes and immoral behaviour of the Olympian gods as portrayed by Homer and Hesiod. Such portrayals were particularly condemned for their subjectivity, since they represented gods in the image of their votaries; the concept of divinity needed to be rethought. In Xenophanes' own account there is one god, motionless, intelligent, seeing and hearing 'as a whole', and activating everything by the power of thought.

It is unlikely that Xenophanes put forward a comprehensive cosmology on Milesian lines. The few fragments on the subject, dealing mainly with the importance of earth, may have had their place in the general revision of the old theology. But another contribution he did make to the history of philosophy was the distinction between knowledge and opinion. He regarded knowledge - of gods and of the other subjects of which he spoke - to be unattainable by men; they could only assent to what was probable, and act according to opinion and belief.

A final quatrain of elegiacs gives an anecdote about Pythagoras recognising the voice of a friend in the yelp of a dog. It is important as the earliest evidence on Pythagoras, and for the confirmation that transmigration was a well-known Pythagorean tenet.

The significance of Xenophanes for the Presocratics has long been disputed. Plato said that the Eleatic ἔθνος started with him and even earlier (*Soph.* 242d5), Aristotle that he was reportedly the teacher of Parmenides and the first to 'one-ify' (ἑνίζειν), but he then dismissed him along with Melissus as being rather crude (*Metaph.* 986b24). The Eleatic connection is probably due to hindsight, especially as there was a tendency to see the history of philosophy in terms of master-pupil relationships between well-known individuals. Xenophanes emerges more as a distinct personality with vigorous and independent views, deserving respect in his own right.

Heraclitus of Ephesus

Heraclitus ('dark and obscure' as he was called even in antiquity), like Anaximander and Anaximenes, wrote just one book, and in prose; a considerable part is extant. It has an elaborate and carefully-balanced opening, and then presents its message in a series of enigmatic sentences, exactingly contrived and immediately memorable, which makes full use of the resources of the Greek language to reveal layers of explicit and implicit meaning. He is contemptuous of the religious cant and intellectual lethargy of his contemporaries, and strives to rouse them with startling explanations of the structure and functioning of the cosmos, and of divine and human reason. His ideas signal the philosophical beginnings of epistemology, psychology and ethics.

Heraclitus starts with the λόγος, the true analysis and description of the way things are, but which passes men unnoticed, as the waking world is unnoticed by the sleeper. Such a λόγος, which accounts for the world being as it is, has divine status as the instantiation of wisdom and power; and true understanding of it is possible for men if they shake themselves out of their private lives. What is required is not the so-called wisdom of the poets, or the πολυμαθία of a Xenophanes, but individual effort to be aware of the workings of the world, and the motivation to align oneself with its rule of law.

The λόγος, like the Delphic oracle, requires an interpreter to reveal its hidden meaning, contained here in the unseen but powerful ἁρμονία that characterises the underlying nature of things. This ἁρμονία is to be understood as the exact tension maintained between opposed forces, as well as a fitting together of opposite functions, which results in an overall unity. Anaximander's idea of warring factions restrained and controlled to produce a cosmic ἰσονομία is reinterpreted by Heraclitus. In one illustration after another he shows the mutual dependence of opposites, as necessary to each other, or complementary, or in some instances 'the same' in that opposite predicates can be truly applied to one subject.

The gods for the Greeks were οἱ ἀθάνατοι - 'the deathless ones'. The Milesians had looked at the beginnings, and realised that what is immortal would need to be sempiternal, without birth as well as death. Xenophanes stripped divinity of anthropomorphic attributes and emphasised intelligence and effortless power in their stead. Adapting and furthering these concepts, Heraclitus expounds the unseen ἁρμονία in divine terms, with the complementary consequences that god is manifest in concurrent and successive opposite states, and that opposite states are unified in the divine principle.

In addition, Heraclitus identifies the divine principle with the physical structure of the world, in terms of ever-living, intelligent and all-controlling fire. Fire takes its place in the cycle of the changes of the world masses, but is also the standard by which the transitions are regulated, as gold is exchanged in barter but sets the standard for the measure of the exchange. In this the sun plays a crucial part as a primary concentration of fire, controlling the times of the days and the seasons, and the distances of the solstices. The 'formula' sense of λόγος is also relevant here, in the proportions that are measured and balanced out at different times and places to ensure the permanence of the cosmos.

According to Heraclitus, continuous warfare between opposites is essential for the maintenance of the *status quo*. Keen observation and heightened awareness are needed to grasp this fundamental aspect of reality, and with it its complement - that all things are constantly changing. Fire keeps a local identity, but in itself it can never be still since its preservation depends on the continual intake and transformation of fuel. The temporal and spatial successions of the 'turnings' of cosmic fire had no beginning, never pause, and will have no end, and so this fire is both the paradigmatic example and the complete instantiation of the perpetual mobility which was summarised in the tag :

πάντα ῥεῖ.

The second and crucial example of πάντα ῥεῖ is to be found in rivers, where the unceasing movement and continual replacement of the waters is the means whereby the river's identity is maintained. This observable fact is the key to understanding the general theory of all things being constantly changing and yet ever the same.

The simultaneous and antithetical 'turnings' of fire - through water to earth and back through water to fire - are repeated on a small scale in the individual ψυχή. But here the individual has some control over the process. The indulgence of desire and anger results in an increase of moisture, and to be drunk is literally to have a wet ψυχή, with the consequent sacrifice of coherent language and direction of the limbs. Conversely, it is in the individual's power to dry out his soul by resisting θυμός, and best of all is to choose glory and die in battle in the prime of life.

The fiery soul in the best state is also the wise soul, and in another cluster of ideas it is suggested that there is within the soul an inexhaustible capacity for understanding. As well as waking to a realisation of the true nature of the external world, the individual must, like Heraclitus, engage in self-searching, drawing on the soul's limitless resources for ever increasing enlightenment.

Parmenides of Elea

One result of the migration to the west after the Persian conquests was the foundation of the Ionian colony of Elea in south Italy. Parmenides was in the second generation of the new citizens, and made the little town so famous that his philosophy could be known simply as

'Eleatic'; Zeno, his younger contemporary and adjutant, confirmed the tradition.

Parmenides did not continue in the new medium of prose writing, but presented his material in the restrictive form of the Homeric hexameter. His one poem divides into three sections - a long prologue (preserved entire), some preliminaries and the main argument of the Ἀλήθεια or 'Road of Truth' (most of which is extant), and the Δόξα or 'Road of Human Opinion', of which only a little remains. Apart from the heightened solemnity given to the work by the use of the metre of Homer and Hesiod, a verse form may have been chosen as an *aide-mémoire* for an argument in which every step is essential. The lines of Parmenides have little to offer the literary critic; the interest in general lies in the original way in which the traditional form is developed.

The prologue describes a journey taken by a κοῦρος, presumably the young Parmenides, in a chariot driven by the daughters of Helios. The chariot tracks the visible path of the sun, coming up from the east, crossing the vault of the sky 'far from the path of men' and descending into the west, where great double gates mark the meeting of night and day. The Heliades persuade the goddess Δίκη to unbar the gates, and the chariot drives through, along a broad highway; the goal is reached when the κοῦρος is greeted by an unnamed goddess. She assures him that his journey is sanctioned by θέμις and δίκη, and gives him instructions to master two programmes - the unshaken heart of truth and the opinions of mortals. The rest of the poem consists of her exposition of them.

The exact meaning of the prologue and even the path of the journey have been much disputed. The move from the house of night into light would seem an obvious allegory for that from ignorance to knowledge, except that the chariot continues beyond the western setting of the sun. The journey is rather to the land of the dead (which explains the persuasion needed for a living man to cross the threshold), a κατάβασις below the extreme west to the nadir of the sphere, from which the Heliades would bring up the chariot for the next day's dawn, and restore the κοῦρος to the world above. Eventually the Road of Truth in its denial of the reality of human phenomena implicitly denies all that was given in the prologue - chariot, Heliades, even the goddess herself. But arguments against the evidence of the senses and the common misuse of language still have to be spoken, and within a commonly intelligible framework - hence the prologue and the pervasive metaphor of the road, its travellers and its destination.

The Ἀλήθεια is the first sustained stretch of argument in European literature, and many would claim that philosophy as such only begins with Parmenides. The section starts from the most basic assumption - that thought requires something to think about. It is impossible to think a blank or converse about nothing, and, since reasoning and intelligent speech therefore require an object, whatever it is that can be thought ('is there for thinking') can be ('is there for being'). This fundamental premise is expressed by ἔστι. The opposite - οὐκ ἔστι - has to be rejected outright as literally a non-starter, that gets one nowhere, for to say or think something that is not there to be spoken or thought of is peculiarly self-refuting.

Once ἔστι is established and its opposite rejected a series of deductions can be made. First there can be no generation or destruction, i.e. no temporal beginning or end, since that would involve a coming from and passing into the (unallowable) 'is not'. And also, in an adaptation of Anaximander's argument, if there is no sufficient reason to start or stop at one time rather than another, there will be no starting or stopping. It then follows that, because there is no generation or destruction of what there is, *a fortiori* there cannot be a series of generations and destructions of a succession of entities, marked off from each other by a temporal stretch of 'is not'; so that what there is has to be continuous and indivisible.

Next comes the denial of movement and change. Any alteration in the present state requires the end of that state as such and the beginning of another, but, since there is no generation or destruction, what is not the case cannot come to be so, and what is true at one time cannot not be true at another. (The implication here is that there is no way of distinguishing past from future, and Parmenides' ἔστι needs to be understood in terms of a tenseless present.) In addition, no deficiency can be attributed to what there is, for a deficiency is a gap, the intervention of what is not.

Finally it is deduced that with the denial of movement comes the denial of room for movement. Since what there is has no gaps, there is no alteration in its consistency, and it is 'equal to itself' in every direction. It is compared to the 'mass of a well-rounded sphere', both in the perfect balance of a solid sphere around its centre, and in its being 'the same all over', from whatever direction it is regarded.

Earlier, another 'road' had been mentioned, that trodden to and fro by the majority of men, who are described as 'dazed, uncritical crowds'. In accepting the world presented to the senses, these people are misled by eye and ear, and do not understand the basic contradictions involved in their assumptions. Such a world is described in the last section of the poem, prefaced by the repetition of the former warning of the falsity of the account. Once the most basic wrong move is allowed, of having two entities and not one, a plausible cosmos can be generated, in this case from two entities which have the characteristics of fire and night. It is clear from the few extant lines that this cosmos was explained in detail. Its most interesting features build on Heraclitean foundations - the presentation of a controlling deity, advances in understanding the concept of 'element', and the development of a physical correlation between the thinking subject and the object thought.

Parmenides perhaps started his composition with the material of the *Doxa*, constructing a cosmology in the Milesian tradition, and then, after becoming aware of the logical inadequacies of the exercise, made a fresh beginning. He may still have considered his original explanation of a perceptible world worth including, while denying its veracity. The reason the goddess gives the κοῦρος for its inclusion is as a dialectical device, to win the argument on all counts 'so that no man's thinking shall outstrip you'.

Zeno of Elea

At the beginning of the dialogue named after Parmenides, Plato describes a visit to Athens by the distinguished Eleatic when in his mid-sixties, accompanied by his younger friend Zeno. While there, Zeno gave a reading of some of his arguments which Socrates heard, and questioned him about afterwards. Zeno explained that the purpose of his book was to offer assistance to Parmenides against those who mocked him for the ridiculous and contradictory consequences of accepting the premise εἰ ἕν ἐστι. Zeno pays the mockers back with interest by showing that even more absurd conclusions follow from the assumption of more than one thing.

Very few of Zeno's original words are extant, but the arguments preserved in Simplicius illustrate the method Plato describes. Zeno takes the hypothesis εἰ πολλά ἐστι, and draws contradictory conclusions from this seemingly innocuous premise. For example, 'many things' can be shown to have no size at all, and to be infinitely big. And if one asks how many there are, they will be found to be both a definite number and an unlimited plurality. Such arguments introduced difficulties concerned with spatial extension, numerical series and infinite regress which were to exercise logical minds over the centuries.

Further puzzles, of which there are only indirect reports, also deal with these topics. The Millet Seed set out a series from one to a bushel, and poses the problem of marking a division on it such that less than that number of seeds makes no sound when falling, and more than that number an audible sound. (If the answer given is one, then a similar question can be asked about the parts of the one.) The most important of the others are the four dealing with moving objects - the Dichotomy, Achilles, Arrow and Stadium. In these, confused thinking about temporal as well as spatial finite and infinite divisibility in the assumption of plurality generates the following paradoxes: it is impossible to traverse a set distance, Achilles cannot overtake a tortoise, a flying arrow is at rest, and a given time is equal to twice that time.

Zeno's aim throughout is polemical. He subjects the obvious and generally accepted assumption that there are lots of things in existence to a devastating analysis; the resulting contradictory or absurd conclusions require a rejection of that assumption. This is as far as his support of Parmenides went. There is no evidence that Zeno positively advocated monism, but some to suggest that he was moving towards the realisation that there are logical difficulties about hypothesising and characterising even one thing.

Melissus of Samos

Eleaticism sped eastwards, and found an advocate in the energetic Samian Melissus, who is said to have engaged and sunk the Athenian fleet in 441 B.C. Melissus wrote one book in prose, in which he adopted the main arguments of Parmenides' Ἀλήθεια, but introduced some modifications and developments of his own. The ten fragments, of varying length, are all from Simplicius.

Melissus agreed with Parmenides in the elimination of generation and destruction; they involve prior and posterior states of nothingness, which is inadmissible. What there is must therefore be eternal. It was then understood that nothingness, interpreted spatially, would be emptiness (κενόν), and, since this is not allowable as an enclosing limit, there would be no limit; so what there is must also be boundlessly extended. And if this is the case, there can be no second thing, as either would be a limit to the other.

The long seventh fragment continues in the same style, deducing a series of denials. Parmenides had previously eradicated movement and change, as well as variation in density; Melissus covers any alteration in arrangement or structure, since the minimum possible change would involve ultimate destruction 'in the whole of time'. In addition pain is denied, as a deterioration, and an intimation of mortality.

If there *were* many things, as our sensible experience

suggests, then each would be as completely immutable as Melissus claims one to be. But he is ready with a lively refutation of the senses. If we see or hear anything correctly, and as it is, then it should stay as it was first seen and heard. But the senses record constant change - cold to hot, hard to soft, living to dead (and the reverse processes), transformations in the world masses, and the wearing away of the hardest substances. We cannot be perceiving things both statically as they are and as constantly changing, so there is something basically unsound about sense-perception, which makes it unreliable as evidence for plurality and change.

The most controversial sentence denies σῶμα - 'body'. If what there is extends limitlessly in space, is 'full' and homogeneous, how can it be said to be without σῶμα? But it has no parts, and so no bulk; there is no means of apprehension or awareness of it through touch or sight; and because of its unlimited extension it has no shape, to make it recognisable as a distinct entity.

Empedocles of Acragas

First reactions to the Eleatic thesis came from Sicily, in the two poems of Empedocles, roughly contemporary with the supportive works of Zeno and Melissus. Empedocles took over some of Parmenides' conclusions as basic postulates of his scheme; other arguments he adapted or modified, and even where he was opposed to Parmenides, Empedocles on occasion retained the wording of his predecessor, as well as the medium of the epic hexameter.

In the poem on nature (the *Physics*), Empedocles agreed that continuity in time and extension in space could not be broken up by μὴ ὄν, and that any naming of γένεσις and ὄλεθρος is unjustifiable. But he attempted to effect a compromise between Parmenides' logic and the sensible world by admitting the existence of more than one thing, in fact a limited plurality of four, which could not be increased or diminished in any way. Perceptible γένεσις and ὄλεθρος are to be explained as the arrangement and rearrangement of these four eternally existing 'roots' - earth, air, fire and water - in movements initiated by φιλία and νεῖκος, the cosmic principles of attraction and repulsion. Change is allowed in so far as the roots unite and disperse, but denied in that they are independent equals, each eternal and homogeneous, never losing or altering its character. Empedocles' god, which is identified with the complete uniting of all into one, meets Eleatic criteria of self-sufficiency, uniqueness, steadfastness and uniformity. It is however actually spherical rather than similar to a σφαῖρα, and its state of perfection comes to an end at an appointed time.

The details of the patterns of balance and antithesis in Empedocles' world scheme are the subject of continuing controversy. It seems however that he first described the four elements held apart from each other as a result of the dominance of νεῖκος. With the advance of φιλία they began to come together, and some strange compounds were formed, but, as the power of φιλία increased, all life was absorbed into one in the perfection of the sphere. At the time prescribed by a 'broad oath', νεῖκος in turn began to advance, causing the elements in the mixture to separate out and move towards their like parts. 'Whole-nature forms' arose, and, when these became fully articulated, the present generation of men and women appeared. Even this, however, will eventually disintegrate as the elements separate further into independent groupings, kept apart again by νεῖκος.

The discussion of the present generation includes a long section (here omitted) on the structure and functioning of organic life. Empedocles was a pioneer in morphology and embryology, and his physiological interests centred in particular on respiration, the movement of blood in the body, and the mechanism of perception and thought. And it is the relationship shown between the physical structure of the thinking subject and the external object that is crucial to understanding Empedocles' second poem as an interpretation of the first. In the *Katharmoi* a more popular version of the theme is presented, not to a privileged student but to the citizen body as a whole.

Any part of a 'root' has soul, in that it is alive and can be aware of and respond to a simple unit of its own kind. Plants and animals have a complex structure and can therefore respond to external objects that are both simple and compound. Man is more sophisticated and more aware, for the heart-blood which contains and controls his intellectual functioning is an almost perfect combination of elements. Most superior is the divine state, apparent in the cosmos when the elements are completely intermingled in perfect harmony, and also in the individual who, in the highest ranks of human life, and as a result of pure intention and intellectual endeavour, attains to an apprehension of the divine and eventual assimilation to it.

Anaxagoras of Clazomenae

Anaximenes had first related the physical constituent of the ψυχή to an encircling and controlling substance of like character. Heraclitus continued the relationship between the internal and external intelligence in a form of fire, and encouraged the individual to improve the quality and capacity of his thought. Parmenides was in the same tradition in having thinking dependent on the mixture of two forms in the body at any given time, with the possibility available to each man of increasing the range of symmetrical contact with the outside world. And Empedocles saw himself as achieving a daimonic status which would unite him with the φρὴν ἱερή. The explicit connection of νοῦς with a force of knowledge and power which directs and arranges all things belongs to Anaxagoras.

He was the first philosopher to find a home in Athens, settling there from the Ionian city of Clazomenae. During his stay he wrote one book in prose, which Socrates says was on sale in the agora for a drachma. He was however eventually brought to trial on a charge of impiety (ostensibly for calling the sun a large hot stone, but his association with Pericles is likely to have been the determining cause), and he spent the rest of his life in Lampsacus. According to Aristotle Anaxagoras was older than Empedocles but τοῖς ἔργοις ὕστερος, which most obviously means that his philosophy was produced later.[3] In his theories both of motive cause and the structure of matter he is working from Empedocles' position, as well as considering the latest developments from the Eleatics.

In the past, Anaxagoras states in his first sentence, 'all things were together'. This would seem to mean that there was a complete and uniform fusion of all the elementary components of the cosmos, in contrast to Empedocles' 'sphere' mixture of particles of earth, air, fire and water which retain their individual characteristics. The enigmatic denials of an ultimate small or large show in effect the irrelevance of size to the complexity of material – any part of the original homogeneity, whatever the size and however small, contains 'all things'.

νοῦς initiated a rotation in this initial 'wash' of ingre-

---

[3] Cf. *Metaph.* 984a11, given in the Appendix.

dients, and as a result predominantly heavy parts came towards the centre of the vortex to form the earth, and parts that were mainly air and αἰθήρ moved out to encircle it, so that a recognisable cosmos eventually emerged. Unlike the traditional world picture, however, no spatial or temporal limits were set to the process, so that the 'rippling' continues indefinitely outwards. In the movements of division and accretion on the earth itself there is further articulation, but all the separating parts of whatever size still keep the complexity of the original fusion, so are able to develop in unlimited ways.

This allows Anaxagoras his most controversial point, that 'in everything there is a portion of everything'. Given the Eleatic denial of absolute generation and destruction, he explained growth, change and the variety of visible transformations not by a re-positioning of parts of a limited number of elements (for 'how could hair have come from what is not hair, and flesh from what is not flesh?') but by the emergence in a new arrangement of a predominance of ingredients that had always been present. And what had always been present was a total mingling of portions of inanimate substances, 'seeds' of plants, animals and animal tissues, and the traditional opposites.

The processes of separation and articulation eventually result in a quantity of dissimilar objects, some with and some without life, and each showing the character of the predominating portions. All the other ingredients are still there, but imperceptible, and any are likely to become accessible to the senses when a different grouping brings different ingredients to the fore. In the insistence here on infinite divisibility and the impossibility of isolating any 'bit' of hot or cold, Anaxagoras is moving towards a realisation that the opposites are not substances but qualities characterising substances and inseparable from them. This perhaps is his most significant advance.

Only νοῦς has no admixture, and it is this independence from the material it works on which would give νοῦς its power to initiate the original rotation, to control the consequent separatings and to arrange the whole into an ordered cosmos. But Socrates (and Aristotle) complained that although such a comprehensive and intelligent ordering was implied in Anaxagoras' scheme, it was not explained in detail or worked to its conclusion.

The Atomists

Although roughly contemporary with Socrates and the sophists, the atomists are usually included in any survey of the Presocratics, because they produced a physical theory which brought to a natural finish the investigation of the structure of the cosmos which began with the Milesians. There are particular difficulties with the evidence here, since there is only one sentence extant from the shadowy figure of Leucippus, and only two brief mentions of atoms in the hundreds of sayings attributed to Democritus. Epicurus, who took over the theory with some modifications, gives no credit for his borrowings. Probably Leucippus initiated the theory, using a rather exotic vocabulary, and further details and supporting arguments were provided by Democritus, but the two men are usually taken together. They were both (probably) from Abdera, and Democritus visited Athens, where he was disappointed to find that no one had heard of him.

Like Empedocles and Anaxagoras, the atomists accepted the denial of γένεσις and ὄλεθρος. Pluralism has to be understood in the strict sense that, since many cannot come from one, the many things are ever existing. These are ἄτομα, unlimited numbers of uncuttable units - solid, eternal, immutable, of different shapes and sizes but having no qualitative differences, and physically if not theoretically indivisible. To be able to move, and so account for perceptible change, they require room for movement. Here μὴ ὄν, denied by Parmenides, and in its spatial application as κενόν by Empedocles and Melissus, is given a blatantly paradoxical existence - nothing (τὸ μηδέν) is as real as thing (τὸ δέν).

No satisfactory explanation seems to have been offered of why or how the infinite number of atoms move in unlimited empty space. There is however a hint of a solution in an analogy with motes in a sunbeam, where a variety of movements can be seen resulting from constant impacts and collisions. The present world order arose as a result of a rotation in a group of atoms, and of the consequent assortment - of the heavier to the centre and the lighter outwards, with the whole held together in an envelope of enclosing atoms. Given limitless material and space, it is obvious that world orders other than ours are forming and disintegrating elsewhere.

Such movements and groupings of atoms in space are the result of λόγος and ἀνάγκη, but the atomists break with all previous thinking in attributing no morality, intelligence or divinity to the workings of the natural law. There is no δίκη in their mechanistic system, and gods, as all else, could only be temporary structures of atomic arrangements.

Individual atoms are distinguished by size and shape, but overall they are too small to be seen. (A late notice allowing very large atoms can be discounted.) In somewhat the same way as the *Iliad* is actually a limited number of letters in different groupings with different spacings, the variety of phenomena is to be explained as arrangements and rearrangements of basic units and empty spaces. Qualities such as colours and tastes are merely νόμῳ, in reality there are only ἄτομα καὶ κενόν.

Since atoms are too small to be seen and void is intangible, the senses are no reliable guide to what there really is. They can only record the results of the interaction of the elemental units in space, and so provide a 'bastard' kind of knowledge, expressed in arbitrary and conventional language. Here the atomists mark the transition from Parmenides' criticism of deceptive senses and unchallenged habit to the great sophistic debate on the conflicting claims of νόμος and φύσις.

THE SOURCES OF THE FRAGMENTS

Fragments of the Presocratics are compiled from quotations from later authors, who refer to their predecessors in different contexts and for widely differing purposes, and who vary considerably in accuracy and general reliability. There is also a network of doxography, i.e. reports, summaries and paraphrases of views attributed to the Presocratics on a range of topics. Most of this is descended, directly or indirectly, from the Φυσικῶν δόξαι, a history of early philosophy written by Theophrastus, the student and successor of Aristotle at the Lyceum.

Even with direct quotations it is often difficult to tell where the original words begin and end, and how much of his own terminology, bias and interpretation the reporting author has interposed. In some cases the quotation was from memory, or the original work was not available; and the problem is further compounded by different and sometimes conflicting manuscript readings.

The following are the main sources, with a note of the fragments taken from them:

Aetius (1st-2nd century A.D.)

This is the name given to a second-hand summary of Theophrastus' Φυσικῶν δόξαι. The source was reconstructed by Diels from parts common to Stobaeus and the pseudo-Plutarch *Placita*, and published in his *Doxographi Graeci*. (E.1 and 3; L.1.)

Aristotle (384-322 B.C.)

Aristotle often takes his predecessors' opinions as a

starting point for his own discussions. He is inclined to use his own terminology, and to see others as tackling a problem from his own point of view. He can be brusque, and sometimes, especially in the case of the Eleatics, unsympathetic or unfair, but he stands preeminent as a source. Apart from some direct quotations, his most valuable contribution for the present purposes is his summary of Presocratic explanations of the world in the first book of the *Metaphysics*, when he looks to his predecessors for confirmation of his own theory of causation. The main sections of this are given (with a translation) in the Appendix; it includes the earliest extant account of the atomists. We are also indebted to Aristotle for the first presentation and criticism of Zeno's four puzzles (cf. Z. 5). Direct quotations are from *Nicomachean Ethics* (H. 48); *Metaphysics* (P. 16; E. 5 and 14); *De anima* (E. 13; D. 14) and *De generatione et corruptione* (cf. L. 2).

Clement of Alexandria (1st-2nd century A.D.)

One of the most erudite of the early Church fathers, Clement was a convert to Christianity who retained his interest in Greek literature. The *Stromateis*, a miscellaneous collection in eight books of comparisons between paganism and Christianity, is a treasure-house of quotations from Greek poets and philosophers. (X. 2-4 and 6; H. 5, 10, 18-19, 21, 49, 53, 59, 63-64, 67 and 73-75; P. 3-4 and 10; E.16 and 22). Two fragments are from his *Protrepticus* (and 'Exhortation to the Greeks') (H. 28-29).

Diogenes Laertius (3rd century A.D.)

The name (sometimes given as Laertes Diogenes) is attached to a compendium with the title: *Lives and Opinions of Famous Philosophers*. The ten books of biography, anecdote, summary and report cover the spectrum from Thales to Epicurus. However unreliable and uncritical a historian,

Diogenes frequently names his primary and secondary sources, and quotes extensively (X. 18; H. 4, 14-15, 23 and 65; Z. 4; D. 4).

Hippolytus (2nd-3rd century A.D.)

In his chief work, *Refutation of all Heresies*, Hippolytus, Bishop of Rome, sets out to combat different heresies by showing their kinship with particular pagan philosophies. He is a main source for Heraclitus, whose theories he matches to the heresy of Mardonius (H. 2, 8, 16-17, 32, 34, 37, 39-40, 46, 51, 54-55 and 68; E. 4, 19 and 20).

Plutarch (50-120+ A.D.)

As well as his *Lives* of Greek and Roman political leaders, Plutarch wrote numerous essays on ethical themes, known collectively as *Moralia*. These essays are packed with quotations from philosophers, but often inadequately remembered, and interspersed with Plutarch's own comment. Essays of relevant interest here are: *Symposium* (X. 15), *De superstitione* (H. 3), *De Pythiae oraculis* (H. 30 and 31), *De E apud Delphos* (H. 58 and 60), *Adversus Colotem* (H. 62; P. 14; D. 8), *De facie in orbe lunae* (P. 15; A. 16), *De exilio* (E. 19), *De sollertia animalium* (D. 16).

Sextus Empiricus (2nd-3rd century A.D.)

Sextus is the main source for ancient scepticism. He quoted extensively, but not all of his material fits the general sceptical framework. There are important Presocratic fragments in books 7 and 9 of his *Adversus mathematicos* (also known as the first books of *Against the Logicians* and *Against the Physicists*) (X. 1, 7, 11 and 16; H. 1, 9 and 13; P. 1 and 7; A. 18 and 20; D. 1-3, 5-6 and 11-12).

Simplicius (6th century A.D.)

Simplicius' commentaries on Aristotle's *Physics* and *De caelo* are monumental works of erudition. When Aristotle refers to a Presocratic, Simplicius usually gives the relevant quotation, sometimes at greater length than necessary where the original was rare and worth preserving. He has a Neoplatonic bias, which tends to interpret all philosophies in terms of a dichotomy between κόσμος νοητός and κόσμος αἰσθητός. (*In Aristotelis Physica commentaria*: X. 8-10; P. 6, 8-9. 12 and 13; Z. 1-3; M. 1-5 and 9-10; E. 2, 6-9 and 12; A. 1-7, 9-15 and 19; D. 10. *In Aristotelis De caelo commentaria*: P. 11 and 17; M. 6 and 8; E. 8 and 10.)

Stobaeus (fifth century A.D.)

John Stobaeus compiled an anthology of quotations from Greek writers as a course of instruction for his son in various topics. The collection is in four books, under the titles of *Florilegium* and *Eclogae*. It relies heavily on earlier extracts and summaries, which circulated widely in the first centuries A.D. (X. 5; H. 6-7, 12, 22, 44, 66, and 70-72; E. 15; D. 17-20).

Other Sources (in roughly chronological order):

Arius Didymus (H. 61), Galen (D. 5). Marcus Aurelius (H. 11 and 20), Proclus (P. 2 and 5), Origen (H. 26 and 35), Aelian (E. 21), Porphyry (H. 41 and 52), Achilles (X. 12), Themistius (H. 33), Ammonius (E. 17), Tzetzes (H. 45). In addition there is some material in the ancient dictionaries, Hesychius, for example, and *Etymologicum Magnum*, and also in the scholia, i.e. anonymous marginal notes on the manuscripts of ancient works.

SELECTIVE BIBLIOGRAPHY

The main fragment and source collection is

H. DIELS: *Die Fragmente der Vorsokratiker*, rev. W. KRANZ, vols. I and II (Berlin 1961, 10th ed.),

supplemented by

H. DIELS: *Doxographi Graeci* (Berlin 1879, repr. 1958).

There is an English version of the fragments in the ordering of Diels / Kranz in

K. FREEMAN: *Ancilla to the Pre-Socratic Philosophers* (Oxford 1946).

An interesting start on the literature can be made by consulting *The Encyclopedia of Philosophy*, ed. P. EDWARDS (New York 1967) s.v. *Pre-Socratic Philosophy* and the names of the individual philosophers.

General works are

J. BURNET: *Early Greek Philosophy* (London 1930, 4th ed.);

W.K.C. GUTHRIE: *A History of Greek Philosophy*, vol. I (Cambridge 1962), vol. II (Cambridge 1965);

while a more philosophical approach is provided compactly by

E. HUSSEY: *The Presocratics* (London 1972),

and more extensively by

J. BARNES: *The Presocratic Philosophers*, vols. I and II (London 1979, one-volume paperback 1982).

Essay collections containing various key articles are

D.J. FURLEY and R.E. ALLEN (edd.): *Studies in Presocratic Philosophy*, vol. I (London 1970), vol. II (London 1975);

A.P.D. MOURELATOS (ed.): *The Pre-Socratics* (New York 1974);

K. ROBB (ed.): *Language and Thought in Early Greek Philosophy* (Illinois 1983, Monist Library of Philosophy).

Detailed bibliographies will be found in

G.B. KERFERD: 'Recent Work on Presocratic Philosophy', *American Philosophical Quarterly* 2 (1965), 130-40 (for the years 1953-62);

E.L. MINAR: 'A Survey of Recent Work in Pre-Socratic Philosophy', *The Classical Weekly* 47 (1954), 161-70, 177-82 (for 1945-52);

E.L. MINAR: 'Pre-Socratic Studies 1953-1966', *The Classical World* 60 (1966), 143-63.

The books by J. Barnes, W.K.C. Guthrie and A.P.D. Mourelatos mentioned above also have comprehensive bibliographies; new works, as they appear, are noticed in *Phronesis* and *Greece and Rome*.

Some books on specific topics are

J.I. BEARE: *Greek Theories of Elementary Cognition* (Oxford 1906);

E.R. DODDS: *The Greeks and the Irrational* (Berkeley 1951);

W. JAEGER: *The Theology of the Early Greek Philosophers* (Oxford 1947);

G.E.R. LLOYD: *Polarity and Analogy* (Cambridge 1966);

M.L. WEST: *Early Greek Philosophy and the Orient* (Oxford 1971).

For an introduction with some texts and translations,,see

G.S. KIRK and J.E. RAVEN: *The Presocratic Philosophers* (Cambridge 1957 , rev. G.S. KIRK and M. SCHOFIELD 1984).

The following is a list of works on the individual philosophers:

Heraclitus

C.H. KAHN: *The Art and Thought of Heraclitus* (Cambridge 1979)

G.S. KIRK: *Heraclitus: The Cosmic Fragments* (Cambridge 1962)

E. HUSSEY: 'Epistemology and Meaning in Heraclitus' in *Language and Logic*, edd. M. SCHOFIELD and M. NUSSBAUM (Cambridge 1982), 33-59;

M. MARCOVICH: *Heraclitus* (Merida 1967).

Parmenides

G. CASERTANO: *Parmenide* (Naples 1978);

A.H. COXON: 'The Philosophy of Parmenides', *Classical Quarterly* 28 (1934), 134-44;

A.P.D. MOURELATOS: *The Route of Parmenides* (New Haven 1970);

L. TARAN: *Parmenides* (Princeton 1965).

Zeno

H.D.P. LEE: *Zeno of Elea* (Cambridge 1967);

G. RYLE: *Dilemmas* (Cambridge 1954), ch.3;

W.C. SALMON: *Zeno's Paradoxes* (Indianapolis 1973).

Empedocles

J. BOLLACK: *Empédocle* (Paris 1965-9) 3 vols.;

N. VAN DER BEN: *The Proem of Empedocles' Peri Physios* (Amsterdam 1975);

M.R. WRIGHT: *Empedocles: The Extant Fragments* (New Haven 1981);

G. ZUNTZ: *Persephone* (Oxford 1971), Book 2: 'Empedokles' *Katharmoi*'.

Anaxagoras

M. SCHOFIELD: *An Essay on Anaxagoras* (Cambridge 1980);

D. SIDER: *The Fragments of Anaxagoras* (Meisenheim 1981);

C. STRANG: 'The Physical Theory of Anaxagoras', *Arch. Geschichte Philosophie* 45 (1963), 102-18;

S.T. TEODORSSON: *Anaxagoras' Theory of Matter* (Göteborg 1982).

Atomists

T.A. COLE: *Democritus and the Sources of Greek Anthropology* (Cleveland 1967);

G. VLASTOS: 'Ethics and Physics in Democritus', *Philosophical Review* 54 (1945), 578-92 and 55 (1946), 53-64.

NOTE

A number in parentheses after a fragment number gives the ordering according to H. Diels / W. Kranz, *Die Fragmente der Vorsokratiker* (6th and subsequent editions) where it differs from the present arrangement. Fragments included in the present collection are subsequently referred to by the philosopher's initial and the number given in the arrangement of this collection, other fragments according to their number in Diels / Kranz, prefixed by B.

Abbreviations for the titles of ancient works generally follow the system used by Liddell and Scott, *Greek - English Lexicon* (rev. by H.S. Jones), hereafter *LSJ*. Modern works listed in the Selective Bibliography are referred to in the notes by the surname of the author. References in the form '*G*. 1397' are to the relevant sections of W.W. Goodwin, *A Greek Grammar* (London, 1951).

XENOPHANES

1(11)

πάντα θεοῖσ' ἀνέθηκαν Ὅμηρός θ' Ἡσίοδός τε,
ὅσσα παρ' ἀνθρώποισιν ὀνείδεα καὶ ψόγος ἐστίν,
κλέπτειν μοιχεύειν τε καὶ ἀλλήλους ἀπατεύειν.

2(14)

ἀλλ' οἱ βροτοὶ δοκέουσι γεννᾶσθαι θεούς,
τὴν σφετέρην ἐσθῆτά τ' ἔχειν φωνήν τε δέμας τε.

3(15)

ἀλλ' εἰ τοι χεῖράς <γ'> εἶχον βόες ἠὲ λέοντες
ἢ γράψαι χείρεσσι καὶ ἔργα τελεῖν ἅπερ ἄνδρες,
ἵπποι μέν θ' ἵπποισι βόες δέ τε βουσὶν ὁμοίας
καί <κε> θεῶν ἰδέας ἔγραφον καὶ σώματ' ἐποίουν
τοιαῦθ' οἷόν περ καὐτοὶ δέμας εἶχον <ἕκαστοι>.

4(16)

Αἰθίοπές τε <θεοὺς σφετέρους> σιμοὺς μέλανάς τε
Θρῆκές τε γλαυκοὺς καὶ πυρρούς <φασι πέλεσθαι>.

* * *

5(18)

οὔτοι ἀπ' ἀρχῆς πάντα θεοὶ θνητοῖσ' ὑπέδειξαν,
ἀλλὰ χρόνῳ ζητοῦντες ἐφευρίσκουσιν ἄμεινον.

6(23)

εἷς θεός, ἔν τε θεοῖσι καὶ ἀνθρώποισι μέγιστος,
οὔτι δέμας θνητοῖσιν ὁμοίιος οὐδὲ νοήμα.

7(24)

οὖλος ὁρᾷ, οὖλος δὲ νοεῖ, οὖλος δέ τ' ἀκούει.

8(26)

αἰεὶ δ' ἐν ταὐτῷ μίμνει κινούμενος οὐδέν,
οὐδὲ μετέρχεσθαί μιν ἐπιπρέπει ἄλλοτε ἄλλῃ.

9(25)

ἀλλ' ἀπάνευθε πόνοιο νόου φρενὶ πάντα κραδαίνει.

* * *

10(29)

γῆ καὶ ὕδωρ πάντ' ἐσθ' ὅσα γίνοντ' ἠδὲ φύονται.

11(27)

ἐκ γαίης γὰρ πάντα καὶ εἰς γῆν πάντα τελευτᾷ.

12(28)

γαίης μὲν τόδε πεῖρας ἄνω παρὰ ποσσὶν ὁρᾶται
ἠέρι προσπλάζον, <τὸ> κάτω δ' ἐς ἄπειρον ἱκνεῖται.

* * *

13(30)

πηγὴ δ' ἐστὶ θάλασσ' ὕδατος, πηγὴ δ' ἀνέμοιο·
οὔτε γὰρ ἐν νέφεσιν <γίνοιτό κε ἴς ἀνέμοιο
ἐκπνείοντος> ἔσωθεν ἄνευ πόντου μεγάλοιο
οὔτε ῥοαὶ ποταμῶν οὔτ' αἰθέρος ὄμβριον ὕδωρ,
ἀλλὰ μέγας πόντος γενέτωρ νεφέων ἀνέμων τε
καὶ ποταμῶν.

14(32)

ἥν τ' Ἶριν καλέουσι, νέφος καὶ τοῦτο πέφυκε,

πορφύρεον καὶ φοινίκεον καὶ χλωρὸν ἰδέσθαι.

* * *

15(35)

ταῦτα δεδοξάσθω μὲν ἐοικότα τοῖς ἐτύμοισι ...

16(34)

καὶ τὸ μὲν οὖν σαφὲς οὔτις ἀνὴρ ἴδεν οὐδέ τις ἔσται
εἰδὼς ἀμφὶ θεῶν τε καὶ ἅσσα λέγω περὶ πάντων·
εἰ γὰρ καὶ τὰ μάλιστα τύχοι τετελεσμένον εἰπών,
αὐτὸς ὅμως οὐκ οἶδε· δόκος δ' ἐπὶ πᾶσι τέτυκται.

17(38)

εἰ μὴ χλωρὸν ἔφυσε θεὸς μέλι, πολλὸν ἔφασκον
γλύσσονα σῦκα πέλεσθαι.

* * *

18(7)

καί ποτέ μιν στυφελιζομένου σκύλακος παριόντα
φασὶν ἐποικτῖραι καὶ τόδε φάσθαι ἔπος·
'παῦσαι μηδὲ ῥάπιζ', ἐπεὶ ἦ φίλου ἀνέρος ἐστίν
ψυχή, τὴν ἔγνων φθεγξαμένης ἀίων'.

HERACLITUS

1(1)

τοῦ δὲ λόγου τοῦδ' ἐόντος αἰεὶ ἀξύνετοι γίνονται ἄνθρωποι καὶ πρόσθεν ἢ ἀκοῦσαι καὶ ἀκούσαντες τὸ πρῶτον· γινομένων γὰρ πάντων κατὰ τὸν λόγον τόνδε ἀπείροισιν ἐοίκασι, πειρώμενοι καὶ ἐπέων καὶ ἔργων τοιούτων, ὁκοίων ἐγὼ διηγεῦμαι, κατὰ φύσιν διαιρέων ἕκαστον καὶ φράζων ὅκως ἔχει. τοὺς δὲ ἄλλους ἀνθρώπους λανθάνει ὁκόσα ἐγερθέντες ποιοῦσιν, ὅκωσπερ ὁκόσα εὕδοντες ἐπιλανθάνονται.

2(50)

οὐκ ἐμοῦ, ἀλλὰ τοῦ λόγου ἀκούσαντας ὁμολογεῖν σοφόν ἐστιν ἓν πάντα εἶναι.

3(89)

τοῖς ἐγρηγορόσιν ἕνα καὶ κοινὸν κόσμον εἶναι.

4(41)

ἓν τὸ σοφόν, ἐπίστασθαι γνώμην, ὅκῃ κυβερνᾶται πάντα διὰ πάντων.

5(32)

ἓν τὸ σοφὸν μοῦνον λέγεσθαι οὐκ ἐθέλει καὶ ἐθέλει Ζηνὸς ὄνομα.

* * *

6(113)

ξυνόν ἐστι πᾶσι τὸ φρονέειν.

7(116)

ἀνθρώποισι πᾶσι μέτεστι γινώσκειν ἑωυτοὺς καὶ σωφρονεῖν.

8(55)

ὅσων ὄψις ἀκοὴ μάθησις, ταῦτα ἐγὼ προτιμέω.

9(2)

τοῦ λόγου δ' ἐόντος ξυνοῦ ζώουσιν οἱ πολλοὶ ὡς ἰδίαν ἔχοντες φρόνησιν.

10(17)

οὐ γὰρ φρονέουσι τοιαῦτα πολλοὶ ὁκοίοις ἐγκυρεῦσιν, οὐδὲ μαθόντες γινώσκουσιν, ἑωυτοῖσι δὲ δοκέουσι.

11(72)

ᾧ μάλιστα διηνεκῶς ὁμιλοῦσι, τούτῳ διαφέρονται, καὶ οἷς καθ' ἡμέραν ἐγκυροῦσι, ταῦτα αὐτοῖς ξένα φαίνεται.

12(108)

ὁκόσων λόγους ἤκουσα, οὐδεὶς ἀφικνεῖται ἐς τοῦτο, ὥστε γινώσκειν ὅτι σοφόν ἐστι πάντων κεχωρισμένον.

* * *

13(107)

κακοὶ μάρτυρες ἀνθρώποισιν ὀφθαλμοὶ καὶ ὦτα βαρβάρους ψυχὰς ἐχόντων.

14(40)

πολυμαθίη νόον οὐ διδάσκει· Ἡσίοδον γὰρ ἂν ἐδίδαξε καὶ Πυθαγόρην, αὖτίς τε Ξενοφάνεά τε καὶ Ἑκαταῖον.

15(42)

τὸν Ὅμηρον ἄξιον ἐκ τῶν ἀγώνων ἐκβάλλεσθαι καὶ ῥαπίζεσθαι.

16(56)

ἐξηπάτηνται οἱ ἄνθρωποι πρὸς τὴν γνῶσιν τῶν φανερῶν παραπλησίως Ὁμήρῳ, ὃς ἐγένετο τῶν Ἑλλήνων σοφώτερος πάντων, ἐκεῖνον γὰρ παῖδες φθεῖρας κατακτείνοντες ἐξηπάτησαν εἰπόντες· ὅσα εἴδομεν καὶ ἐλάβομεν, ταῦτα ἀπολείπομεν, ὅσα δὲ οὔτε εἴδομεν οὔτ' ἐλάβομεν, ταῦτα φέρομεν.

17(57)

διδάσκαλος δὲ πλείστων Ἡσίοδος· τοῦτον ἐπίστανται πλεῖστα εἰδέναι, ὅστις ἡμέρην καὶ εὐφρόνην οὐκ ἐγίνωσκεν· ἔστι γὰρ ἕν.

* * *

18(21)

θάνατός ἐστιν ὁκόσα ἐγερθέντες ὁρέομεν, ὁκόσα δὲ εὕδοντες ὕπνος.

19(26)

ἄνθρωπος ἐν εὐφρόνῃ φάος ἅπτεται ἑαυτῷ ἀποσβεσθεὶς ὄψεις, ζῶν δὲ ἅπτεται τεθνεῶτος εὕδων, ἐγρηγορὼς ἅπτεται εὕδοντος.

20(75)

τοὺς καθεύδοντας ἐργάτας εἶναι.

21(20)

γενόμενοι ζώειν ἐθέλουσι μόρους τ' ἔχειν, καὶ παῖδας καταλείπουσι μόρους γενέσθαι.

22(114)

ξὺν νόῳ λέγοντας ἰσχυρίζεσθαι χρὴ τῷ ξυνῷ πάντων, ὅκωσπερ νόμῳ πόλις, καὶ πολὺ ἰσχυροτέρως. τρέφονται γὰρ πάντες οἱ ἀνθρώπειοι νόμοι ὑπὸ ἑνὸς τοῦ θείου· κρατεῖ γὰρ τοσοῦτον ὁκόσον ἐθέλει καὶ ἐξαρχεῖ πᾶσι καὶ περιγίνεται.

23(44)

μάχεσθαι χρὴ τὸν δῆμον ὑπὲρ τοῦ νόμου ὅκωσπερ τείχεος.

24(49)

εἷς <ἐμοὶ> μύριοι, ἐὰν ἄριστος ᾖ.

* * *

25(78)

ἦθος γὰρ ἀνθρώπειον μὲν οὐκ ἔχει γνώμας, θεῖον δὲ ἔχει.

26(79)

ἀνὴρ νήπιος ἤκουσε πρὸς δαίμονος ὅκωσπερ παῖς πρὸς ἀνδρός.

27(5)

καθαίρονται δ' ἄλλως αἵματι μιαινόμενοι, ὁκοῖον εἴ τις εἰς πηλὸν ἐμβὰς πηλῷ ἀπονίζοιτο· μαίνεσθαι δ' ἂν δοκέοι, εἴ τίς μιν ἀνθρώπων ἐπιφράσαιτο οὕτω ποιέοντα. καὶ τοῖς ἀγάλμασι δὲ τουτέοισιν εὔχονται, ὁκοῖον εἴ τις δόμοισι λεσχηνεύοιτο, οὔ τι γινώσκων θεοὺς οὐδ' ἥρωας οἵτινές εἰσι.

28(14)

τὰ νομιζόμενα κατ' ἀνθρώπους μυστήρια ἀνιερωστὶ μυεῦνται.

29(15)

εἰ μὴ Διονύσῳ πομπὴν ἐποιοῦντο καὶ ὕμνεον ᾆσμα αἰδοίοισιν, ἀναιδέστατα εἴργασται· ὡυτὸς δὲ Ἀίδης καὶ Διόνυσος, ὅτεῳ μαίνονται καὶ ληναΐζουσιν.

30(92)

Σίβυλλα μαινομένῳ στόματι ἀγέλαστα [καὶ ἀκαλλώπιστα καὶ ἀμύριστα] φθεγγομένη.

31(93)

ὁ ἄναξ, οὗ τὸ μαντεῖόν ἐστι τὸ ἐν Δελφοῖς, οὔτε λέγει οὔτε κρύπτει, ἀλλὰ σημαίνει.

32(54)

ἁρμονίη ἀφανὴς φανερῆς κρείσσων.

33(123)

φύσις κρύπτεσθαι φιλεῖ.

* * *

34(53)

πόλεμος πάντων μὲν πατήρ ἐστι, πάντων δὲ βασιλεύς, καὶ τοὺς μὲν θεοὺς ἔδειξε τοὺς δὲ ἀνθρώπους, τοὺς μὲν δούλους ἐποίησε τοὺς δὲ ἐλευθέρους.

35(80)

εἰδέναι δὲ χρὴ τὸν πόλεμον ἐόντα ξυνόν, καὶ δίκην ἔριν, καὶ γινόμενα πάντα κατ' ἔριν καὶ χρεώμενα.

36(10)

συλλάψιες ὅλα καὶ οὐχ ὅλα, συμφερόμενον διαφερόμενον, συνᾷδον διᾷδον· ἐκ πάντων ἓν καὶ ἐξ ἑνὸς πάντα.

37(51)

οὐ ξυνιᾶσιν ὅκως διαφερόμενον ἑωυτῷ ὁμολογέει· παλίντονος ἁρμονίη ὅκωσπερ τόξου καὶ λύρης.

38(48)

τῷ οὖν τόξῳ ὄνομα βίος, ἔργον δὲ θάνατος.

39(59)

γραφείῳ ὁδὸς εὐθεῖα καὶ σκολιή.

40(60)

ὁδὸς ἄνω κάτω μία καὶ ὡυτή.

41(103)

ξυνὸν ἀρχὴ καὶ πέρας ἐπὶ κύκλου [περιφέρειας].

42(125)

καὶ ὁ κυκεὼν διίσταται <μὴ> κινούμενος.

43(61)

θάλασσα ὕδωρ καθαρώτατον καὶ μιαρώτατον, ἰχθύσι μὲν πότιμον καὶ σωτήριον, ἀνθρώποις δὲ ἄποτον καὶ ὀλέθριον.

44(111)

νοῦσος ὑγιείην ἐποίησεν ἡδὺ καὶ ἀγαθόν, λιμὸς κόρον, κάματος ἀνάπαυσιν.

45(126)

τὰ ψυχρὰ θέρεται, θερμὸν ψύχεται, ὑγρὸν αὐαίνεται, καρφαλέον νοτίζεται.

* * *

46(62)

ἀθάνατοι θνητοί, θνητοὶ ἀθάνατοι, ζῶντες τὸν ἐκείνων θάνατον, τὸν δὲ ἐκείνων βίον τεθνεῶτες.

47(88)

ταὐτό τ' ἔνι ζῶν καὶ τεθνηκὸς καὶ τὸ ἐγρηγορὸς καὶ τὸ καθεῦδον καὶ νέον καὶ γηραιόν· τάδε γὰρ μεταπεσόντα ἐκεῖνά ἐστι, κἀκεῖνα πάλιν μεταπεσόντα ταῦτα.

48(8)

τὸ ἀντίξουν συμφέρον καὶ ἐκ τῶν διαφερόντων καλλίστην ἁρμονίαν.

49(23)

Δίκης ὄνομα οὐκ ἂν ᾔδεσαν, εἰ ταῦτα μὴ ἦν.

50(124)

ὥσπερ σάρμα εἰκῆ κεχυμένων ὁ κάλλιστος κόσμος.

51(67)

ὁ θεὸς ἡμέρη εὐφρόνη, χειμὼν θέρος, πόλεμος εἰρήνη, κόρος λιμός, ἀλλοιοῦται δὲ ὅκωσπερ <πῦρ>, ὁπόταν συμμιγῇ θυώμασιν, ὀνομάζεται καθ' ἡδονὴν ἑκάστου.

52(102)

τῷ μὲν θεῷ καλὰ πάντα [καὶ ἀγαθὰ] καὶ δίκαια, ἄνθρωποι δὲ ἃ μὲν ἄδικα ὑπειλήφασιν, ἃ δὲ δίκαια.

* * *

53(30)

κόσμον τόνδε, τὸν αὐτὸν ἁπάντων, οὔτε τις θεῶν οὔτε ἀνθρώπων ἐποίησεν, ἀλλ' ἦν ἀεὶ καὶ ἔστιν καὶ ἔσται πῦρ ἀείζωον, ἁπτόμενον μέτρα καὶ ἀποσβεννύμενον μέτρα.

54(64)

τὰ δὲ πάντα οἰακίζει κεραυνός.

55(66)

πάντα τὸ πῦρ ἐπελθὸν κρινεῖ καὶ καταλήψεται.

56(94)

ἥλιος ούχ ὑπερβήσεται μέτρα· εἰ δὲ μή, Ἐρινύες μιν Δίκης ἐπίκουροι ἐξευρήσουσιν.

57(99)

εἰ μὴ ἥλιος ἦν, ἕνεκα τῶν ἄλλων ἄστρων εὐφρόνη ἂν ἦν.

58(90)

πυρός τε ἀνταμοιβὴ τὰ πάντα καὶ πῦρ ἁπάντων ὅκωσπερ χρυσοῦ χρήματα καὶ χρημάτων χρυσός.

59(31)

πυρὸς τροπαὶ πρῶτον θάλασσα, θαλάσσης δὲ τὸ μὲν ἥμισυ γῆ, τὸ δὲ ἥμισυ πρηστήρ ... θάλασσα διαχέεται καὶ μετρέεται εἰς τὸν αὐτὸν λόγον ὁκοῖος πρόσθεν ἦν ἢ γενέσθαι γῆ.

60(91)

ποταμῷ οὐκ ἔστιν ἐμβῆναι δὶς τῷ αὐτῷ.

61(12)

ποταμοῖσι τοῖσιν αὐτοῖσιν ἐμβαίνουσιν ἕτερα καὶ ἕτερα ὕδατα ἐπιρρεῖ.

* * *

62(101)

ἐδιζησάμην ἐμεωυτόν.

63(35)

χρὴ εὖ μάλα πολλῶν ἵστορας φιλοσόφους ἄνδρας εἶναι.

64(22)

χρυσὸν οἱ διζήμενοι γῆν πολλὴν ὀρύσσουσι καὶ εὑρίσκουσιν ὀλίγον.

65(45)

ψυχῆς πείρατα ἰὼν οὐκ ἂν ἐξεύροιο, πᾶσαν ἐπιπορευόμενος ὁδόν· οὕτω βαθὺν λόγον ἔχει.

66(115)

ψυχῆς ἐστι λόγος ἑαυτὸν αὔξων.

67(36)

ψυχῇσιν θάνατος ὕδωρ γενέσθαι, ὕδατι δὲ θάνατος γῆν γενέσθαι, ἐκ γῆς δὲ ὕδωρ γίνεται, ἐξ ὕδατος δὲ ψυχή.

68(52)

αἰὼν παῖς ἐστι παίζων, πεσσεύων· παιδὸς ἡ βασιληίη.

69(85)

θυμῷ μάχεσθαι χαλεπόν· ὃ γὰρ ἂν θέλῃ, ψυχῆς ὠνεῖται.

70(117)

ἀνὴρ ὁκόταν μεθυσθῇ, ἄγεται ὑπὸ παιδὸς ἀνήβου σφαλλόμενος, οὐκ ἐπαΐων ὅκη βαίνει, ὑγρὴν τὴν ψυχὴν ἔχων.

71(118)

αὔη ψυχὴ σοφωτάτη καὶ ἀρίστη.

72(119)

ἦθος ἀνθρώπῳ δαίμων.

73(29)

αἱρεῦνται ἓν ἀντὶ ἁπάντων οἱ ἄριστοι, κλέος ἀέναον θνητῶν· οἱ δὲ πολλοὶ κεκόρηνται ὅκωσπερ κτήνεα.

74(24)

ἀρηιφάτους θεοὶ τιμῶσι καὶ ἄνθρωποι.

75(27)

ἀνθρώπους μένει ἀποθανόντας ἅσσα οὐκ ἔλπονται οὐδὲ δοκέουσιν.

76(63)

†ἔνθα δ' ἐόντι† ἐπανίστασθαι καὶ φύλακας γίνεσθαι ἐγερτὶ ζώντων καὶ νεκρῶν.

PARMENIDES

1

ἵπποι ταί με φέρουσιν, ὅσον τ' ἐπὶ θυμὸς ἱκάνοι,
πέμπον, ἐπεί μ' ἐς ὁδὸν βῆσαν πολύφημον ἄγουσαι
δαίμονος, ἣ κατὰ πάντ' ἄστη φέρει εἰδότα φῶτα·
τῇ φερόμην· τῇ γάρ με πολύφραστοι φέρον ἵπποι
ἅρμα τιταίνουσαι, κοῦραι δ' ὁδὸν ἡγεμόνευον.
ἄξων δ' ἐν χνοίῃσιν <ἵει> σύριγγος ἀυτήν
αἰθόμενος (δοιοῖς γὰρ ἐπείγετο δινωτοῖσιν
κύκλοις ἀμφοτέρωθεν), ὅτε σπερχοίατο πέμπειν
Ἡλιάδες κοῦραι, προλιποῦσαι δώματα Νυκτός
εἰς φάος, ὠσάμεναι κράτων ἄπο χερσὶ καλύπτρας.
ἔνθα πύλαι Νυκτός τε καὶ Ἤματός εἰσι κελεύθων,
καί σφας ὑπέρθυρον ἀμφὶς ἔχει καὶ λάινος οὐδός·
αὐταὶ δ' αἰθέριαι πλῆνται μεγάλοισι θυρέτροις·
τῶν δὲ Δίκη πολύποινος ἔχει κληῖδας ἀμοιβούς.
τὴν δὴ παρφάμεναι κοῦραι μαλακοῖσι λόγοισιν
πεῖσαν ἐπιφραδέως, ὥς σφιν βαλανωτὸν ὀχῆα
ἀπτερέως ὤσειε πυλέων ἄπο· ταὶ δὲ θυρέτρων
χάσμ' ἀχανὲς ποίησαν ἀναπτάμεναι πολυχάλκους
ἄξονας ἐν σύριγξιν ἀμοιβαδὸν εἱλίξασαι
γόμφοις καὶ περόνῃσιν ἀρηρότε· τῇ ῥα δι' αὐτέων
ἰθὺς ἔχον κοῦραι κατ' ἀμαξιτὸν ἅρμα καὶ ἵππους.
καί με θεὰ πρόφρων ὑπεδέξατο, χεῖρα δὲ χειρί
δεξιτερὴν ἕλεν, ὧδε δ' ἔπος φάτο καί με προσηύδα·
ὦ κοῦρ', ἀθανάτοισι συνάορος ἡνιόχοισιν

ἵπποις ταί σε φέρουσιν, ἱκάνων ἡμέτερον δῶ,
χαῖρ', ἐπεὶ οὔτι σε μοῖρα κακὴ προύπεμπε νέεσθαι
τήνδ' ὁδόν (ἦ γὰρ ἀπ' ἀνθρώπων ἐκτὸς πάτου ἐστίν),
ἀλλὰ θέμις τε δίκη τε. χρεὼ δέ σε πάντα πυθέσθαι
ἠμὲν 'Αληθείης εὐκυκλέος ἀτρεμὲς ἦτορ
ἠδὲ βροτῶν δόξας, ταῖς οὐκ ἔνι πίστις ἀληθής.
ἀλλ' ἔμπης καὶ ταῦτα μαθήσεαι, ὡς τὰ δοκοῦντα
χρῆν δοκίμως εἶναι διὰ παντὸς πάντα περ ὄντα.

* * *

2

εἰ δ' ἄγ' ἐγὼν ἐρέω, κόμισαι δὲ σὺ μῦθον ἀκούσας,
αἵπερ ὁδοὶ μοῦναι διζήσιός εἰσι νοῆσαι·
ἡ μὲν ὅπως ἐστίν τε καὶ ὡς οὐκ ἔστι μὴ εἶναι
Πειθοῦς ἐστι κέλευθος ('Αληθείῃ γὰρ ὀπηδεῖ),
ἡ δ' ὡς οὐκ ἔστιν τε καὶ ὡς χρεών ἐστι μὴ εἶναι,
τὴν δή τοι φράζω παναπευθέα ἔμμεν ἀταρπόν·
οὔτε γὰρ ἂν γνοίης τό γε μὴ ἐὸν (οὐ γὰρ ἀνυστόν)
οὔτε φράσαις.

3

τὸ γὰρ αὐτὸ νοεῖν ἐστίν τε καὶ εἶναι.

4

λεῦσσε δ' ὅμως ἀπεόντα νόῳ παρεόντα βεβαίως·
οὐ γὰρ ἀποτμήξει τὸ ἐὸν τοῦ ἐόντος ἔχεσθαι
οὔτε σκιδνάμενον πάντῃ πάντως κατὰ κόσμον
οὔτε συνιστάμενον.

5

ξυνὸν δέ μοί ἐστιν
ὁππόθεν ἄρξωμαι· τόθι γὰρ πάλιν ἵξομαι αὖθις.

* * *

6

χρὴ τὸ λέγειν τε νοεῖν τ᾽ ἐὸν ἔμμεναι. ἔστι γὰρ εἶναι,
μηδὲν δ᾽ οὐκ ἔστιν· τά σ᾽ ἐγὼ φράζεσθαι ἄνωγα.
πρώτης γάρ σ᾽ ἀφ᾽ ὁδοῦ ταύτης διζήσιος <εἴργω>,
αὐτὰρ ἔπειτ᾽ ἀπὸ τῆς, ἣν δὴ βροτοὶ εἰδότες οὐδέν
πλάττονται, δίκρανοι· ἀμηχανίη γὰρ ἐν αὐτῶν
στήθεσιν ἰθύνει πλακτὸν νόον· οἱ δὲ φοροῦνται
κωφοὶ ὁμῶς τυφλοί τε, τεθηπότες, ἄκριτα φῦλα,
οἷς τὸ πέλειν τε καὶ οὐκ εἶναι ταὐτὸν νενόμισται
κοὐ ταὐτόν, πάντων δὲ παλίντροπός ἐστι κέλευθος.

7

οὐ γὰρ μήποτε τοῦτο δαμῇ εἶναι μὴ ἐόντα·
ἀλλὰ σὺ τῆσδ᾽ ἀφ᾽ ὁδοῦ διζήσιος εἶργε νόημα
μηδέ σ᾽ ἔθος πολύπειρον ὁδὸν κατὰ τήνδε βιάσθω,
νωμᾶν ἄσκοπον ὄμμα καὶ ἠχήεσσαν ἀκουὴν
καὶ γλῶσσαν, κρῖναι δὲ λόγῳ πολύδηριν ἔλεγχον
ἐξ ἐμέθεν ῥηθέντα.

8

᾿ΑΛΗΘΕΙΑ

μόνος δ᾽ ἔτι μῦθος ὁδοῖο
λείπεται, ὡς ἔστιν. ταύτῃ δ᾽ ἐπὶ σήματ᾽ ἔασι
πολλὰ μάλ᾽, ὡς ἀγένητον ἐὸν καὶ ἀνώλεθρόν ἐστιν,

οὖλον μουνογενές τε καὶ ἀτρεμὲς ἠδ' ἀτέλεστον·
οὐδέ ποτ' ἦν οὐδ' ἔσται, ἐπεὶ νῦν ἔστιν ὁμοῦ πᾶν,
ἕν, ξυνεχές.
(i) τίνα γὰρ γένναν διζήσεαι αὐτοῦ;
πῇ πόθεν αὐξηθέν; οὐδ' ἐκ μὴ ἐόντος ἐάσσω
φάσθαι σ' οὐδὲ νοεῖν· οὐ γὰρ φατὸν οὐδὲ νοητόν
ἔστιν ὅπως οὐκ ἔστι. τί δ' ἄν μιν καὶ χρέος ὦρσεν
ὕστερον ἢ πρόσθεν, τοῦ μηδενὸς ἀρξάμενον, φῦν;
οὕτως ἢ πάμπαν πέλεναι χρεών ἐστιν ἢ οὐχί.
οὐδέ ποτ' ἐκ μὴ ἐόντος ἐφήσει πίστιος ἰσχύς
γίνεσθαί τι παρ' αὐτό· τοῦ εἵνεκεν οὔτε γενέσθαι
οὔτ' ὄλλυσθαι ἀνῆκε Δίκη χαλάσασα πέδῃσιν,
ἀλλ' ἔχει· ἡ δὲ κρίσις περὶ τούτων ἐν τῷδ' ἐστίν·
ἔστιν ἢ οὐκ ἔστιν· κέκριται δ' οὖν, ὥσπερ ἀνάγκη,
τὴν μὲν ἐᾶν ἀνόητον ἀνώνυμον (οὐ γὰρ ἀληθής
ἔστιν ὁδός), τὴν δ' ὥστε πέλειν καὶ ἐτήτυμον εἶναι.
πῶς δ' ἂν ἔπειτ' ἀπόλοιτο ἐόν; πῶς δ' ἄν κε γένοιτο;
εἰ γὰρ ἔγεντ', οὐκ ἔστ', οὐδ' εἴ ποτε μέλλει ἔσεσθαι.
τὼς γένεσις μὲν ἀπέσβεσται καὶ ἄπυστος ὄλεθρος.
(ii) οὐδὲ διαιρετόν ἐστιν, ἐπεὶ πᾶν ἐστιν ὁμοῖον,
οὐδέ τι τῇ μᾶλλον, τό κεν εἴργοι μιν συνέχεσθαι,
οὐδέ τι χειρότερον· πᾶν δ' ἔμπλεόν ἐστιν ἐόντος.
τῷ ξυνεχὲς πᾶν ἐστιν, ἐὸν γὰρ ἐόντι πελάζει.
(iii) αὐτὰρ ἀκίνητον μεγάλων ἐν πείρασι δεσμῶν
ἔστιν ἄναρχον, ἄπαυστον, ἐπεὶ γένεσις καὶ ὄλεθρος
τῆλε μαλ' ἐπλάγχθησαν, ἀπῶσε δὲ πίστις ἀληθής.
ταὐτόν τ' ἐν ταὐτῷ τε μένον καθ' ἑαυτό τε κεῖται,

χοὕτως ἔμπεδον αὖθι μένει· κρατερὴ γὰρ 'Ανάγκη
πείρατος ἐν δεσμοῖσιν ἔχει, τό μιν ἀμφὶς ἐέργει.
οὕνεκεν οὐκ ἀτελεύτητον τὸ ἐὸν θέμις εἶναι·
ἔστι γὰρ οὐκ ἐπιδεές· μὴ ἐὸν δ' ἂν παντὸς ἐδεῖτο.
(ταὐτὸν δ' ἐστὶ νοεῖν τε καὶ οὕνεκέν ἐστι νόημα·
οὐ γὰρ ἄνευ τοῦ ἐόντος, ἐν ᾧ πεφατισμένον ἐστίν,
εὑρήσεις τὸ νοεῖν· οὐδὲν γὰρ <ἢ> ἔστιν ἢ ἔσται
ἄλλο πάρεξ τοῦ ἐόντος, ἐπεὶ τό γε Μοῖρ' ἐπέδησεν
οὖλον ἀκίνητον τ' ἔμεναι. τῷ πάντ' ὄνομ' ἔσται,
ὅσσα βροτοὶ κατέθεντο πεποιθότες εἶναι ἀληθῆ,
γίγνεσθαί τε καὶ ὄλλυσθαι, εἶναί τε καὶ οὐχί,
καὶ τόπον ἀλλάσσειν, διά τε χρόα φανὸν ἀμείβειν.)
(iv) αὐτὰρ ἐπεὶ πεῖρας πύματον, τετελεσμένον ἐστί
πάντοθεν, εὐκύκλου σφαίρης ἐναλίγκιον ὄγκῳ,
μεσσόθεν ἰσοπαλὲς πάντῃ· τὸ γὰρ οὔτε τι μεῖζον
οὔτε τι βαιότερον πελέναι χρεόν ἐστι τῇ ἢ τῇ.
οὔτε γὰρ οὐκ ἐόν ἐστι, τό κεν παύοι μιν ἱκνεῖσθαι
εἰς ὁμόν, οὔτ' ἐόν ἐστιν ὅπως εἴη κεν ἐόντος
τῇ μᾶλλον τῇ δ' ἧσσον, ἐπεὶ πᾶν ἐστιν ἄσυλον·
οἷ γὰρ πάντοθεν ἶσον, ὁμῶς ἐν πείρασι κύρει.

ΔΟΞΑ

ἐν τῷ σοι παύω πιστὸν λόγον ἠδὲ νόημα
ἀμφὶς ἀληθείης· δόξας δ' ἀπὸ τοῦδε βροτείας
μάνθανε, κόσμον ἐμῶν ἐπέων ἀπατηλὸν ἀκούων.
μορφὰς γὰρ κατέθεντο δύο γνώμας ὀνομάζειν·
τῶν μίαν οὐ χρεών ἐστιν, ἐν ᾧ πεπλανημένοι εἰσίν·

τάντία δ' ἐκρίναντο δέμας καὶ σήματ' ἔθεντο
χωρὶς άπ' ἀλλήλων, τῇ μὲν φλογὸς αἰθέριον πῦρ,
ἤπιον ὄν, μέγ' [άραιὸν] ἐλαφρόν, ἑωυτῷ πάντοσε τωὐτόν,
τῷ δ' ἑτέρῳ μὴ τωὐτόν· ἀτὰρ κἀκεῖνο κατ' αὐτό
τάντία νύκτ' ἀδαῆ, πυκινὸν δέμας ἐμβριθές τε.
τόν σοι ἐγὼ διάκοσμον ἐοικότα πάντα φατίζω,
ὡς οὐ μή ποτέ τίς σε βροτῶν γνώμη παρελάσσῃ.

* * *

9

αὐτὰρ ἐπειδὴ πάντα φάος καὶ νὺξ ὀνόμασται
καὶ τὰ κατὰ σφετέρας δυνάμεις ἐπὶ τοῖσί τε καὶ τοῖς,
πᾶν πλέον ἐστὶν ὁμοῦ φάεος καὶ νυκτὸς ἀφάντου
ἴσων ἀμφοτέρων, ἐπεὶ οὐδετέρῳ μέτα μηδέν.

10

εἴσῃ δ' αἰθερίαν τε φύσιν τά τ' ἐν αἰθέρι πάντα
σήματα καὶ καθαρᾶς εὐαγέος ἠελίοιο
λαμπάδος ἔργ' ἀίδηλα καὶ ὁππόθεν ἐξεγένοντο,
ἔργα τε κύκλωπος πεύσῃ περίφοιτα σελήνης
καὶ φύσιν, εἰδήσεις δὲ καὶ οὐρανὸν ἀμφὶς ἔχοντα
ἔνθεν ἔφυ τε καὶ ὥς μιν ἄγουσ' ἐπέδησεν 'Ανάγκη
πείρατ' ἔχειν ἄστρων.

11

πῶς γαῖα καὶ ἥλιος ἠδὲ σελήνη
αἰθήρ τε ξυνὸς γάλα τ' οὐράνιον καὶ ὄλυμπος
ἔσχατος ἠδ' ἄστρων θερμὸν μένος ὡρμήθησαν
γίγνεσθαι.

* * *

12

αἱ γὰρ στεινότεραι πλῆντο πυρὸς ἀκρήτοιο,
αἱ δ' ἐπὶ ταῖς νυκτός, μετὰ δὲ φλογὸς ἵεται αἶσα·
ἐν δὲ μέσῳ τούτων δαίμων ἣ πάντα κυβερνᾷ·
πάντα γὰρ <ἣ> στυγεροῖο τόκου καὶ μίξιος ἄρχει,
πέμπουσ' ἄρσενι θῆλυ μιγῆν τό τ' ἐναντίον αὖτις
ἄρσεν θηλυτέρῳ.

13

πρώτιστον μὲν Ἔρωτα θεῶν μητίσατο πάντων

14

νυκτιφαὲς περὶ γαῖαν ἀλώμενον ἀλλότριον φῶς

15

αἰεὶ παπταίνουσα πρὸς αὐγὰς ἠελίοιο.

* * *

16

ὡς γὰρ ἑκάστοτ' ἔχει κρᾶσις μελέων πολυπλάγκτων,
τὼς νόος ἀνθρώποισι παρίσταται· τὸ γὰρ αὐτό
ἔστιν ὅπερ φρονέει μελέων φύσις ἀνθρώποισιν
καὶ πᾶσιν καὶ πάντι· τὸ γὰρ πλέον ἐστὶ νόημα.

* * *

17(19)

οὕτω τοι κατὰ δόξαν ἔφυ τάδε καὶ νῦν ἔασι
καὶ μετέπειτ' ἀπὸ τοῦδε τελευτήσουσι τραφέντα·
τοῖς δ' ὄνομ' ἄνθρωποι κατέθεντ' ἐπίσημον ἑκάστῳ.

ZENO

1(1/2)

εἰ μὴ ἔχοι μέγεθος τὸ ὄν, οὐδ' ἂν εἴη.
εἰ γὰρ ἄλλῳ ὄντι προσγένοιτο, οὐδὲν ἂν μεῖζον ποιήσειεν· μεγέθους γὰρ μηδενὸς ὄντος, προσγενομένου δέ, οὐδὲν οἷόν τε εἰς μέγεθος ἐπιδοῦναι. καὶ οὕτως ἂν ἤδη τὸ προσγινόμενον οὐδὲν εἴη.
εἰ δὲ ἀπογινομένου τὸ ἕτερον μηδὲν ἔλαττον ἔσται μηδὲ αὖ προσγινομένου αὐξήσεται, δῆλον ὅτι τὸ προσγενόμενον οὐδὲν ἦν οὐδὲ τὸ ἀπογενόμενον.

2(1)

εἰ δέ ἐστιν, ἀνάγκη ἕκαστον μέγεθός τι ἔχειν καὶ πάχος καὶ ἀπέχειν αὐτοῦ τὸ ἕτερον ἀπὸ τοῦ ἑτέρου. καὶ περὶ τοῦ προύχοντος ὁ αὐτὸς λόγος. καὶ γὰρ ἐκεῖνο ἕξει μέγεθος καὶ προέξει αὐτοῦ τι. ὅμοιον δὴ τοῦτο ἅπαξ τε εἰπεῖν καὶ ἀεὶ λέγειν· οὐδὲν γὰρ αὐτοῦ τοιοῦτον ἔσχατον ἔσται οὔτε ἕτερον πρὸς ἕτερον οὐκ ἔσται.
οὕτως εἰ πολλά ἐστιν, ἀνάγκη αὐτὰ μικρά τε εἶναι καὶ μεγάλα· μικρὰ μὲν ὥστε μὴ ἔχειν μέγεθος, μεγάλα δὲ ὥστε ἄπειρα εἶναι.

3

εἰ πολλά ἐστιν, ἀνάγκη τοσαῦτα εἶναι ὅσα ἐστὶ καὶ οὔτε πλείονα αὐτῶν οὔτε ἐλάττονα. εἰ δὲ τοσαῦτά ἐστιν ὅσα ἐστί, πεπερασμένα ἂν εἴη.
εἰ πολλά ἐστιν, ἄπειρα τὰ ὄντα ἐστίν· ἀεὶ γὰρ ἕτερα μεταξὺ τῶν ὄντων ἐστί, καὶ πάλιν ἐκείνων ἕτερα μεταξύ. καὶ οὕτως ἄπειρα τὰ ὄντα ἐστί.

4

τὸ κινούμενον οὔτ' ἐν ᾧ ἔστι τόπῳ κινεῖται οὔτ' ἐν ᾧ μὴ ἔστι.

5(A25-8)

τέτταρες δ' εἰσὶν οἱ λόγοι περὶ κινήσεως Ζήνωνος οἱ παρέχοντες τὰς δυσκολίας τοῖς λύουσιν·

(i) πρῶτος μὲν ὁ περὶ τοῦ μὴ κινεῖσθαι διὰ τὸ πρότερον εἰς τὸ ἥμισυ δεῖν ἀφικέσθαι τὸ φερόμενον ἢ πρὸς τὸ τέλος.

(ii) δεύτερος δ' ὁ καλούμενος Ἀχιλλεύς· ἔστι δ' οὗτος, ὅτι τὸ βραδύτατον οὐδέποτε καταληφθήσεται θέον ὑπὸ τοῦ ταχίστου. ἔμπροσθεν γὰρ ἀναγκαῖον ἐλθεῖν τὸ διῶκον ὅθεν ὥρμησεν τὸ φεῦγον, ὥστε ἀεί τι προέχειν ἀναγκαῖον τὸ βραδύτερον.

(iii) τρίτος δ' ὁ νῦν ῥηθείς, ὅτι ἡ ὀϊστὸς φερομένη ἕστηκεν. (*cf.* εἰ γὰρ αἰεὶ ἠρεμεῖ πᾶν ὅταν ᾖ κατὰ τὸ ἴσον, ἔστιν δ' αἰεὶ τὸ φερόμενον ἐν τῷ νῦν, ἀκίνητον τὴν φερομένην εἶναι ὀϊστόν.)

(iv) τέταρτος δ' ὁ περὶ τῶν ἐν τῷ σταδίῳ κινουμένων ἐξ ἐναντίας ἴσων ὄγκων παρ' ἴσους, τῶν μὲν ἀπὸ τέλους τοῦ σταδίου τῶν δ' ἀπὸ μέσου, ἴσῳ τάχει, ἐν ᾧ συμβαίνειν οἴεται ἴσον εἶναι χρόνον τῷ διπλασίῳ τὸν ἥμισυν.

MELISSUS

1

ἀεὶ ἦν ὅ τι ἦν, καὶ ἀεὶ ἔσται. εἰ γὰρ ἐγένετο, ἀναγκαῖόν ἐστι πρὶν γενέσθαι εἶναι μηδέν· εἰ τοίνυν μηδὲν ἦν, οὐδαμὰ ἂν γένοιτο οὐδὲν ἐκ μηδενός.

2

ὅτε τοίνυν οὐκ ἐγένετο, ἔστι τε καὶ ἀεὶ ἦν καὶ ἀεὶ ἔσται καὶ ἀρχὴν οὐκ ἔχει οὐδὲ τελευτήν, ἀλλ' ἄπειρόν ἐστιν. εἰ μὲν γὰρ ἐγένετο, ἀρχὴν ἂν εἶχεν (ἤρξατο γὰρ ἄν ποτε γενόμενον) καὶ τελευτήν (ἐτελεύτησε γὰρ ἄν ποτε γενόμενον)· ὅτε δὲ μήτε ἤρξατο μήτε ἐτελεύτησεν, ἀεί τε ἦν καὶ ἀεὶ ἔσται <καὶ> οὐκ ἔχει ἀρχὴν οὐδὲ τελευτήν· οὐ γὰρ ἀεὶ εἶναι ἀνυστόν, ὅ τι μὴ πᾶν ἐστι.

3

ἀλλ' ὥσπερ ἐστὶν ἀεί, οὕτω καὶ τὸ μέγεθος ἄπειρον ἀεὶ χρὴ εἶναι.

4

ἀρχήν τε καὶ τέλος ἔχον οὐδὲν οὔτε ἀίδιον οὔτε ἄπειρόν ἐστιν.

5

εἰ μὴ ἓν εἴη, περανεῖ πρὸς ἄλλο.

6

εἰ γὰρ <ἄπειρον> εἴη, ἓν εἴη ἄν· εἰ γὰρ δύο εἴη, οὐκ ἂν δύναιτο ἄπειρα εἶναι, ἀλλ' ἔχοι ἂν πείρατα πρὸς ἄλληλα.

* * *

7

(i) οὕτως οὖν ἀίδιόν ἐστι καὶ ἄπειρον καὶ ἓν καὶ ὅμοιον πᾶν.

(ii) καὶ οὔτ' ἂν ἀπόλοιτο οὔτε μεῖζον γίνοιτο οὔτε μετακοσμέοιτο οὔτε ἀλγεῖ οὔτε ἀνιᾶται· εἰ γάρ τι τούτων πάσχοι, οὐκ ἂν ἔτι ἓν εἴη. εἰ γὰρ ἑτεροιοῦται, ἀνάγκη τὸ ἐὸν μὴ ὁμοῖον εἶναι, ἀλλὰ ἀπόλλυσθαι τὸ πρόσθεν ἐόν, τὸ δὲ οὐκ ἐὸν γίνεσθαι. εἰ τοίνυν τριχὶ μιῇ μυρίοις ἔτεσιν ἑτεροῖον γίνοιτο τὸ πᾶν, ὄλοιτο ἂν ἐν τῷ παντὶ χρόνῳ.

(iii) ἀλλ' οὐδὲ μετακοσμηθῆναι ἀνυστόν· ὁ γὰρ κόσμος ὁ πρόσθεν ἐὼν οὐκ ἀπόλλυται οὔτε ὁ μὴ ἐὼν γίνεται. ὅτε δὲ μήτε προσγίνεται μηδὲν μήτε ἀπόλλυται μήτε ἑτεροιοῦται, πῶς μετακοσμηθὲν τῶν ἐόντων ἤ; εἰ μὲν γάρ τι ἐγίνετο ἑτεροῖον, ἤδη ἂν καὶ μετακοσμηθείη.

(iv) οὐδὲ ἀλγεῖ· οὐ γὰρ ἂν πᾶν εἴη ἀλγέον· οὐ γὰρ ἂν δύναιτο ἀεὶ εἶναι χρῆμα ἀλγέον· οὐδὲ ἔχει ἴσην δύναμιν τῷ ὑγιεῖ· οὐδ' ἂν ὁμοῖον εἴη εἰ ἀλγέοι· ἀπογινομένου γάρ τευ ἂν ἀλγέοι ἢ προσγινομένου, κοὐκ ἂν ἔτι ὁμοῖον εἴη.

(v) οὐδ' ἂν τὸ ὑγιὲς ἀλγῆσαι δύναιτο· ἀπὸ γὰρ ἂν ὄλοιτο τὸ ὑγιὲς καὶ τὸ ἐόν, τὸ δὲ οὐκ ἐὸν γένοιτο.

(vi) καὶ περὶ τοῦ ἀνιᾶσθαι ὡυτὸς λόγος τῷ ἀλγέοντι.

(vii) οὐδὲ κενεόν ἐστιν οὐδέν· τὸ γὰρ κενεὸν οὐδέν ἐστιν· οὐκ ἂν οὖν εἴη τό γε μηδέν.

(viii) οὐδὲ κινεῖται· ὑποχωρῆσαι γὰρ οὐκ ἔχει οὐδαμῇ, ἀλλὰ πλέων ἐστίν. εἰ μὲν γὰρ κενεὸν ἦν, ὑπεχώρει ἂν εἰς τὸ κενόν· κενοῦ δὲ μὴ ἐόντος οὐκ ἔχει ὄκῃ ὑποχωρήσει.

(ix) πυκνὸν δὲ καὶ ἀραιὸν οὐκ ἂν εἴη. τὸ γὰρ ἀραιὸν οὐκ ἀνυστὸν πλέων εἶναι ὁμοίως τῷ πυκνῷ, ἀλλ' ἤδη τὸ ἀραιόν γε κενεώτερον γίνεται τοῦ πυκνοῦ.

(x) κρίσιν δὲ ταύτην χρὴ ποιήσασθαι τοῦ πλέω καὶ τοῦ μὴ πλέω· εἰ μὲν οὖν χωρεῖ τι ἢ εἰσδέχεται, οὐ πλέων· εἰ δὲ μήτε χωρεῖ μήτε εἰσδέχεται, πλέων.

(xi) ἀνάγκη τοίνυν πλέων εἶναι, εἰ κενὸν μὴ ἔστιν. εἰ τοίνυν πλέων ἐστίν, οὐ κινεῖται.

* * *

8

(i) μέγιστον μὲν οὖν σημεῖον οὗτος ὁ λόγος, ὅτι ἓν μόνον ἐστίν· ἀτὰρ καὶ τάδε σημεῖα.

(ii) εἰ γὰρ ἦν πολλά, τοιαῦτα χρὴ αὐτὰ εἶναι, οἷόν περ ἐγώ φημι τὸ ἓν εἶναι. εἰ γάρ ἐστι γῆ καὶ ὕδωρ καὶ ἀὴρ καὶ πῦρ καὶ σίδηρος καὶ χρυσός, καὶ τὸ μὲν ζῶον τὸ δὲ τεθνηκός, καὶ μέλαν καὶ λευκὸν καὶ τὰ ἄλλα, ὅσα φασὶν οἱ ἄνθρωποι εἶναι ἀληθῆ, εἰ δὴ ταῦτά ἐστι, καὶ ἡμεῖς ὀρθῶς ὁρῶμεν καὶ ἀκούομεν, εἶναι χρὴ ἕκαστον τοιοῦτον, οἷόν περ τὸ πρῶτον ἔδοξεν ἡμῖν, καὶ μὴ μεταπίπτειν μηδὲ γίνεσθαι ἑτεροῖον, ἀλλὰ ἀεὶ εἶναι ἕκαστον, οἷόν πέρ ἐστιν.

(iii) νῦν δέ φαμεν ὀρθῶς ὁρᾶν καὶ ἀκούειν καὶ συνιέναι. δοκεῖ δὲ ἡμῖν τό τε θερμὸν ψυχρὸν γίνεσθαι καὶ τὸ ψυχρὸν θερμὸν καὶ τὸ σκληρὸν μαλθακὸν καὶ τὸ μαλθακὸν σκληρὸν καὶ τὸ ζῶον ἀποθνῄσκειν καὶ ἐκ μὴ ζῶντος γίνεσθαι, καὶ ταῦτα πάντα ἑτεροιοῦσθαι, καὶ ὅ τι ἦν τε καὶ ὃ νῦν οὐδὲν ὁμοῖον εἶναι, ἀλλ' ὅ τε σίδηρος σκληρὸς ἐὼν τῷ δακτύλῳ κατατρίβεσθαι ὁμουρέων, καὶ χρυσὸς καὶ λίθος καὶ ἄλλο ὅ τι ἰσχυρὸν δοκεῖ εἶναι πᾶν, ἐξ ὕδατός τε γῆ καὶ λίθος γίνεσθαι. [ὥστε συμβαίνει μήτε ὁρᾶν μήτε τὰ ὄντα γινώσκειν.]

(iv) οὐ τοίνυν ταῦτα ἀλλήλοις ὁμολογεῖ. φαμένοις γὰρ εἶναι πολλὰ καὶ ἀίδια καὶ εἴδη τε καὶ ἰσχὺν ἔχοντα, πάντα ἑτεροιοῦσθαι ἡμῖν δοκεῖ καὶ μεταπίπτειν ἐκ τοῦ ἑκάστοτε ὁρωμένου.

(v) δῆλον τοίνυν, ὅτι οὐκ ὀρθῶς ἑωρῶμεν οὐδὲ ἐκεῖνα πολλὰ ὀρθῶς δοκεῖ εἶναι· οὐ γὰρ ἂν μετέπιπτεν, εἰ ἀληθῆ ἦν, ἀλλ' ἦν οἷόν περ ἐδόκει ἕκαστον τοιοῦτον. τοῦ γὰρ ἐόντος ἀληθινοῦ κρεῖσσον οὐδέν.

(vi) ἢν δὲ μεταπέσῃ, τὸ μὲν ἐὸν ἀπώλετο, τὸ δὲ οὐκ ἐὸν γέγονεν. οὕτως οὖν, εἰ πολλὰ εἴη, τοιαῦτα χρὴ εἶναι, οἷόν περ τὸ ἕν.

9

εἰ μὲν οὖν εἴη, δεῖ αὐτὸ ἓν εἶναι· ἓν δ' ἐὸν δεῖ αὐτὸ σῶμα μὴ ἔχειν. εἰ δὲ ἔχοι πάχος, ἔχοι ἂν μόρια, καὶ οὐκέτι ἓν εἴη.

10

εἰ διῄρηται τὸ ἐόν, κινεῖται· κινούμενον δὲ οὐκ ἂν εἴη.

EMPEDOCLES

1(6)

τέσσαρα γὰρ πάντων ῥιζώματα πρῶτον ἄκουε·
Ζεὺς ἀργὴς Ἥρη τε φερέσβιος ἠδ' Ἀϊδωνεύς
Νῆστίς θ' ἣ δακρύοις τέγγει κρούνωμα βρότειον.

2(17)

δίπλ' ἐρέω· τοτὲ μὲν γὰρ ἓν ηὐξήθη μόνον εἶναι
ἐκ πλεόνων, τοτὲ δ' αὖ διέφυ πλέον' ἐξ ἑνὸς εἶναι.
δοιὴ δὲ θνητῶν γένεσις, δοιὴ δ' ἀπόλειψις.
τὴν μὲν γὰρ πάντων σύνοδος τίκτει τ' ὀλέκει τε,
ἡ δὲ πάλιν διαφυομένων θρεφθεῖσα διέπτη.
καὶ ταῦτ' ἀλλάσσοντα διαμπερὲς οὐδαμὰ λήγει,
ἄλλοτε μὲν φιλότητι συνερχόμεν' εἰς ἓν ἅπαντα,
ἄλλοτε δ' αὖ δίχ' ἕκαστα φορεύμενα νείκεος ἔχθει.
<οὕτως ᾗ μὲν ἓν ἐκ πλεόνων μεμάθηκε φύεσθαι>
ἠδὲ πάλιν διαφύντος ἑνὸς πλέον' ἐκτελέθουσι,
τῇ μὲν γίγνονταί τε καὶ οὔ σφισιν ἔμπεδος αἰών·
ᾗ δὲ διαλλάσσοντα διαμπερὲς οὐδαμὰ λήγει,
ταύτῃ δ' αἰὲν ἔασιν ἀκίνητοι κατὰ κύκλον.
ἀλλ' ἄγε μύθων κλῦθι, μάθη γάρ τοι φρένας αὔξει·
ὡς γὰρ καὶ πρὶν ἔειπα πιφαύσκων πείρατα μύθων
δίπλ' ἐρέω· τοτὲ μὲν γὰρ ἓν ηὐξήθη μόνον εἶναι
ἐκ πλέονων, τοτὲ δ' αὖ διέφυ πλέον' ἐξ ἑνὸς εἶναι,
πῦρ καὶ ὕδωρ καὶ γαῖα καὶ ἠέρος ἄπλετον ὕψος·
νεῖκός τ' οὐλόμενον δίχα τῶν, ἀτάλαντον ἁπάντῃ,
καὶ φιλότης ἐν τοῖσιν, ἴση μῆκός τε πλάτος τε·

τὴν σὺ νόῳ δέρκευ, μηδ' ὄμμασιν ἧσο τεθηπώς·
ἥτις καὶ θνητοῖσι νομίζεται ἔμφυτος ἄρθροις,
τῇ τε φίλα φρονέουσι καὶ ἄρθμια ἔργα τελοῦσι,
Γηθοσύνην καλέοντες ἐπώνυμον ἠδ' 'Αφροδίτην·
τὴν οὔ τις μετὰ τοῖσιν ἑλισσομένην δεδάηκε
θνητὸς ἀνήρ· σὺ δ' ἄκουε λόγου στόλον οὐκ ἀπατηλόν.
ταῦτα γὰρ ἶσά τε πάντα καὶ ἥλικα γένναν ἔασι,
τιμῆς δ' ἄλλης ἄλλο μέδει, πάρα δ' ἦθος ἑκάστῳ,
ἐν δὲ μέρει κρατέουσι περιπλομένοιο χρόνοιο.
καὶ πρὸς τοῖς οὐδ' †ἄρ τι† ἐπιγίγνεται οὐδ' ἀπολήγει·
εἴτε γὰρ ἐφθείροντο διαμπερές, οὐκέτ' ἂν ἦσαν.
τοῦτο δ' ἀπαυξήσειε τὸ πᾶν τί κε, καὶ πόθεν ἐλθόν;
πῇ δέ κε κήξαπόλοιτο, ἐπεὶ τῶνδ' οὐδὲν ἐρῆμον;
ἀλλ' αὔτ' ἔστιν ταῦτα, δι' ἀλλήλων δὲ θέοντα
γίγνεται ἄλλοτε ἄλλα καὶ ἠνεκὲς αἰὲν ὁμοῖα.

3(8)

ἄλλο δέ τοι ἐρέω· φύσις οὐδενός ἐστιν ἁπάντων
θνητῶν, οὐδέ τις οὐλομένου θανάτοιο τελευτή,
ἀλλὰ μόνον μίξις τε διάλλαξίς τε μιγέντων
ἔστι, φύσις δ' ἐπὶ τοῖς ὀνομάζεται ἀνθρώποισιν.

* * *

4(29/28)

οὐ γὰρ ἀπὸ νώτοιο δύο κλάδοι ἀίσσονται,
οὐ πόδες, οὐ θοὰ γοῦν', οὐ μήδεα γεννήεντα,
ἀλλ' ὅ γε πάντοθεν ἶσος <ἐοῖ> καὶ πάμπαν ἀπείρων,
σφαῖρος κυκλοτερὴς μονίῃ περιηγέι γαίων.

5(30)

αὐτὰρ ἐπεὶ μέγα νεῖκος ἐνὶ μελέεσσιν ἐθρέφθη
εἰς τιμάς τ' ἀνόρουσε τελειομένοιο χρόνοιο,
ὅς σφιν ἀμοιβαῖος πλατέος παρ' ἐλήλαται ὅρκου

6(31)

πάντα γὰρ ἑξείης πελεμίζετο γυῖα θεοῖο.

7(22)

ἄρθμια μὲν γὰρ ταῦτα ἑαυτῶν πάντα μέρεσσιν,
ἠλέκτωρ τε χθών τε καὶ οὐρανὸς ἠδὲ θάλασσα,
ὅσσα φιν ἐν θνητοῖσιν ἀποπλαχθέντα πέφυκεν.

* * *

8(35)

αὐτὰρ ἐγὼ παλίνορσος ἐλεύσομαι ἐς πόρον ὕμνων,
τὸν πρότερον κατέλεξα, λόγου λόγον ἐξοχετεύων
κεῖνον· ἐπεὶ νεῖκος μὲν ἐνέρτατον ἵκετο βένθος
δίνης, ἐν δὲ μέσῃ φιλότης στροφάλιγγι γένηται,
ἐν τῇ δὴ τάδε πάντα συνέρχεται ἓν μόνον εἶναι,
οὐκ ἄφαρ, ἀλλὰ θελημὰ συνιστάμεν' ἄλλοθεν ἄλλα.
τῶν δέ τε μισγομένων χεῖτ' ἔθνεα μυρία θνητῶν·
πολλὰ δ' ἄμικτ' ἕστηκε κεραιομένοισιν ἐναλλάξ,
ὅσσ' ἔτι νεῖκος ἔρυκε μετάρσιον· οὐ γὰρ ἀμεμφέως
πῶ πᾶν ἐξέστηκεν ἐπ' ἔσχατα τέρματα κύκλου,
ἀλλὰ τὰ μέν τ' ἐνέμιμνε μελέων τὰ δέ τ' ἐξεβεβήκει.
ὅσσον δ' αἰὲν ὑπεκπροθέοι, τόσον αἰὲν ἐπῄει
ἠπιόφρων φιλότητος ἀμεμφέος ἄμβροτος ὁρμή·
αἶψα δὲ θνήτ' ἐφύοντο, τὰ πρὶν μάθον ἀθάνατ' εἶναι,

ζωρά τε πρὶν κέκρητο, διαλλάξαντα κελεύθους.
τῶν δέ τε μισγομένων χεῖτ' ἔθνεα μυρία θνητῶν,
παντοίαις ἰδέῃσιν ἀρηρότα, θαῦμα ἰδέσθαι.

* * *

9(96)

ἡ δὲ χθὼν ἐπίηρος ἐν εὐστέρνοις χοάνοισι
τὼ δύο τῶν ὀκτὼ μερέων λάχε Νήστιδος αἴγλης,
τέσσαρα δ' Ἡφαίστοιο· τὰ δ' ὀστέα λεύκα γένοντο,
ἁρμονίης κόλλῃσιν ἀρηρότα θεσπεσίηθεν.

10(57)

ᾗ πολλαὶ μὲν κόρσαι ἀναύχενες ἐβλάστησαν,
γυμνοὶ δ' ἐπλάζοντο βραχίονες εὔνιδες ὤμων,
ὄμματά τ' οἶ' ἐπλανᾶτο πενητεύοντα μετώπων.

11(59)

αὐτὰρ ἐπεὶ κατὰ μεῖζον ἐμίσγετο δαίμονι δαίμων,
ταῦτά τε συμπίπτεσκον ὅπῃ συνέκυρσεν ἕκαστα,
ἄλλα τε πρὸς τοῖς πολλὰ διηνεκῆ ἐξεγένοντο.

* * *

12(62)

νῦν δ' ἄγ', ὅπως ἀνδρῶν τε πολυκλαύτων τε γυναικῶν
ἐννυχίους ὄρπηκας ἀνήγαγε κρινόμενον πῦρ,
τῶνδε κλύ'· οὐ γὰρ μῦθος ἀπόσκοπος οὐδ' ἀδαήμων.
οὐλοφυεῖς μὲν πρῶτα τύποι χθονὸς ἐξανέτελλον,
ἀμφοτέρων ὕδατός τε καὶ εἴδεος αἶσαν ἔχοντες·
τοὺς μὲν πῦρ ἀνέπεμπε θέλον πρὸς ὁμοῖον ἱκέσθαι,

οὔτε τί πω μελέων ἐρατὸν δέμας ἐμφαίνοντας,
οὔτ' ἐνοπὴν οὔτ' αὖ ἐπιχώριον ἀνδράσι γυῖον.

* * *

13(109)

γαίῃ μὲν γὰρ γαῖαν ὀπώπαμεν, ὕδατι δ' ὕδωρ,
αἰθέρι δ' αἰθέρα δῖον, ἀτὰρ πυρὶ πῦρ ἀίδηλον,
στοργὴν δὲ στοργῇ, νεῖκος δέ τε νείκεϊ λυγρῷ.

14(108)

ὅσσον <δ'> ἀλλοῖοι μετέφυν, τόσον ἄρ σφισιν αἰεὶ
καὶ τὸ φρονεῖν ἀλλοῖα παρίσταται.

15(105)

αἵματος ἐν πελάγεσσι τεθραμμένη ἀντιθορόντος,
τῇ τε νόημα μάλιστα κικλήσκεται ἀνθρώποισιν·
αἷμα γὰρ ἀνθρώποις περικάρδιόν ἐστι νόημα.

* * *

16(133)

οὐκ ἔστιν πελάσασθαι ἐν ὀφθαλμοῖσιν ἐφικτὸν
ἡμετέροις ἢ χερσὶ λαβεῖν, ᾗπέρ τε μεγίστη
πειθοῦς ἀνθρώποισιν ἀμαξιτὸς εἰς φρένα πίπτει.

17(134)

οὔτε γὰρ ἀνδρομέῃ κεφαλῇ κατὰ γυῖα κέκασται,
οὐ πόδες, οὐ θοὰ γοῦν', οὐ μήδεα λαχνήεντα,
ἀλλὰ φρὴν ἱερὴ καὶ ἀθέσφατος ἔπλετο μοῦνον,
φροντίσι κόσμον ἅπαντα καταΐσσουσα θοῇσιν.

* * *

18(110)

εἰ γάρ κεν σφ' ἀδινῇσιν ὑπὸ πραπίδεσσιν ἐρείσας
εὐμενέως καθαρῇσιν ἐποπτεύσῃς μελέτῃσιν,
ταῦτά τέ σοι μάλα πάντα δι' αἰῶνος παρέσονται,
ἄλλα τε πόλλ' ἀπὸ τῶνδε κτήσεαι· αὐτὰ γὰρ αὔξει
ταῦτ' εἰς ἦθος ἕκαστον, ὅπῃ φύσις ἐστὶν ἑκάστῳ.
εἰ δὲ σύ γ' ἀλλοίων ἐπορέξεαι, οἷα κατ' ἄνδρας
μυρία δειλὰ πέλονται ἅ τ' ἀμβλύνουσι μερίμνας,
ἦ σ' ἄφαρ ἐκλείψουσι περιπλομένοιο χρόνοιο
σφῶν αὐτῶν ποθέοντα φίλην ἐπὶ γένναν ἱκέσθαι·
πάντα γὰρ ἴσθι φρόνησιν ἔχειν καὶ νώματος αἶσαν.

* * *

19(115)

ἔστιν ἀνάγκης χρῆμα, θεῶν ψήφισμα παλαιόν,
ἀίδιον, πλατέεσσι κατεσφρηγισμένον ὅρκοις·
εὖτέ τις ἀμπλακίῃσι φόβῳ φίλα γυῖα μιήνῃ
†ὃς καὶ† ἐπίορκον ἁμαρτήσας ἐπομόσσῃ,
δαίμονες οἵτε μακραίωνος λελάχασι βίοιο,
τρίς μιν μυρίας ὧρας ἀπὸ μακάρων ἀλάλησθαι,
φυόμενον παντοῖα διὰ χρόνου εἴδεα θνητῶν
ἀργαλέας βιότοιο μεταλλάσσοντα κελεύθους.
αἰθέριον μὲν γάρ σφε μένος πόντονδε διώκει,
πόντος δ' ἐς χθονὸς οὖδας ἀπέπτυσε, γαῖα δ' ἐς αὐγὰς
ἠελίου φαέθοντος, ὁ δ' αἰθέρος ἔμβαλε δίναις·
ἄλλος δ' ἐξ ἄλλου δέχεται, στυγέουσι δὲ πάντες.

τῶν καὶ ἐγὼ νῦν εἰμί, φυγὰς θεόθεν καὶ ἀλήτης,

νείκεϊ μαινομένῳ πίσυνος.

20(117)

ἤδη γάρ ποτ' ἐγὼ γενόμην κοῦρός τε κόρη τε

θάμνος τ' οἰωνός τε καὶ ἔξαλος ἔλλοπος ἰχθύς.

* * *

21(127)

ἐν θήρεσσι λέοντες ὀρειλεχέες χαμαιεῦναι

γίγνονται, δάφναι δ' ἐνὶ δένδρεσιν ἠυκόμοισιν.

22(146)

εἰς δὲ τέλος μάντεις τε καὶ ὑμνόπολοι καὶ ἰητροί

καὶ πρόμοι ἀνθρώποισιν ἐπιχθονίοισι πέλονται·

ἔνθεν ἀναβλαστοῦσι θεοὶ τιμῇσι φέριστοι.

ANAXAGORAS

1

ὁμοῦ πάντα χρήματα ἦν, ἄπειρα καὶ πλῆθος καὶ σμικρότητα· καὶ γὰρ τὸ σμικρὸν ἄπειρον ἦν. καὶ πάντων ὁμοῦ ἐόντων οὐδὲν ἔνδηλον ἦν ὑπὸ σμικρότητος· πάντα γὰρ ἀήρ τε καὶ αἰθὴρ κατεῖχεν, ἀμφότερα ἄπειρα ἐόντα. [ταῦτα γὰρ μέγιστα ἔνεστιν ἐν τοῖς σύμπασι καὶ πλήθει καὶ μεγέθει.]

2

καὶ γὰρ ἀήρ τε καὶ αἰθὴρ ἀποκρίνονται ἀπὸ τοῦ πολλοῦ τοῦ περιέχοντος, καὶ τό γε περιέχον ἄπειρόν ἐστι τὸ πλῆθος.

3

οὔτε γὰρ τοῦ σμικροῦ ἐστι τό γε ἐλάχιστον, ἀλλ' ἔλασσον ἀεί (τὸ γὰρ ἐὸν οὐκ ἔστι τὸ μὴ οὐκ εἶναι)· ἀλλὰ καὶ τοῦ μεγάλου ἀεί ἐστι μεῖζον, καὶ ἴσον ἐστι τῷ σμικρῷ πλῆθος· πρὸς ἑαυτὸ δὲ ἕκαστόν ἐστι καὶ μέγα καὶ σμικρόν.

4

(i) τούτων δὲ οὕτως ἐχόντων, χρὴ δοκεῖν ἐνεῖναι πολλά τε καὶ παντοῖα ἐν πᾶσι τοῖς συγκρινομένοις καὶ σπέρματα πάντων χρημάτων καὶ ἰδέας παντοίας ἔχοντα καὶ χροιὰς καὶ ἡδονάς.

(ii) καὶ ἀνθρώπους τε συμπαγῆναι καὶ τὰ ἄλλα ζῷα ὅσα ψυχὴν ἔχει. καὶ τοῖς γε ἀνθρώποισιν εἶναι καὶ πόλεις συνῳκημένας καὶ ἔργα κατεσκευασμένα, ὥσπερ παρ' ἡμῖν, καὶ ἠέλιόν τε αὐτοῖσιν εἶναι καὶ σελήνην καὶ τὰ ἄλλα, ὥσπερ παρ' ἡμῖν, καὶ τὴν γῆν αὐτοῖσι φύειν πολλά τε καὶ παντοῖα, ὧν ἐκεῖνοι τὰ ὀνήιστα συνενεγκάμενοι εἰς τὴν οἴκησιν χρῶνται. ταῦτα μὲν οὖν μοι λέλεκται περὶ τῆς ἀποκρίσιος, ὅτι οὐκ ἂν παρ' ἡμῖν μόνον ἀποκριθείη, ἀλλὰ καὶ ἄλλῃ.

(iii) πρὶν δὲ ἀποκριθῆναι [ταῦτα] πάντων ὁμοῦ ἐόντων οὐδὲ χροιὴ ἔνδηλος ἦν οὐδεμία· ἀπεκώλυε γὰρ ἡ σύμμιξις πάντων χρημάτων, τοῦ τε διεροῦ καὶ τοῦ ξηροῦ καὶ τοῦ θερμοῦ καὶ τοῦ ψυχροῦ καὶ τοῦ λαμπροῦ καὶ τοῦ ζοφεροῦ, καὶ γῆς πολλῆς ἐνεούσης καὶ σπερμάτων ἀπείρων πλῆθος, οὐδὲν ἐοικότων ἀλλήλοις. οὐδὲ γὰρ τῶν ἄλλων οὐδὲν ἔοικε τὸ ἕτερον τῷ ἑτέρῳ.

(iv) τούτων δὲ οὕτως ἐχόντων ἐν τῷ σύμπαντι χρὴ δοκεῖν ἐνεῖναι πάντα χρήματα.

* * *

5

τούτων δὲ οὕτω διακεκριμένων, γινώσκειν χρὴ ὅτι πάντα οὐδὲν ἐλάσσω ἐστὶν οὐδὲ πλείω (οὐ γὰρ ἀνυστὸν πάντων πλείω εἶναι), ἀλλὰ πάντα ἴσα ἀεί.

6

καὶ ὅτε δὲ ἴσαι μοῖραί εἰσι τοῦ τε μεγάλου καὶ τοῦ σμικροῦ πλῆθος, καὶ οὕτως ἂν εἴη ἐν παντὶ πάντα· οὐδὲ χωρὶς ἔστιν εἶναι, ἀλλὰ πάντα παντὸς μοῖραν μετέχει. ὅτε τοὐλάχιστον μὴ ἔστιν εἶναι, οὐκ ἂν δύναιτο χωρισθῆναι, οὐδ' ἂν ἐφ' ἑαυτοῦ γενέσθαι, ἀλλ' ὅπωσπερ ἀρχὴν εἶναι καὶ νῦν πάντα ὁμοῦ. ἐν πᾶσι δὲ πολλὰ ἔνεστι καὶ τῶν ἀποκρινομένων ἴσα πλῆθος ἐν τοῖς μείζοσί τε καὶ ἐλάσσοσι.

7(8)

οὐ κεχώρισται ἀλλήλων τὰ ἐν τῷ ἑνὶ κόσμῳ οὐδὲ ἀποκέκοπται πελέκει οὔτε τὸ θερμὸν ἀπὸ τοῦ ψυχροῦ οὔτε τὸ ψυχρὸν ἀπὸ τοῦ θερμοῦ.

8(10)

πῶς γὰρ ἂν ἐκ μὴ τριχὸς γένοιτο θρὶξ καὶ σὰρξ ἐκ μὴ σαρκός;

* * *

9(11)

ἐν παντὶ παντὸς μοῖρα ἔνεστι πλὴν νοῦ, ἔστιν οἷσι δὲ καὶ νοῦς ἔνι.

10(12)

(i) τὰ μὲν ἄλλα παντὸς μοῖραν μετέχει, νοῦς δέ ἐστιν ἄπειρον καὶ αὐτοκρατὲς καὶ μέμεικται οὐδενὶ χρήματι, ἀλλὰ μόνος αὐτὸς ἐπ' ἑωυτοῦ ἐστιν. εἰ μὴ γὰρ ἐφ' ἑαυτοῦ ἦν, ἀλλά τεῳ ἐμέμεικτο ἄλλῳ, μετεῖχεν ἂν ἁπάντων χρημάτων, εἰ ἐμέμεικτό τεῳ· ἐν παντὶ γὰρ παντὸς μοῖρα ἔνεστιν, ὥσπερ ἐν τοῖς πρόσθεν μοι λέλεκται· καὶ ἂν ἐκώλυεν αὐτὸν τὰ συμμεμειγμένα, ὥστε μηδενὸς χρήματος κρατεῖν ὁμοίως ὡς καὶ μόνον ἐόντα ἐφ' ἑαυτοῦ.

(ii) ἔστι γὰρ λεπτότατόν τε πάντων χρημάτων καὶ καθαρώτατον, καὶ γνώμην γε περὶ παντὸς πᾶσαν ἴσχει καὶ ἰσχύει μέγιστον· καὶ ὅσα γε ψυχὴν ἔχει καὶ τὰ μείζω καὶ τὰ ἐλάσσω, πάντων νοῦς κρατεῖ.

(iii) καὶ τῆς περιχωρήσιος τῆς συμπάσης νοῦς ἐκράτησεν, ὥστε περιχωρῆσαι τὴν ἀρχήν. καὶ πρῶτον ἀπό του σμικροῦ ἤρξατο περιχωρεῖν, ἐπὶ δὲ πλέον περιχωρεῖ, καὶ περιχωρήσει ἐπὶ πλέον.

(iv) καὶ τὰ συμμισγόμενά τε καὶ ἀποκρινόμενα καὶ διακρινόμενα πάντα ἔγνω νοῦς. καὶ ὁποῖα ἔμελλεν ἔσεσθαι καὶ ὁποῖα ἦν, ἅσσα νῦν μὴ ἔστι, καὶ ὅσα νῦν ἔστι καὶ ὁποῖα ἔσται, πάντα διεκόσμησε νοῦς, καὶ τὴν περιχώρησιν ταύτην, ἣν νῦν περιχωρέει τά τε ἄστρα καὶ ὁ ἥλιος καὶ ἡ σελήνη καὶ ὁ ἀὴρ καὶ ὁ αἰθὴρ οἱ ἀποκρινόμενοι. ἡ δὲ περιχώρησις αὐτὴ ἐποίησεν ἀποκρίνεσθαι.

(v) καὶ ἀποκρίνεται ἀπό τε τοῦ ἀραιοῦ τὸ πυκνὸν καὶ ἀπὸ τοῦ ψυχροῦ τὸ θερμὸν καὶ ἀπὸ τοῦ ζοφεροῦ τὸ λαμπρὸν καὶ ἀπὸ τοῦ διεροῦ τὸ ξηρόν.

(vi) μοῖραι δὲ πολλαὶ πολλῶν εἰσι. παντάπασι δὲ οὐδὲν ἀποκρίνεται οὐδὲ διακρίνεται ἕτερον ἀπὸ τοῦ ἑτέρου πλὴν νοῦ. νοῦς δὲ πᾶς ὅμοιός ἐστι καὶ ὁ μείζων καὶ ὁ ἐλάσσων. ἕτερον δὲ οὐδέν ἐστιν ὅμοιον [οὐδενί], ἀλλ' ὅτων πλεῖστα ἔνι, ταῦτα ἐνδηλότατα ἓν ἕκαστόν ἐστι καὶ ἦν.

* * *

11(13)

καὶ ἐπεὶ ἤρξατο ὁ νοῦς κινεῖν, ἀπὸ τοῦ κινουμένου παντὸς

ἀπεκρίνετο, καὶ ὅσον ἐκίνησεν ὁ νοῦς, πᾶν τοῦτο διεκρίθη· κινουμένων δὲ καὶ διακρινομένων ἡ περιχώρησις πολλῷ μᾶλλον ἐποίει διακρίνεσθαι.

12(14)

ὁ δὲ νοῦς, †ὅσα ἐστί τε κάρτα†, καὶ νῦν ἐστιν ἵνα καὶ τὰ ἄλλα πάντα, ἐν τῷ πολλῷ περιέχοντι καὶ ἐν τοῖς προσκριθεῖσι καὶ ἐν τοῖς ἀποκεκριμένοις.

13(15)

τὸ μὲν πυκνὸν καὶ διερὸν καὶ ψυχρὸν καὶ τὸ ζοφερὸν ἐνθάδε συνεχώρησεν, ἔνθα νῦν <ἡ γῆ>, τὸ δὲ ἀραιὸν καὶ τὸ θερμὸν καὶ τὸ ξηρὸν ἐξεχώρησεν εἰς τὸ πρόσω τοῦ αἰθέρος.

14(9)

οὕτω τούτων περιχωρούντων τε καὶ ἀποκρινομένων ὑπὸ βίης τε καὶ ταχυτῆτος – βίην δὲ ἡ ταχυτὴς ποιεῖ – ἡ [δὲ] ταχυτὴς αὐτῶν οὐδενὶ ἔοικε χρήματι τὴν ταχυτῆτα τῶν νῦν ἐόντων χρημάτων ἐν ἀνθρώποις, ἀλλὰ πάντως πολλαπλασίως ταχύ ἐστι.

15(16)

ἀπὸ τουτέων ἀποκρινομένων συμπήγνυται γῆ· ἐκ μὲν γὰρ τῶν νεφελῶν ὕδωρ ἀποκρίνεται, ἐκ δὲ τοῦ ὕδατος γῆ, ἐκ δὲ τῆς γῆς λίθοι συμπήγνυνται ὑπὸ τοῦ ψυχροῦ, οὗτοι δὲ ἐκχωρέουσι μᾶλλον τοῦ ὕδατος.

16(18)

ἥλιος ἐντίθησι τῇ σελήνῃ τὸ λαμπρόν.

17(19)

Ἶριν δὲ καλέομεν τὸ ἐν τῇσιν νεφέλῃσιν ἀντιλάμπον τῷ ἡλίῳ.

* * *

18(21)

ὑπ᾽ ἀφαυρότητος αὐτῶν οὐ δυνατοί ἐσμεν κρίνειν τἀληθές.

19(17)

τὸ δὲ γίνεσθαι καὶ ἀπόλλυσθαι οὐκ ὀρθῶς νομίζουσιν οἱ Ἕλληνες· οὐδὲν γὰρ χρῆμα γίνεται οὐδὲ ἀπόλλυται, ἀλλ᾽ ἀπὸ ἐόντων χρημάτων συμμίσγεταί τε καὶ διακρίνεται. καὶ οὕτως ἂν ὀρθῶς καλοῖεν τό τε γίνεσθαι συμμίσγεσθαι καὶ τὸ ἀπόλλυσθαι διακρίνεσθαι.

20(21a)

ὄψις τῶν ἀδήλων τὰ φαινόμενα.

LEUCIPPUS

1(2)

οὐδὲν χρῆμα μάτην γίνεται, ἀλλὰ πάντα ἐκ λόγου τε καὶ ὑπ' ἀνάγκης.

2(A7)

Λεύκιππος δ' ἔχειν ᾠήθη λόγους οἵτινες πρὸς τὴν αἴσθησιν ὁμολογούμενα λέγοντες οὐκ ἀναιρήσουσιν οὔτε γένεσιν οὔτε φθορὰν οὔτε κίνησιν καὶ τὸ πλῆθος τῶν ὄντων. ὁμολογήσας δὲ ταῦτα μὲν τοῖς φαινομένοις, τοῖς δὲ τὸ ἓν κατασκευάζουσιν ὡς οὐκ ἂν κίνησιν οὖσαν ἄνευ κενοῦ, τό τε κενὸν μὴ ὂν καὶ τοῦ ὄντος οὐθὲν μὴ ὄν φησιν εἶναι· τὸ γὰρ κυρίως ὂν παμπλῆρες ὄν. ἀλλ' εἶναι τὸ τοιοῦτον οὐχ ἕν, ἀλλ' ἄπειρα τὸ πλῆθος καὶ ἀόρατα διὰ σμικρότητα τῶν ὄγκων. ταῦτα δ' ἐν τῷ κενῷ φέρεσθαι (κενὸν γὰρ εἶναι), καὶ συνιστάμενα μὲν γένεσιν ποιεῖν, διαλυόμενα δὲ φθοράν.

DEMOCRITUS

1(6)

γιγνώσκειν τε χρὴ ἄνθρωπον τῷδε τῷ κανόνι, ὅτι ἐτεῆς ἀπήλλακται.

2(7)

δηλοῖ μὲν δὴ καὶ οὗτος ὁ λόγος, ὅτι ἐτεῇ οὐδὲν ἴσμεν περὶ οὐδενός, ἀλλ' ἐπιρυσμίη ἑκάστοισιν ἡ δόξις.

3(11)

γνώμης δὲ δύο εἰσὶν ἰδέαι, ἡ μὲν γνησίη, ἡ δὲ σκοτίη· καὶ σκοτίης μὲν τάδε σύμπαντα, ὄψις, ἀκοή, ὀδμή, γεῦσις, ψαῦσις. ἡ δὲ γνησίη, ἀποκεκριμένη δὲ ταύτης.

4(117)

ἐτεῇ δὲ οὐδὲν ἴδμεν· ἐν βυθῷ γὰρ ἡ ἀλήθεια.

5(9)

νόμῳ χροιή, νόμῳ γλυκύ, νόμῳ πικρόν, ἐτεῇ δ' ἄτομα καὶ κενόν.

6(9)

ἡμεῖς δὲ τῷ μὲν ἐόντι οὐδὲν ἀτρεκὲς συνίεμεν, μεταπῖπτον δὲ κατά τε σώματος διαθήκην καὶ τῶν ἐπεισιόντων καὶ τῶν ἀντιστηριζόντων.

7(125)

(ἐποίησε τὰς αἰσθήσεις λεγούσας πρὸς τὴν διάνοιαν οὕτως·) 'τάλαινα φρήν, παρ' ἡμέων λαβοῦσα τὰς πίστεις ἡμέας καταβάλλεις; πτῶμά τοι τὸ κατάβλημα'.

* * *

8(156)

μὴ μᾶλλον τὸ δὲν ἢ τὸ μηδὲν εἶναι.

9(A37)

Δημόκριτος ἡγεῖται τὴν τῶν ἀιδίων φύσιν εἶναι μικρὰς οὐσίας πλῆθος ἀπείρους· ταύταις δὲ τόπον ἄλλον ὑποτίθησιν ἄπειρον τῷ μεγέθει. προσαγορεύει δὲ τὸν μὲν τόπον τοῖσδε τοῖς ὀνόμασι τῷ τε κενῷ καὶ τῷ οὐδενὶ καὶ τῷ ἀπείρῳ, τῶν δὲ οὐσιῶν ἑκάστην τῷ τε δενὶ καὶ τῷ ναστῷ καὶ τῷ ὄντι.

νομίζει δὲ εἶναι οὕτω μικρὰς τὰς οὐσίας, ὥστε ἐκφυγεῖν τὰς ἡμετέρας αἰσθήσεις. ὑπάρχειν δὲ αὐταῖς παντοίας μορφὰς καὶ σχήματα παντοῖα καὶ κατὰ μέγεθος διαφοράς. ἐκ τούτων οὖν ἤδη καθάπερ ἐκ στοιχείων γεννᾷ καὶ συγκρίνει τοὺς ὀφθαλμοφανεῖς καὶ τοὺς αἰσθητοὺς ὄγκους.

10(167)

δῖνον ἀπὸ τοῦ παντὸς ἀποκριθῆναι παντοίων ἰδεῶν.

11(164)

καὶ γὰρ ζῷα ὁμογενέσι ζῴοις συναγελάζεται ὡς περιστεραὶ περιστεραῖς καὶ γέρανοι γεράνοις καὶ ἐπὶ τῶν ἄλλων ἀλόγων ὡσαύτως. ὣς δὲ καὶ ἐπὶ τῶν ἀψύχων, καθάπερ ὁρᾶν πάρεστιν ἐπί τε τῶν κοσκινευομένων σπερμάτων καὶ ἐπὶ τῶν παρὰ ταῖς κυματωγαῖς ψηφίδων· ὅπου μὲν γὰρ κατὰ τὸν τοῦ κοσκίνου δῖνον διακριτικῶς φακοὶ μετὰ φακῶν τάσσονται καὶ κριθαὶ μετὰ κριθῶν καὶ πυροὶ μετὰ πυρῶν, ὅπου δὲ κατὰ τὴν τοῦ κύματος κίνησιν αἱ μὲν ἐπιμήκεις ψηφῖδες εἰς τὸν αὐτὸν τόπον ταῖς ἐπιμήκεσιν ὠθοῦνται, αἱ δὲ περιφερεῖς ταῖς περιφερέσιν ὡς ἂν συναγωγόν τι ἐχούσης τῶν πραγμάτων τῆς ἐν τούτοις ὁμοιότητος.

* * *

12(166)

Δημόκριτος δὲ εἴδωλά τινά φησιν ἐμπελάζειν τοῖς ἀνθρώποις καὶ τούτων τὰ μὲν εἶναι ἀγαθοποιὰ τὰ δὲ κακοποιά· ἔνθεν καὶ εὔχετο εὐλόγχων τυχεῖν εἰδώλων.

13(67A29)

εἴδωλα γάρ τινα ὁμοιόμορφα ἀπὸ τῶν ὁρωμένων συνεχῶς ἀπορρέοντα καὶ ἐμπίπτοντα τῇ ὄψει τοῦ ὁρᾶν ᾐτιῶντο.

τοιοῦτοι δὲ ἦσαν οἵ τε περὶ Λεύκιππον καὶ Δημόκριτον, οἳ καὶ ἐκ τῆς τῶν ἀορατῶν διὰ μικρότητα παραθέσεως τὴν τῶν μεταξὺ χρωμάτων φαντασίαν ἐποίουν.

14(A122)

(Δημόκριτος οἰόμενος) εἰ γένοιτο κενὸν τὸ μεταξύ, ὁρᾶσθαι ἂν ἀκριβῶς, εἰ μύρμηξ ἐν τῷ οὐρανῷ εἴη.

* * *

15(155)

εἰ κῶνος τέμνοιτο παρὰ τὴν βάσιν ἐπιπέδῳ, τί χρὴ διανοεῖσθαι τὰς τῶν τμημάτων ἐπιφανείας, ἴσας ἢ ἀνίσους γιγνομένας; ἄνισοι μὲν γὰρ οὖσαι τὸν κῶνον ἀνώμαλον παρέξουσι πολλὰς ἀποχαράξεις λαμβάνοντα βαθμοειδεῖς καὶ τραχύτητας, ἴσων δ' οὐσῶν ἴσα τμήματα ἔσται καὶ φανεῖται τὸ τοῦ κυλίνδρου πεπονθὼς ὁ κῶνος, ἐξ ἴσων συγκείμενος καὶ οὐκ ἀνίσων κύκλων, ὅπερ ἐστὶν ἀτοπώτατον.

* * *

16(154)

(τῶν ζῴων) μαθητὰς ἐν τοῖς μεγίστοις γεγονότας ἡμᾶς· ἀράχνης ἐν ὑφαντικῇ καὶ ἀκεστικῇ, χελιδόνος ἐν οἰκοδομίᾳ, καὶ τῶν λιγυρῶν, κύκνου καὶ ἀηδόνος, ἐν ᾠδῇ κατὰ μίμησιν.

17(247)

ἀνδρὶ σοφῷ πᾶσα γῆ βατή· ψυχῆς γὰρ ἀγαθῆς πατρὶς ὁ ξύμπας κόσμος.

18(230)

βίος ἀνεόρταστος μακρὴ ὁδὸς ἀπανδόκευτος.

19(211)

σωφροσύνη τὰ τερπνὰ ἀέξει καὶ ἡδονὴν ἐπιμείζονα ποιεῖ.

20(171)

εὐδαιμονίη οὐκ ἐν βοσκήμασιν οἰκεῖ οὐδὲ ἐν χρυσῷ· ψυχὴ οἰκητήριον δαίμονος.

COMMENTARY

X E N O P H A N E S

Fragments 1-4: Criticism of the gods as presented by Homer and Hesiod.

1(11) Sextus *Adv. math.* 9.193

The grounds of reproaches and blame (ὀνείδεα καὶ ψόγος) are theft, adultery and mutual deceit.

1.1 ἀνέθηκαν: from ἀνατίθημι - 'placed on', 'attributed'.
1.3 ἀπατεύειν: a unique form of the infinitive of ἀπατάω.

2(14) Clement *Strom.* 5.109

Mortals suppose that gods have parents, wear human clothing, and speak and look like men and women.

2.1 ἀλλ' . . . θεούς: the line as it stands is an iambic trimeter (and it is known that Xenophanes wrote in this metre, cf. D.L. 9.18) but it is unsatisfactory in this form and position; perhaps it should be adapted to fit the hexameter, as e.g. ἀλλὰ βροτοὶ δοκέουσι θεοὺς γεννᾶσθαι <ὁμοίως>.
γεννᾶσθαι: post-Homeric verb, meaning both 'to be begotten' from the father and 'to be born' from the mother.
2.2 δέμας: 'physical structure', 'general appearance' as at 3.5.

3(15) Clement *Strom.* 5.110

If animals had hands, they would depict gods in their own animal likenesses.

3.1-4 εἰ εἶχον . . . κε . . . ἔγραφον καὶ . . . ἐποίουν: the condition is present unfulfilled, with imperfect indicatives (cf. *G.* 1397).
3.5 οἷόν περ . . . εἶχον: the imperfect with present sense continues into the relative clause - 'they would sculpt bodies in the same shape as they each have'; other suggestions for completing the line are Karsten's <ἕκαστον> and Mullach's <ὁμοῖον>.

4(16) Clement *Strom.* 7.22

The two lines were reconstructed by Diels from Clement's paraphrase. Men make gods in their own image, black and snub-nosed for the Ethiopians (the one negroid race known to the Greeks), blonde and blue-eyed for the Thracians.

4.2 γλαυκοὺς καὶ πυρρούς: the colours, as generally for the ancients, are ill-defined: γλαυκός for 'bright' eyes (used notably of Athena's), either blue or grey, and πυρρός - 'fiery' for red, auburn or fair hair.

Fragments 5-9: God is one, intelligent and unmoving.

5(18) Stobaeus 1.8.2

Knowledge is not gained by divine revelation but by human perseverance.

5.2 χρόνῳ ζητοῦντες: time and personal research are necessary conditions for progress.
ἄμεινον: ambiguous between the adverb - 'they find out in a better way', and the object - 'they find out a better thing'.

6(23) Clement *Strom.* 5.109

Among gods and men there can be only one (true) god, unlike men in appearance and intelligence. Positive argument complements the negative criticisms of frs. 1-4.

6.1 εἷς θεός: the verb is a common omission in this form of expression; the possible meanings are - 'one is god', 'god is one' or 'there is one god'.
ἔν τε θεοῖσι καὶ ἀνθρώποισι μέγιστος: a general expression - 'greatest in heaven and earth', 'greatest of all'. Any minor deities implicit in ἐν θεοῖσι do not conflict with Xenophanes' basic monotheism.
6.2 οὔτι δέμας . . . νόημα: the accusatives give the reference for the adj. (cf. *G.* 1058). οὔτις is preferred by the poets to οὐδείς (cf. 16.1) - 'not at all like men in body or thought'.

7(24) Sextus *Adv. math.* 9.144

The god has no specific organs of perception and thought, but he sees, hears and thinks as a totality.

7.1 οὖλος: Ionic for ὅλος - 'all over', 'wholly'.

8(26) Simplicius *In Phys.* 23.11

The god always stays in the same place, appropriately motionless.

8.1 κινούμενος οὐδέν: the participle is middle - 'not moving (himself) at all'.
8.2 οὐδὲ . . . ἐπιπρέπει: impersonal verb - 'it is not fitting', 'appropriate', almost 'it is not possible'.
ἄλλοτε ἄλλῃ: 'at one time in one direction, at another time in another'.

9(25) Simplicius *In Phys*. 23.20

The god is separate from all things, but, by the working of his own, non-human thought, he effortlessly causes their movement.

νόου φρενί: 'by the instrument of his thought'; φρήν (or φρένες) was a physical organ used for whole or part of the chest region of diaphragm, heart and lungs, and connected with the related activities of perception and thought. But Xenophanes' god has no human organs (cf. frs. 6 and 7); his 'means of thought' are all-pervasive, responsible for the movement of things, but distinct from them.
κραδαίνει: 'brandishes', 'shakes', 'causes to vibrate', as both surrounding and (perhaps) permeating.

Fragments 10-12: Earth the source and end of all things.

10(29) Simplicius *In Phys*. 189.1

A similar line to this and the following, or perhaps another version, is B.33: πάντες γὰρ γαίης τε καὶ ὕδατος ἐκγενόμεσθα. The common origin of life, and the main component of living things, is moist earth.

11(27) Sextus *Adv. math*. 10.313

'From earth all comes and into earth all ends'; a general, rather obvious statement, acceptable to myth and tradition, and without any implication of earth being the one and only world origin and element. The line is thought suspect by some.

12(28) Achilles *Isag*. 4.

Air bounds the upper limit of earth.

12.2 ἠέρι (or αἰθέρι): The former is Diels', the latter Karsten's emendation for the MSS καὶ ῥεῖ.

προσπλάζον: 'reaching to' (as of the water up to Tantalus' beard, Homer, *Od.* 11.583).
ἐς ἄπειρον: not necessarily 'to infinity', but indefinitely downwards - the 'bottom' of the earth is seemingly unreachable.
ἱκνεῖται: for the short iota cf. P. 8.46. <τὸ> or <τὰ> is usually supplied to complete the line, and the original εἰς then shortened.

Fragments 13-14: On some natural phenomena.

13(30) Schol. Genav. ad *Il.* 21.196

The doxography attributes a considerable number of statements on astronomy and meteorology to Xenophanes, although the ideas summarised are simple, and in the Milesian tradition. Apart from an incomplete quotation on the sun 'swinging over' the earth and warming it, this and the following fragment are the only direct words extant on the subject. Here the sea is shown to be the source of clouds, wind, rain and rivers. The completion of the lacuna in lines 2-3 is Diels'.

13.2 οὔτε . . . γίνοιτό κε: 'there would not occur . . .' - potential optative with κε (cf. *G.* 1329).
ἲς ἀνέμοιο: Homeric phrase for the wind's force.

14(32) Schol. Eustathius ad *Il.* 11.27

She who is called Iris (goddess and rainbow) is a coloured cloud.

14.1 ἥν τ': τε in Epic can be appended to relatives without affecting the meaning; on a relative without an antecedent, cf. *G.* 1026.
14.2 πορφύρεον . . .: the colours are again uncertain - perhaps violet (the nearest shade to purple on the spectrum), red and yellow. (χλωρός can also be green but cf. fr. 17 below).
ἰδέσθαι: poetic use of the middle voice of ὁράω for the active.

Fragments 15-17: Preliminary distinctions between knowledge and opinion, reality and appearance.

15(35) Plutarch *Symp.* 746b

The line recalls the contrast with τὰ ἔτυμα in Homer, *Od.* 19.203 and in Hesiod, *Theogony* 27.

δεδοξάσθω: Wilamowitz' reading for the MSS δεδοξάσθαι; Karsten suggested δεδόξασται. With the aorist passive imperative of δοκέω the sense is - 'let this be taken as opinion, resembling truth', or perhaps 'let these be accepted as appearances resembling true things'; cf. on δόκος, 16.4.

16(34) Sextus *Adv. math.* 7.49

There can be only opinion, not knowledge, of divinity and related matters.

16.1 ἴδεν . . . ἔσται εἰδώς: the vocabulary of seeing and knowing
-2 merges in the basic verb *εἴδω from which are derived the
aorist εἶδον (ἴδεν unaugmented) and perfect οἶδα (here in a periphrastic future with the participle) - 'what is certain about the gods no man has seen nor will anyone be knowledgeable on'.

16.3 εἰ . . . τύχοι . . . οὐκ οἶδε: mixed condition - 'for if anyone were, even by the greatest chance (καὶ τὰ μάλιστα is adverbial with τύχοι) to speak the truth (*lit.* 'to say what has come to pass', a Homeric use of τετελεσμένον), still that man does not *know*'.

ἐπὶ πᾶσι: this could be masc. - 'among all men', or neut. - 'over all things'.

τέτυκται: from τεύχω - 'has been produced', 'is found'.

17(38) Herodian Περὶ μονήρους λέξεως 41.5

Judgments dependent on perceptions are limited and relative.

17.1 εἰ μὴ . . . ἔφυσε, . . . ἔφασκον: a mixed condition - 'if god had not made yellow honey, they would say a fig was much sweeter'. (The absence of κε in the apodosis is unremarkable.) θεός has no particular monotheistic emphasis in a context of this kind.

πολλὸν: Ionic form of πολύ.

17.2 γλύσσονα: a unique comparative of γλυκύς.

Fragment 18: Human ψυχή in animal form.

18(7) Diogenes Laertius 8.36

The quatrain is in elegaics, and the speaker is given in the sources as Pythagoras. The fragment is the first extant reference in Greek to transmigration; the implicit irony suggests that the theory was well known.

18.1 μιν: Epic form for all genders of the acc. sing. of the

third person pronoun.
στυφελιζομένου σκύλακος: genitive absolute - 'while a puppy was being beaten'.
18.2 φάσθαι: middle infinitive with active sense.
18.3 ἦ: confirmatory adverb - 'indeed'.
18.4 τὴν: relative pronoun - 'which I recognised'.
ἀΐων: from ἀΐω (epic and lyric verb in pres. and imperf. only) with the genitive of the source of sound given in the participle φθεγξαμένης - 'hearing (it) cry out'.

HERACLITUS

Fragments 1-5: The logos.

1(1) Sextus *Adv. math.* 7.132

Heraclitus' work probably began with this complex and carefully structured fragment. It asserts the existence of the λόγος and its universality and compares men to sleepers in their unawareness of it. The range of meanings of λόγος exploited by Heraclitus include: (i) what is said, an account, report; (ii) what is said to oneself, and so one's thought; (iii) rational explanation; (iv) the objective truth of what is said; (v) universal (common) truth, principle or law; (vi) its instantiation in proportion and measure.

αἰεὶ: the position of the adverb makes the sense deliberately ambiguous between - 'of this λόγος which always is, men are uncomprehending', and - 'of the λόγος being this (i.e. as I explain) men are always uncomprehending'.

πρόσθεν ἢ: like πρίν with an infinitive - 'before hearing it'.

ἀπείροισιν . . . πειρώμενοι: the root meaning of these words is the basis for the contrast - 'they are like untried men when they make trial of . . .'. The preceding genitive absolute is concessive - 'although everything happens . . .'.

ὁκοίων: ὁκ-forms are Ionic for ὁπ-.

κατὰ φύσιν: 'constitution', 'structure' and 'growth' are implicit in φύσις. The approach is scientific - 'analysing each thing according to its nature and describing its actual state'.

ὁκόσα ἐγερθέντες ποιοῦσιν: subject of λανθάνει, whereas ὁκόσα εὕδοντες (ποιοῦσιν) is the object of ἐπιλανθάνονται. Relative clauses tend to assimilate an indefinite antecedent (as the English 'what they do' for 'that which').

2(50) Hippolytus *Ref.* 9.9.1

On hearing (and heeding) the λόγος it is wise to admit a universal unity.

λόγου . . . ὁμολογεῖν: the verb 'to say the same as' is etymologically linked with the noun λόγος, so that the fuller meaning is - 'to be in accord with λόγος and say'. The λόγος here is specifically distinguished from Heraclitus and his account.

ἓν πάντα εἶναι: ambiguous between 'one thing is all things' and 'all things are one'. In this fragment the MSS read δόγματος (λόγου Bernays) and εἰδέναι (εἶναι Miller).

3(89) Plutarch *De superstit.* 166c

A three term ratio, which here relates having understanding to being awake as being awake to asleep, is characteristic of Heraclitus. Plutarch is reporting him indirectly (hence εἶναι), and continues: τῶν δὲ κοιμωμένων ἕκαστον εἰς ἴδιον ἀποστρέφεσθαι - 'but of the sleepers each turns to his private world'. How much of the whole sentence preserves Heraclitus' wording is disputed.

τοῖς ἐγρηγορόσιν: the perfect participle (of ἐγείρω) for the past action and present state - 'for those who have woken up and are now (truly) awake'.
κοινὸν κόσμον: κόσμος has been rejected as anachronistic and Heraclitus elsewhere uses the epic / Ionic ξυνός rather than κοινός, but the phrase, with its sense of 'a world shared in common', could well be basically Heraclitean.

4(41) Diogenes Laertius 9.1

The concept of comprehensive, intelligent control is introduced.

γνώμην: external object - 'to know the reasoning', rather than internal - 'to be skilled in true judgment'.
ὅκῃ κυβερνᾶται: 'by which all things are guided through all things'. This interpretation connects γνώμη with the divine principle but the text is corrupt. For other emendations of the MS ὀτέη κυβερνῆται, cf. Kirk 387-89 and Marcovich 449-52.

5(32) Clement *Strom.* 5.115

The name of Zeus is both appropriate and inappropriate for the divine principle.

ἓν τὸ σοφὸν μοῦνον: ambiguous between 'one, the only wise', and 'one alone, the wise', or, with punctuation after μοῦνον, 'the wise (is) one only'. The reference is to the divine principle, whereas ἓν τὸ σοφόν in the previous fragment seems to be 'the one wisdom (among men)'.
Ζηνὸς: rather than the more common genitive Διός, to connect Zeus with ζῆν - 'to live', 'life'. The name 'Zeus' has the relevant connotations of wisdom, power and eternal life but, as with Xenophanes, anthropomorphic attributes of god are rejected.

Fragments 6-12: Understanding is possible but men are heedless.

6(113) Stobaeus 3.1.179

All have the capacity to think.

ξυνόν: epic / Ionic, equivalent to κοινόν, and a key adjective in Heraclitus, especially for the aural connection with ξὺν νόῳ.
πᾶσι: either neuter - 'for all things' (cf. E. 18.10), or masculine - 'for all men', as in the next fragment.

7(116) Stobaeus 3.5.6

Self-knowledge and sound thinking belong to all men.

μέτεστι: the infinitives are the subject of the verb.
ἑωυτοὺς: Ionic for ἑαυτοὺς.
σωφρονεῖν: both Delphic injunctions (self-knowledge and moderation) are recalled in the fragment and there is also an etymological link with the φρονέειν of the previous fragment.

8(55) Hippolytus *Ref.* 9.9.5

There is value in learning through direct experience.

ὅσων: 'of what things seeing and hearing are the learning', i.e. 'what is learnt through sight and sound'.
μάθησις: one's own learning, to be contrasted with πολυμαθίη, of secondhand information (see fr. 14 below).

9(2) Sextus *Adv. math.* 7.133

Men in their private worlds are unaware of the shared λόγος.

τοῦ λόγου . . . ξυνοῦ: the genitive absolute is concessive - 'although the λόγος is common'; for ξυνός, cf. frs. 6 and 22. Here the adjective is in marked contrast to ἰδίαν.
ὡς: with a participle makes an assertion without implying that it is the speaker's own; so here - 'they live as if having . . .', 'having, as they suppose'.

10(17) Clement *Strom.* 2.8

Men's thoughts do not match their experience, nor do they learn from it.

ὁκοίοις ἐγκυρεῦσιν: Bergk's emendation for the MSS ὁκόσος ἐγκυρσεύουσιν.

οὐδὲ μαθόντες γινώσκουσιν: a paradoxical juxtaposition - even after 'learning' there is no real understanding.
δοκέουσι: sc. γινώσκειν.

11(72) Marcus Aurelius 4.46

This sentence develops the previous fragment. In the second half Aurelius may be paraphrasing rather than quoting Heraclitus directly.

ὁμιλοῦσι . . . διαφέρονται: the contrasting verbs make a paradox - 'what they associate with most regularly they are estranged from'. τούτῳ in the MS has a gloss which may be more Stoic than Heraclitean - λόγῳ τῷ τὰ ὅλα διοικοῦντι.

12(108) Stobaeus 3.1.174

No one has yet understood the separateness of wisdom.

λόγους: here for other people's account, that Heraclitus has heard or heard of.
ὅτι . . . κεχωρισμένον: highly (and no doubt deliberately) ambiguous. Possible interpretations include: 'to understand wisdom, separate from (i.e. unattainable by) all men', 'to understand what is the wise (i.e. the divine principle of fr. 5), separate from all things', or, without punctuation after ἐστί, 'to understand that wisdom is set apart from all (men and/or things)'.

Fragments 13-17: A disparagement of those with a reputation for wisdom.

13(107) Sextus *Adv. math.* 7.126

A modification, not a contradiction, of fr. 8; when not interpreted aright, the evidence of the senses can mislead the ψυχή.

βαρβαροὺς ψυχάς: the onomatopoeic adj. refers, in the early fifth century, to those who do not speak Greek. For Heraclitus, Greeks who have 'barbarian souls' are those who speak and listen to their language without understanding its significance, as well as not appreciating the meaning of what they see.

14(40) Diogenes Laertius 9.1

Some particular examples of men esteemed as wise, but whose

learning did not bring knowledge.

πολυμαθίη νόον: a contrast between the accumulation of information on a range of topics and genuine understanding.

διδάσκει: the verb takes two accusatives, for the subject and the person taught. νόον (in some versions ἔχειν νόον) from the first part of the sentence is to be understood with ἂν ἐδίδαξε, and a second general object (ἀνθρώπους) is implied at the beginning to give: 'much learning does not teach (men) understanding, otherwise it would have taught (understanding) to . . .'. Without this filling, the sense would be: 'much learning does not teach (the) mind . . .'. ἂν ἐδίδαξε is aorist indicative with ἄν for an unrealised state of affairs in the past; cf. *G.* 1338.

αὖτίς τε: Xenophanes and Hecataeus are near contemporaries, Pythagoras a little earlier, and Hesiod two centuries back. Hesiod is criticised again in fr. 17, and in B 129 Pythagoras is accused of plagiarism and his polymathy linked with professional fraud (κακοτεχνία).

15(42) Diogenes Laertius 9.1

Even Homer is disparaged.

ῥαπίζεσθαι: Homer, personified in his rhapsode, should be driven from the competitions (and ἐκβάλλεσθαι implies 'like a bad actor from the stage'), and beaten with the stick that, as ῥάβδος, symbolises his profession. Diogenes adds to this καὶ Ἀρχίλοχον ὁμοίως, and Archilochus is mentioned with Homer and Hesiod as a standard author for official recitations (cf. Plato, *Ion* 531a). In the same vein is B 104 - 'What understanding or sense have they? They believe the poets of the people and take the mob as their teacher . . .'.

16(56) Hippolytus *Ref.* 9.9.6

In being puzzled by the obvious, men are like Homer, who could not solve a child's riddle.

γνῶσιν: 'recognition', the earliest extant occurrence of the noun. The formation of verbal nouns in -σις is characteristic of Heraclitus' style.

φθεῖρας: 'lice', the solution to the riddle - 'What we saw and caught we leave behind, and what we did not see or catch we take with us'. In some versions the boys are fishing or hunting, which makes the answer to the question 'What did you catch?' even more elusive. Traditionally, Homer's physical blindness is emphasised in this context, and he is said to have died of grief at being unable to solve the riddle. For Heraclitus there may have been an additional paradox in the aural connection of φθεῖρας with φθείρω.

κατακτείνοντες: epic / Ionic verb, which gives the narrative a poetic flourish.

17(57) Hippolytus *Ref.* 9.10.2

A specific criticism of Hesiod for not understanding that day and night are one.

ἐπίστανται . . . εἰδέναι . . . ἐγίνωσκεν: the three 'knowing' verbs are in ascending order: the affirmation of people in general, classroom knowledge and true understanding.

εὐφρόνην: the 'kindly time'; Ionic and poetic euphemism for night, now recognised to be, not a positive blackness, but the absence of sunlight, with its length regulated by the length of the day.

Fragments 18-24: Awareness and participation.

18(21) Clement *Strom.* 3.21

Death, sleep and waking are interconnected.

ὕπνος: 'All we see when awake is death, all we see when sleeping is ὕπνος.' A word implying 'life' or 'truth' might be expected at the end to regulate the contrasts, and so Marcovich reads ὕπαρ ('a true vision'), but the unexpected word is in Heraclitus' style.

19(26) Clement *Strom.* 4.141

The relationships in the previous fragment are developed in a sophisticated and suggestive balance of contrasts. A man, unable to see at night and lighting a lamp, illustrates the contact of the living sleeper with the dead, and of the wakeful with the sleeper.

ἀποσβεσθείς: from ἀποσβέννυμι, 'put out' a fire or light. The participle contrasts with ἅπτεται ('kindles (for himself)'), and ὄψεις is a 'retained' accusative (cf. *G.* 1239) - 'having been extinguished in his eyes', i.e. a man in darkness lights a lamp for himself as he cannot see. But ἅπτεται more generally means 'touch' and this word-play, with the ambiguous participles, brings out the next contrast - 'alive, while sleeping, he touches / kindles a dead man / death, awake he touches / kindles a man asleep /sleep'.

20(75) Marcus Aurelius 6.42

'Sleepers are active' has the ring of a Heraclitean paradox, even though Aurelius is quoting indirectly and from memory. He finishes with: καὶ συνεργοὺς τῶν ἐν τῷ κόσμῳ γινομένων.

21(20) Clement *Strom.* 3.14

This enigmatic criticism of the majority's way of life and death may belong here or in the last section of ethical fragments.

μόρους τ' ἔχειν: once born, men wish to live and 'have their portions' but the phrase also suggests 'meet their deaths', as if the so-called 'enjoyment of portions' were a kind of living death. (The verb in Clement's gloss μᾶλλον δὲ ἀναπαύεσθαι after ἔχειν is used for the repose of both sleep and death.)

μόρους γενέσθαι: the infinitive is ambiguous between purpose - 'in order to become (the inheritors of) their portions' - and consequence - 'with the result that they are born to be deaths' (cf. *G.* 1532-33). The mundane life that is a kind of death is passed on from one generation to another; the sense is reflected in the cyclic structure of the fragment, enclosed between γενόμενοι and γενέσθαι.

22(114) Stobaeus 3.1.179

The intelligent must rely on what is common, even more than a city on its walls, for human laws are nourished by the one divine.

ξὺν νόῳ . . . τῷ ξυνῷ: the cognate sounds indicate cognate meaning (cf. frs. 6 and 9). There is further word-play with the infinitve and adverb - 'to put their strength in . . . and more strongly'.

πάντων: to be taken with τῷ ξυνῷ - 'what is common to all'. The gender of these words, as of ἑνὸς τοῦ θείου and πᾶσι later in the sentence, is ambiguous between masculine and neuter.

τρέφονται: 'are nourished', 'sustained', a metaphor suggesting that human laws are children or nurslings of the one divine.

περιγίνεται: 'it (or he) is enough for all and more than enough' but the verb can also mean 'is superior' and 'survives'. Power, sufficiency and immortality are marks of the divine.

23(44) Diogenes Laertius 9.2

The people must fight for their law as for their city-wall.

τοῦ νόμου: 'law (generally)' or 'their (collective) law'. (Some MSS add to νόμου: ὑπὲρ τοῦ γινομένου.)
χρὴ: 'it is their duty and in their interest' is the full meaning.

24(49) Theodorus Prodromus *Epistulae* 1

ἐμοὶ: supplied from Galen's quotation of the apodosis, *De dign. puls*. (8.773K).
μύριοι: an exact number, 10,000; or indefinitely many, cf. 'a man in a million'.
ἄριστος: the word has political connotations, cf. the praise for Bias and Hermodorus in B 39 and B 121, as well as B 33 - 'it is νόμος to obey the counsel of one'.

Fragments 25-33: True divinity and conventional religion.

25(78) Origen *Contra Celsum* 6.12

Understanding belongs to divine not human nature.

ἦθος: character determined by habitual behaviour, ranging from basic nature to individual disposition.
γνώμας: here plural (cf. fr. 4) - 'insights', 'sound thoughts'. Men tend to act irresolutely, because they lack coherent judgment.

26(79) Origen *Contra Celsum* 6.12 (following fr. 25)

ἀνὴρ . . . δαίμονος: the sense shifts between 'a man is a baby compared with god' to 'a man is called silly by god'. For the gnomic aorist, cf. *G*. 1292, and for the sense of ἀκούω as passive of λέγω - 'I am spoken of as', 'I am called', cf. *LSJ* s.v., III.1. The baby is 'silly' in having no clear speech or thought, or control of his body; cf. the drunkard in fr. 70.

27(5) Aristocritus *Theosophia* 68 / Origen *Contra Celsum* 7.62

Some rituals are demonstrably foolish.

αἵματι: to be taken with the verb and the participle: 'they purify themselves in vain with blood / with blood defiled'.
ὁκοῖον εἴ τις: with the optative here and in the following sentence for an absurd situation - 'as if someone were to wash with mud . . . talk to a house'. (To be consistent

with the Ionic forms, ὁκοῖον for οἷον, δοκέοι for δοκοίη and μιν for αὐτόν are read.).
ἀνθρώπων: with εἴ τις - 'if anyone were to notice him'.
λεσχηνεύοιτο: middle verb - 'gossip', 'chat', from λέσχη - 'a meeting place for idlers'. The tone of the fragment is sarcastic and flippant; cf. the contempt for burial rites at B 96 - 'corpses are more discardable (ἐκβλητότεροι) than dung'.

28(14) Clement *Protr.* 22

Clement precedes this quotation with a list of people connected with mysteries, who are sometimes assumed to have been named by Heraclitus. They are μάγοι (Persian wise men), νυκτιπόλοι, βάκχοι and λῆναι (followers of Bacchus), and μύσται (initiates).

νομιζόμενα: 'practised', 'honoured' and 'believed in'.
μυστήρια: the cognate accusative repeats the meaning of the verb (cf. *G.* 1051), an idiom which does not translate easily. ἀνιερωστί is an adverb and the general sense is 'they are sacrilegiously initiated into sacred mysteries'.

29(15) Clement *Protr.* 34

Shamelessness is accepted as reverence in the rites of Dionysus, identifiable with Hades.

εἰ μή: to be taken with the proper name - 'if it were not for Dionysus that they march in procession'.
αἰδοίοισιν: i.e. the phallus, carried aloft in procession and celebrated in song. There is a verbal connection (for Heraclitus a sign of essential connection) between αἰδοῖα ('the shameful parts' and the source of life), ἀναιδέστατα ('shameless', i.e. both 'immodest' and 'lacking reverence') and Ἀΐδης ('unseen' and 'unseeing', the god and place of the dead).
εἴργασται: perfect of ἐργάζομαι with passive sense (and singular with neuter plural as subject) for the apodosis of a mixed condition - 'most shameful acts have been performed'.
ὡυτός: Ionic for ὁ αὐτός; the gods of death and life, and so death and life themselves, are 'the same'.
ληναΐζουσιν: 'celebrate the Lenaia', the winter festival in honour of Dionysus.

30(92) Plutarch *De Pyth. or.* 397a

The Sibyl's ravings are to be taken seriously.

Σίβυλλα: Sibyl, priestess of Apollo; the word is the name

of the original priestess, and used generally for the holder of the office. She acted as a medium, Apollo being thought to possess her and then to speak with her voice. The resulting 'ravings' were ordered and versified by an interpreter.
ἀγέλαστα: active - 'not laughing'; but here more probably passive - 'not to be laughed at', 'serious'. It is not clear whether the bracketed words are from Heraclitus or Plutarch.
φθεγγομένη: probably φθέγγεται in the original words. The sentence in Plutarch concludes: χιλίων ἐτῶν ἐξικνεῖται τῇ φωνῇ διὰ τὸν θεόν.

31(93) Plutarch *De Pyth. or.* 404d

Apollo does not speak out or conceal, but through his oracle gives a sign.

32(54) Hippolytus *Ref.* 9.10.1

The wide range of meanings possible for these four tightly-knit words suggests that Heraclitus is himself deliberately adopting an oracular style as the appropriate method of expressing the complexities and subtleties of his thought.

ἁρμονίη: a literal and metaphorical term from carpentry and music - 'joining', 'connection', 'framework', 'structure', 'attunement', 'agreement'.
ἀφανής: 'hidden', 'invisible', 'underlying', contrasted with 'obvious', 'superficial'.
κρείσσων: 'stronger', 'more powerful', but also 'better', 'superior'.

33(123) Themistius *Orationes* 5.69

This fragment connects with the previous one, and with frs. 62-65, on the searching that is necessary for truth.

φύσις: a notoriously difficult word; here 'nature' personified as a child playing hide-and-seek, but implying also the concealed 'constitution of things'.
φιλεῖ: 'is accustomed to', as well as 'likes to'.
κρύπτεσθαι: middle - 'to hide (itself)', or passive - 'to be hidden'.

Fragments 34-45: Cosmic war and the unity of opposites.

34(53) Hippolytus *Ref.* 9.9.5

War is sovereign.

πόλεμος: as the principle of universal opposition, 'war' is given the rank of the Homeric Zeus, responsible for the generation of all (the gender of πάντων is again ambiguous) and with power over all. More specifically, in the human battlefield, it shows those who are 'gods' (for men who die in battle have a special status; cf. fr. 74) and, of the survivors, some are free and others made slaves.
ἔδειξε . . . ἐποίησε: gnomic aorists (cf. *G.* 1291-92).

35(80) Origen *Contra Celsum* 6.12

Related to this fragment on the universality of war is a reported criticism of Achilles' wish for ἔρις among gods and men to perish (*Il.* 18.107, DK 22A22).

ξυνόν: 'common', 'shared' (cf. frs. 6, 9 and 22).
δίκην ἔριν: a startling juxtaposition - 'justice (i.e. established order and rightness) is strife'.
χρεώμενα: perhaps 'are ordained' (cf. Kahn *Heraclitus* 207) but the participle is difficult and has been emended to χρεών (Diels) and κρινόμενα (Bywater).

36(10) [Aristotle] *De mundo* 396b20

In this general statement it is left ambiguous whether the opposite combinations are to be taken simultaneously (as the first word suggest) or successively (as in the concluding statement). Individual examples of both follow in frs. 37-47.

συλλάψιες: (an alternative reading is συνάψιες) Ionic for the nom. plural συλλήψεις. The noun has both the physical and mental senses of συλλαμβάνω - 'conjunctions to be grasped and understood together', and the three following pairs of opposites are subsumed under this heading.
συμφερόμενον διαφερόμενον: 'the converging, the diverging' includes both locomotion, 'moving together, moving apart', and metaphorically 'agreeing, disagreeing'.
συνᾷδον διᾷδον: present participle of compounds of ᾄδω (a contracted form of ἀείδω) in the neut. sing. for the general musical terms, 'the concordant, the discordant', i.e. 'singing together and in competition', or perhaps something like 'point and counterpoint', 'tune and descant'.

37(51) Hippolytus *Ref.* 9.9.2

The bow and lyre are particular examples of the συμφερόμενον / διαφερόμενον conjunction.

οὐ ξυνιᾶσιν: the verb is a deliberate link with ξυνός and ξὺν νόῳ (cf. frs. 6, 9 and 22).
ὁμολογέει: Zeller and others read συμφέρεται from Plato *Symposium* 187a: τὸ ἓν γάρ φησι διαφερόμενον αὐτὸν αὐτῷ ξυμφέρεσθαι ὥσπερ ἁρμονίαν τόξου τε καὶ λύρας.
παλίντονος: 'back-stretched', 'stretching in opposite directions' is the standard Homeric epithet for the bow. A variant reading, frequently adopted, is παλίντροπος - 'back-turning', less appropriate for the taut string but perhaps better suited to the general context (cf. Parmenides 6.9).
ἁρμονίη: for the structure of the bow and the lyre - how they are put together - as well as the particular 'attunement' of the lyre. The fundamental agreement / disageement in the structure of the instruments, which ensures their functioning, is the exact tension between the component parts, i.e. the string in relation to the wood or shell. If this tension is too slack, the bow does not pull and the lyre is out of tune; if too tight, the string breaks.

38(48) *Etymologicum magnum* s.v. βίος

Names are significant for the truth they reveal.

ὄνομα . . . ἔργον: in the conflict between its name and its function the bow exemplifies a unity of opposites.
βίος: 'life' but, with a change of accent (which would not have been marked on the written word), βιός - a Homeric word for 'bow'.

39(59) Hippolytus *Ref.* 9.10.4

γραφείῳ: a line of writing traces a straight and crooked path - up and down for the letters but in a straight line from left to right. Given the interest in the novelty of writing with the spread of literacy in Heraclitus' time, this is a good example of the concurrence of opposites. But there are other readings and interpretations, notable γνάφων - 'of carding instruments', where wool is straightened by going through combs, or up and over drums or rollers; cf. Kahn *Heraclitus* 191-92. (γναφείῳ, for the screw or screwpress in the fuller's shop, is less likely, as the screw was a later invention.)

40(60) Hippolytus *Ref.* 9.10.4

The famous 'road' fragment has been given metaphysical status and a variety of interpretations in ancient and modern commentary. Most probably it should be taken literally, as an example of opposites predicated of the same subject.

ἄνω κάτω: the road 'up and down' or 'there and back'; the expresssion could also be used for the road inland, to and from the coast.
ὡυτή: Ionic for ἡ αὐτή.

41(103) Porphyry *Quaest. Hom.* ad *Il.* 14.200

Any point on the circumference of a circle is a coincidence of opposites - the beginning and end of that circle. Like the previous fragment, this is sometimes given a broader significance, for cycles of the seasons and the cosmos, as well as of the soul and human generations.

ξυνόν: cf. frs. 6, 9 and 22 for this characteristic adjective.
πέρας: 'limit', 'end' - a key term in Greek philosophy, found elsewhere in Heraclitus only at fr. 65.
περιφέρεια: 'circumference' - a technical word, likely to have been a later addition.

42(125) Theophrastus *De vertigine* 9

An example of the necessity for opposites to interact. If the barley drink is not stirred the dry ingredients settle and the potion as such loses its character and effieciency.

κυκεών: a medicinal drink; the recipe at *Il.* 11.638-40 is for grated goat's cheese and barley-meal stirred into Pramnian wine but there were variations. The point for Heraclitus is that the dry and liquid parts must be stirred together and drunk in combination.
<μή>: supplied by Bernays. μή is used to negate the conditional participle (cf. *G.* 1413).

43(61) Hippolytus *Ref.* 9.10.5

Sea water has opposite attributes producing opposite effects; cf. B 9 ('donkeys prefer rubbish to gold') and B 13/37 ('pigs like to wash in mud').

ὕδωρ: predicative - 'sea: water most pure and most polluted'.

44(111) Stobaeus 3.1.177

Examples of states which can only be understood and appreciated by reference to their opposite.

ἐποίησεν: gnomic aorist (cf. fr. 34).
κάματος ἀνάπαυσιν: 'exhaustion rest'; rest or relaxation only has meaning in the context of its opposite - a spell of hard work.

45(126) Tzetzes *Schol. ad exeg. Il.* 126

The two most obvious sets of opposites which change into and replace each other in the physical world. The four verbs are ambiguous between middle and passive - 'cold things warm themselves' or 'are warmed', 'what is hot cools (itself)' or 'is cooled'.

καρφαλέον νοτίζεται: rare words - 'what is dry gets (itself) wet' or 'is wettened'.

Fragments 46-52: Divine and human reconciliations of opposites.

46(62) Hippolytus *Ref.* 9.10.6

A notoriously difficult fragment on the interconnection between life, death and immortality. The first two pairs of words identify immortals and mortals and the following participles with their accusatives explain the identification. The accusatives are 'internal' or 'limiting', of the kind used with intransitive verbs (cf. *G.* 1051-52). Heraclitus is being startlingly paradoxical and, like Xenophanes, introducing some new thinking on what it means to be an immortal god.

ζῶντες . . . τεθνεῶτες: the participles can and probably should be taken with both subjects - 'immortals living the death of mortals and dying their life, mortals living the death of immortals and dying their life'. βίον τεθνεῶτες is, more exactly, 'being dead in relation to their life'. The death of mortals is in some way necessary to and explicable by the life of gods, and similarly with the death of gods and the life of mortals; cf. the mutual replacement of living and dead in the next fragment, and fr. 67 on the death and birth of ψυχαί.

47(88) [Plutarch] *Consolatio ad Apollonium* 106e

The unity and transposition of the main opposed states in the human (and animal) world.

ἔνι: for ἔνεστι - 'it is the same thing that exists in us as . . .'.
τὸ . . . τὸ: some editors omit these articles, but Heraclitus is not consistent in his use (cf. fr. 45). The neuter participles are all substantive - 'that which is living and that which is dead'.
μεταπεσόντα: from μεταπίπτω, used as the passive of μεταβάλλω - 'these (the first of each pair) transposed are those (the second of each pair), and those (the second of each pair) again transposed are these (the first terms)'. The states

succeed each other, including the living from the dead and the old from the young. In the former the reference is probably not to palingenesis or transmigration, but to natural change, and the latter uses a well-established notion of the grandfather's life being replaced by and continued in that of the grandchild (cf. DK 22A19).

48(8) Aristotle *Eth. Nic.* 1155b4

Aristotle finishes his sentence with: καὶ πάντα κατ' ἔριν γίνεσθαι from fr. 35. The second part similarly is assumed to be a version of fr. 37 but it may well be original, a particular musical application of a general statement.

ἀντίξουν: an Ionic word, having a double sense in combination with συμφέρον - 'opposition is conjunction' and 'the adverse is beneficial'.
ἁρμονίαν (or ἁρμονίην): here for musical concord, produced from notes at variance.

49(23) Clement *Strom.* 4.10

The name (and nature) of Δίκη depends on an opposition.

ὄνομα: for the significance of a name, cf. frs. 5 and 38.
Δίκη: goddess and daughter of Zeus, personifying established order and 'rightness' (cf. B 28).
ταῦτα: from Clement's context, the pronoun appears to refer to τὰ ἄδικα and this would bring out a characteristic Heraclitean opposition - 'men would not know (Sylberg's ᾔδεσαν for the MS ἔδησαν) the name of Justice (i.e. understand and appreciate order and rightness) if there were no injustices or wrongs'; there is also the more obvious sense of there being no lawsuits or penalties if there were no crimes (present unfulfilled condition; cf. *G.* 1397).

50(124) Theophrastus *Metaph.* 15

The fragment is corrupt but if the text is accepted in this form it gives a paradoxical and shocking identification of the cosmos with a pile of litter. Perhaps it is a parody or a sarcastic comment on a Milesian-type cosmogony.

σάρμα εἰκῇ κεχυμένων: 'a rubbish-pile of things heaped up at random'. σάρμα, connecting with σαίρω, is a collective noun for the sweepings pushed together after a room is cleaned out; the word is Diels' suggestion for the MS σάρξ. The participle is sometimes altered to κεχυμένον.
κόσμος: any orderly arrangement, then applied to the world as a whole (cf. fr. 53).

51(67) Hippolytus *Ref.* 9.10.8

God is first presented in terms of four pairs of opposed nouns and is then the subject of a verb of alteration, explained in a complex and obscure comparison with incense-burning.

ἡμέρη . . . λιμός: the oneness of day and night was given in fr. 17, while fr. 44 showed how hunger makes satiety appreciated. The opposites of winter and summer similarly succeed and are understood in terms of each other, and so with war (in its common human sense) and peace. In Heraclitus' manner (e.g. frs. 4, 13 and 36) no connecting verb is given; the precise relationship of the four pairs of opposites to the definition and explanation of ὁ θεός is left unstated.

ὅκωσπερ <πῦρ>: <πῦρ> is Diels' suggested supplement; others are μύρον (Heidel), ἔλαιον (Fränkel), οἶνος and θύωμα. The general sense is that the god undergoes changes, as different scents are given off by different spices. The supplements suggest various bases and aspects: wine with spiced flavourings, oil with scented unguents, or - most generally accepted - fire with types of incense burned. There are opposite aspects of god as the fragrances from the altar fire have different names; for the perception involved, cf. B 7 - 'if all were smoke, the nose could tell the difference'.

καθ' ἡδονὴν ἑκάστου: 'according to the savour (a specialised Ionic meaning of ἡδονή) of each', with an implicit second sense, that the naming is 'according to each man's fancy'.

52(102) Porphyry *Quaest. Hom.* ad *Il.* 4.4

The sentence may not be an exact quotation (and καὶ ἀγαθά, as in most MSS, is best omitted as a cliché after καλά) but there is no reason to doubt the Heraclitean contrast between the divine and human perspective.

τῷ θεῷ: for the divine understanding, cf. frs. 4, 5 and 25.

ὑπειλήφασιν: from ὑπολαμβάνω - 'assume', 'suppose'. The connection between human and divine law was given in fr. 22, that between human justice and injustice in fr. 49.

Fragments 53-61: The cosmic fire and its changes.

53(30) Clement *Strom.* 5.104

The κόσμος is uncreated, an everliving fire, kindled and quenched in measures.

κόσμον: 'arrangement', 'order' and then 'world order'.

τόνδε: supplied from the quotation of the fragment by Plutarch and Simplicius.
τὸν αὐτὸν ἁπάντων: 'the same for all', only in Clement, and possibly his interpolation.
οὔτε τις θεῶν οὔτε ἀνθρώπων: the equivalent of an emphatic 'no one at all'; for the expression, cf. Xenophanes 6 above.
κόσμον . . . ἐποίησεν: almost the equivalent of διεκόσμησεν - the present order did not arise from a previous disorder, nor was any organiser responsible for it but the state of affairs is now as it has always been.
πῦρ ἀείζωον: in apposition to the subject -'it always was and is and will be, fire everliving' - rather than predicative.
ἁπτόμενον . . . μέτρα: the participles are middle and the accusatives 'limiting' (cf. *G.* 1054) - 'kindling (itself) in measures and quenching (itself) in measures'. The 'measures' are probably both temporal and spatial; at different times and in different parts the kindlings and quenchings balance out.

54(64) Hippolytus *Ref.* 9.10.7

Fire as the helmsman.

τὰ δὲ πάντα: perhaps to be read as τάδε πάντα - 'these things, all of them'.
οἰακίζει: 'steers', 'guides', from οἴαξ 'rudder' or 'tiller', a similar metaphor to κυβερνᾶται in fr. 4. The Ionic word would be οἰηκίζει.
κεραυνός: 'thunderbolt', 'lightning flash', the particular weapon of Zeus and an obvious symbol for the universal regulating fire, as Hippolytus explains - κεραυνὸν τὸ πῦρ λέγων τὸ αἰώνιον.

55(66) Hippolytus *Ref.* 9.10.7

A continuation of the description of the role of fire.

ἐπελθὸν κρινεῖ καὶ καταλήψεται: the three verbs show fire as a kind of cosmic policeman and magistrate ('will come upon and judge and convict') but the conviction can also be a 'taking hold of' and so 'absorption' into the fire. The whole fragment is sometimes rejected as Hippolytus' own 'hell-fire' interpretation.

56(94) Plutarch *De exil.* 604a

The Erinyes ensure that the sun's measures are not exceeded.

ἥλιος: 'the sun will not overstep its measures', i.e. it will keep to its set path as the regulator of the day, seasons and year. But elsewhere for Heraclitus there is a new sun every day (B 6) and its size is the width of a foot (B 3). If this is not flippancy, the theory may be that the sun is quenched as it sinks into the ocean in the west and is rekindled in the east.

Δίκης ἐπίκουροι: Δίκη, herself the daughter of Zeus, is represented as ensuring the constant pattern of the sun's movements by the agency of the Erinyes, traditionally the avengers of any violation of the natural order. But ἥλιος here, like κεραυνός in fr. 54, may be a symbol for the universal fire, the kindlings and quenchings of which are guaranteed according to a cosmic justice.

57(99) [Plutarch] *Aqua an ignis utilior* 957a

The sun is responsible for daylight, its absence for night.

ἕνεκα . . . ἄστρων: inserted from a paraphrase of the fragment in Clement, and from Plutarch *De Fortuna* 98c.

εὐφρόνη: cf. fr. 17 for the vocabulary and the sense. The recognition that night was explicable by the absence of sun (as day by its presence) was a recent discovery.

58(90) Plutarch *De E.* 388e

Fire, like gold, is a standard of exchange.

ἀνταμοιβή: the noun, followed by τά, is Diels' generally accepted emendation of the MSS ἀνταμοιβήσετα or ἀνταμείβεται. It is predicative with ἐστι implied - 'all things are an exchange for fire'. The genitives throughout are of price (cf. *G.* 1133), giving the equivalent value.

ὅκωσπερ . . . χρυσός: 'as goods for gold and gold for goods'. It is not that everything is at one time exchanged for fire (and so burned in an ἐκπύρωσις), for all the goods available are not bought up on any one occasion, but sometimes some things are exchanged for (or turned into) fire and at other times fire is given in exchange, i.e. it turns into something else but remains the standard whereby the exchange is assessed (cf. fr. 59 below).

59(31) Clement *Strom.* 5.104

The changes or turnings of fire.

πρῶτον . . . πρηστήρ: the explanation of the subject (πυρὸς τροπαί) is set after it with no connecting verb. The first 'turn' or reversal of fire is into sea, and of sea one half part turns to earth and the other to πρηστήρ (a form of fire associated with water, appearing most commonly as sheet lightning in rain and thus showing the transition from water to fire). The changes of the 'halves' are not total and instantaneous (which would mean the end of the sea) but continuous, with fire, sea and earth each keeping to a constant λόγος.

θάλασσα . . . γῆ: the second part of the fragment (perhaps belonging directly after the first, separated from it by some lines of Clement) gives the constancy of this λόγος in the change of sea to and from earth. θάλασσα is the subject throughout and the sense is 'sea is poured out (from earth) and is measured to the same amount as it was before it became earth'. (Emendations to the text such as adding an initial γῆ, deleting the last three words, or making the last word accusative are unnecessary).

60(91) Plutarch *De E.* 392b

The famous 'river' fragment, often however rejected as a later, short version of fr. 61 (cf. Kirk 368-84, Marcovich 206-14, Guthrie 1.488-92); it illustrates the saying frequently attributed to Heraclitus - πάντα ῥεῖ.

ἔστιν: in the sense of 'it is possible'.
ποταμῷ . . . τῷ αὐτῷ: 'the same river'.

61(12) Arius Didymus (Eusebius *Praeparatio evangelica* 15.20)

The explanation of why the river instantiates and illustrates continual flux. The river stays 'the same' (in the name and place that gives it its identity), but the waters of which it is composed change continually in a constant and regular flow.

ἐμβαίνουσιν: dative of the participle - 'on those who step into . . .'.

Fragments 62-76: The soul and the individual.

62(101) Plutarch *Adv. Col.* 1118c

An ambiguous statement on self-searching.

ἐμεωυτόν: Ionic for ἐμαυτόν. With ἐδιζησάμην the sense is both 'I engaged in search for my (true) self' and also 'I cross-examined myself' (i.e. 'I found out for myself without outside assistance').

63(35) Clement *Strom* 5.140

Philosophy as enquiry.

εὖ μάλα: 'indeed', 'very much so'.
ἵστορας: 'inquirers and observers', 'students'.
φιλοσόφους: the first extant occurrence of the word, here as an adjective with ἄνδρας. The sense is both 'men who love wisdom' and 'men who want to become wise'.

64(22) Clement *Strom.* 4.4

A great deal of effort is needed to produce a small 'nugget'. The individual hard work required of those who would be philosophers is in contrast with the polymath's secondhand learning.

οἱ διζήμενοι: the verb of fr. 62, here without ambiguity - 'seekers after gold', 'gold-miners'.

65(45) Diogenes Laertius 9.7

The limitless resources of soul.

πείρατα ἰὼν: Diels' emendation of the MSS πειραταιον - 'in your going you would not discover limits to soul'.
ἐπιπορευόμενος: the participle is used for the protasis, equivalent to εἰ and the optative - 'if you were to travel all the way'. πᾶσαν ὁδόν could also be taken as 'along every way' but this is less likely; the metaphor, continued in οὕτω βαθὺν λόγον, is of a seemingly bottomless pit or well.

66(115) Stobaeus 3.1.180

The increase of the soul's λόγος.

ψυχῆς ἐστι: 'there belongs to soul', 'soul has'.
ἑαυτὸν αὔξων: equivalent to αὐξόμενος ('increasing'), explaining why the λόγος is so deep. The human intellect has an inexhaustible capacity to extend the range of its understanding.

67(36) Clement *Strom.* 6.17

The changes of soul (like the 'turnings' of fire in fr. 59) are through water to earth and back from earth through water to soul.

ψυχῇσιν θάνατος: a deliberate paradox, assigning death to the life principle - 'death for souls is the birth of water, and death for water the birth of earth'. (For the translation 'it is death to souls to become water' something like the Neoplatonic variant ὑγρῇσι γένεσθαι is needed.) The admission of water into the physical structure of the individual soul is a beginning of death,

and the reduction of the moisture a corresponding increase of the life resources. It would seem that the transformations are continuous and dependent to some extent on individual motivation and effort.
ψυχή: an example of 'ring composition', with the sentence returning at its end to the noun of the starting point. There may be a distinction between the (plural) individual souls and the (singular) general life principle.

68(52) Hippolytus *Ref.* 9.9.4

An enigmatic fragment, usually understood in terms of a cosmic player eternally moving on his board such pieces as life / death, waking / sleeping, young / old (cf. fr. 47). But αἰών in its earlier uses is for one's life force or life time; so that it is perhaps the individual who is playing a game which he tries to win through a combination of chance and skill.

πεσσεύων: playing πεσσεία, a board game like backgammon, involving (probably) chance in the throw of a dice and skill in the movement of pieces.
παιδὸς ἡ βασιληίη: a trivialisation not of the divine steering (cf. frs. 3-5, 25 and 54), but of human values. A king can move people like pieces, but his own power is a temporary position.

69(85) Plutarch *Coriolanus* 22

The gains of θυμός are at the expense of soul.

θυμῷ: θυμός is the impulse to act, motivated and affected by desire and anger.
ὃ ἂν θέλῃ: general and indefinite - 'whatever it wants'.
ψυχῆς: genitive of the price paid.

70(117) Stobaeus 3.5.7

A drunkard literally has a wet ψυχή, which affects his perception and control of his body.

μεθυσθῇ: aor. pass. subj. of μεθύσκω - 'whenever he is drunk'.
ἐπαΐων: the range of meanings of the verb covers 'seeing', 'perceiving' and 'understanding'.
ὅκη: also written ὅκῃ - 'in what direction'.
ὑγρὴν . . . ἔχων: the adj. is predicative and the participle causal - 'because he has his soul wet', or (more exactly) 'watery'.

71(118) Stobaeus 3.5.8

Soul in its wisest and best state.

αὔη: a dry soul (awake, intelligent and active) is wisest, in contrast to the 'wet' soul of the drunkard in the previous fragment. An alternative reading (advocated by Kahn 245-54) is αὐγὴ ξηρὴ ψυχή, ambiguous between 'a beam of light is the dry soul' and 'a dry beam of light is soul'.

72(119) Stobaeus 4.40.23

Character determines destiny.

δαίμων: god, guardian god, or destiny. Here in the last sense: what happens to a man can be attributed to his ἦθος, the personality resulting from the habit of certain kinds of thoughts and actions which affects the physical composition of the soul.

73(29) Clement *Strom.* 5.59

The contrasted choices of the best and the many.

αἱρεῦνται: = αἱρέονται
ἀέναον: 'ever-flowing' and so 'unfailing', 'everlasting', contrasted with the adjacent θνητῶν. The best men exchange everything for one thing - immortal glory among mortal men, as did Achilles and Leonidas (cf. *Il.* 9.410-16 and Simonides fr. 4). A less likely interpretation of θνητῶν takes it as neut. plural with a second ἀντί understood - 'immortal glory instead of mortal things'.
κτήνεα: of any collection of farm animals - cattle, sheep, and, most appropriately here, pigs.

74(24) Clement *Strom.* 4.16

Those who die in battle are honoured.

ἀρηϊφάτους: Homeric compound from the root φεν - ('slain by Ares', i.e. in battle). Such men have a special status; they die in their prime, choosing everlasting glory in honourable combat (cf. fr. 34).

75(27) Clement *Strom.* 4.144

After death is the unexpected.

ἅσσα: Ionic for ἅτινα. The relative clause with its implied antecedent is the subject of μένει - 'what (i.e. things which) they do not expect . . . await men'.
ἔλπονται: 'hope' (which would imply a threat: there will

not be the good things they hope for) but also more neutrally 'expect', 'suppose' (cf. B 25 μόροι μέζονες μέζονας μοῖρας λαγχάνουσι).

76(63) Hippolytus *Ref*. 9.10.6

The guardians.

ἔνθα δ' ἐόντι: sometimes accepted as a reference to god - 'before the one who is there' - but the phrase is probably corrupt.

ἐπανίστασθαι: no subject is given, nor any verb to account for the infinitive, to show whether it is Heraclitus' view or one reported. The general sense is that 'they' (presumably some souls after death) arise and become guardians of the living, like Hesiod's golden race (*Erga* 121-25).

ἐγερτί: adverb meaning 'wakefully', ambiguously placed, to be taken with φύλακας γίνεσθαι 'they become watchful guardians') or with ζώντων ('of those who live wakefully') or with both.

καὶ νεκρῶν: perhaps Hippolytus' addition, given the disparaging reference to corpses in B. 96.

P A R M E N I D E S

Fragment 1: The journey to the goddess and her greeting.

Sextus *Adv. math.* 7.111

1.1-10: The young Parmenides is conveyed in a chariot driven by the daughters of Helios, the sun-god, in their journey along the sun's path.

1.1 ταί: = αἵ, an epic use of the article, in the form beginning with *tau*, as a relative pronoun; the gender shows that ἵπποι are mares.

φέρουσιν: 'in general, Parmenides in this fragment uses present tenses for permanent features, imperfects to denote the continuing activities of his journey, aorists to denote events that took place before these activities, and then aorists for the particular actions involved in his reception by the goddess.' (D.J. Furley, *Exegesis and Argument* 2-3)

ἱκάνοι: the optative is not iterative (the journey for Parmenides is only made once) but potential without ἄν/κε as often in Homer - 'as far as the θυμός might reach', i.e. 'as far as the heart's desire'.

1.2 πέμπον: unaugmented, as, in epic style, are most of the past verbs in this passage. φέρω, πέμπω and ἄγω are used of the mares pulling the chariot in which the κοῦρος sits, ἡγεμονεύω (5) and πέμπω again (8) of the charioteers.

ἐς ὁδὸν βῆσαν: 'tmesis' (cf. *G.* 1222), with ἐσβαίνω causal - 'put on the road'.

1.3 δαίμονος: 'of the goddess' (the road brings the κοῦρος eventually to the unidentified θεά of 22); or 'of the god', i.e. Helios. Stein emends to δαίμονες for the as yet unmentioned Heliades; ἥ . . . τῇ refers to the road. κατὰ πάντ' ἄστη seems to contradict 27; if correct, the phrase would mean 'over all the towns', as is the sun's path.

εἰδότα φῶτα: the κοῦρος does not yet 'know', so the sense may be 'the initiate', or, generally, 'the wise man'.

1.4 πολύφραστοι: 'much-perceiving', 'clever', or perhaps 'much-attending', 'careful'.

1.5 τιταίνουσαι: fem. plural participle - 'pulling (at full stretch)'.

1.6-8 'and the axle, glowing in the naves, gave out (<ἵει> supplied by Diels) the sound of a pipe, for it was pressed on both sides by two whirling wheels'.

1.8 ὅτε σπερχοίατο πέμπειν: 'whenever they hurried to drive' - the journey is habitual for the Heliades.

1.10 εἰς φάος: having left the house of Night 'for the region of light'. ὠσάμεναι (and ὦσειε 17) from ὠθέω.

1.11-21: The journey continues through the gate which lies across the routes of Night and Day; it is opened by Δίκη.

1.11 πύλαι: one gate with double leaves, which is set across the one road travelled alternately by Night and Day.
1.13 αἰθέριαι: 'sky-high'; the gate is tall, but clearly defined by its lintel and stone threshold.
1.14 κληῖδας ἀμοιβούς: 'the keys that fit them', or 'the keys that open and close'. The 'keys' are probably pins securing the fastened bar (βαλανῶτον ὀχῆα 16) across the double leaves.
1.15 παρφάμεναι: from παράφημι - 'beguiling', 'cajoling'.
1.17 ταὶ δὲ . . . ἀρηρότε: 'and they (the doors of the gate),
-20 flying open, revealed a wide gap between their leaves as they turned (ειλιξάσαι from ἑλίσσω) on their hinges, one after the other, the bronze jambs fitted with bolts and pins'.
1.21 ἔχον: unaugmented imperfect, here 'held in their control', 'guided'.

1.22-32: the goddess explains that the young man will learn both truth and human opinion.

1.22 θεά: the goddess is not identified, being neither Δίκη (who was left behind at the gate) nor Ἀνάγκη, referred to in the third person in fr. 8.30.
1.25 δῶ: short epic form for δῶμα - 'coming to our house'.
1.26 μοῖρα κακή: presumably death, which brings its victims on a far journey.
1.27 ἐκτὸς πάτου: 'far from the beaten track' - the English idiom is similar to the Greek.
1.28 χρεώ: sc. ἐστί - 'there is a need that you . . .', i.e. 'you must'.
1.29 εὐκυκλέος: 'well-rounded'; other readings are εὐπειθέος - 'well-persuading' and εὐφεγγέος -'bright'.
ἀτρεμὲς: 'unshaken', with an alternative reading ἀτρεκὲς - 'sure', 'precise'.
1.31 ἔμπης: epic for ἔμπας - 'nevertheless'.
μαθήσεαι: 2nd sing. future middle form; the object ταῦτα refers back to the βροτῶν δόξαι, which are then spelled out in the following ὡς clause.
1.31 ὡς . . . περ ὄντα: '(namely) that what seems must certainly
-32 exist, being indeed everything' (or, with the alternative reading περῶντα, 'going through everything'). Diels' δοκιμῶσ(αι) for δοκίμως, giving some such meaning as 'how one should examine what seems to exist', is now generally rejected.

Fragments 2 and 3: The Two Roads: ἔστι and οὐκ ἔστι.

2 Proclus *In Timaeum*. 1 (345.18)

These lines are likely to have continued immediately after fr. 1, with the goddess explaining the options to the κοῦρος, before proceeding to the main exposition of the Road of Truth.

2.1 ἐγὼν: epic form of ἐγώ before initial vowel (Karsten's emendation; ἄγε τῶν in Proclus). εἰ δ' ἄγ' is an epic formula of encouragement - 'come now'.
κόμισαι: aorist imperative middle as the active, with the composite meaning - 'take in, study and keep safe'.
2.2 διζήσιος: 'of enquiry', cf. fr. 7.2; this is a rare abstract noun from δίζημαι - the metaphor being of paths travelled in a search.
νοῆσαι: an early dative use of the infinitive with a general sense of purpose. This tends to be active in Greek, passive in English - 'is for thinking', i.e. 'can be thought about' (cf. *G.* 1532).
2.3 ὅπως ἐστίν: the first road - 'that "it is" and "there is an impossibility for it not to be"'; the second ἐστί in the line has the particular sense of possibility, cf. *LSJ* s.v. εἰμί, A.VI. The initially indefinite subject is defined by stages, starting with fr. 3 - 'what can be thought about'.
2.5 ὡς οὐκ ἔστιν: the second road - 'that "it is not" and "there is a necessity for it not to be"'. On the pattern of 1.3 οὐκ ἔστιν is restated as μὴ εἶναι with the modal χρεών ἐστι.
2.6 ἔμμεν: epic form of εἶναι.
παναπευθέα ἀταρπόν: 'a path completely unknowable'; the sense is preserved in the colloquialism - 'it gets you nowhere'; cf. also οὐ γὰρ ἀνυστόν in the next line - 'it is not accomplishable', 'it can't be done'.
2.7 οὔτε ἂν γνοίης . . . οὔτε φράσαις: the 'strong' form of the potential optative, equivalent to an absolute future (cf. *G.* 1329); it is impossible to know or speak intelligently about τὸ μὴ ἐόν - 'what does not exist'. (Parmenides consistently negatives this participle with μή, whatever its grammatical function.)

3 Clement *Strom*. 6.23

This is usually taken as the completion of fr. 2.

τὸ γὰρ αὐτὸ . . . εἶναι: 'the same thing is for thinking and for being', i.e. 'what can be thought can exist' - 'dative' or 'purpose' infinitives as in fr. 2.2. (The sentence is highly controversial. Other interpretations suggest 'knowing and being are the same', or 'to think means that what you think exists', but these are harder to reconcile with the argument of fr. 6.)

Fragment 4: The continuity of τὸ ἐόν.

Clement *Strom.* 5.15

A general connection is made between thinking and what there is. It is uncertain whether the lines should be taken temporally (as by Clement who quotes them), spatially, or both, i.e. of past and future events as well as of distant objects. The ambiguity may be deliberate at this initial stage.

4.1 νόῳ: probably instrumental dat., and active in sense - 'by thinking (about it)', rather than with παρεόντα 'present to the mind'.

4.2 ἀποτμήξει: 2nd sing. of the future middle (sometimes emended to ἀποτμήξῃ) rather than 3rd sing. future active with νόος understood from the previous line as subject. With the unusual construction of a following infinitive the sense is 'cut off and prevent'.

4.3 σκιδνάμενον: from σκίδνημι; the participle is present and causal - 'since by no means and in no way is it in a process of dispersing or collecting together in a world order'. (For κατὰ κόσμον, cf. B. 3; the goddess flatly contradicts Ionian-type cosmologies.) The statement is argued out in fr. 8.22-25 and 45-49.

Fragment 5: The start of the argument.

Proclus *In Parmenidem* 1 (708.16)

A general comment linking fragments 3, 6 and 8. Parmenides is not saying that the argument is circular but that entry at any stage in the discussion involves first a return to the starting point: 'engagement in rational discourse requires the existence of something to be talked about'; then the deductions follow down to the point of entry.

Fragment 6: The Road of Human Opinion

Simplicius *In Phys.* 86.27 and 117.3

To the two Roads of the second fragment is added a third, a confusion of ἔστι and οὐκ ἔστι, the road trodden by the unthinking majority of men.

6.1 χρὴ . . . ἔστιν: τὸ λέγειν τε νοεῖν τ' ἐὸν is the subject
-2 of the infinitive ἔμμεναι (epic for εἶναι) after χρή, and the construction follows that of frs. 2.2 and 3: 'it

must be the case that what there is for talking and thinking about exists' or in the more idiomatic passive ' . . . that what can be talked and thought about exists'. The argument continues: 'for it is possible for that to exist but it is not possible for nothing to'. For symmetry ἔστι should have the same sense - 'it is possible' in both clauses; εἶναι is understood at the end, as in the translation 'it is not possible for nothing to (exist)'.

6.2 ἄνωγα: epic perf. with pres. sense, and τά is pronominal - 'this (the complex argument of the previous one and a half lines) I ask you to think about'.

6.3 πρώτης . . . ἀφ' ὁδοῦ ταύτης: the first wrong road is οὐκ ἔστιν, understood from the previous line as μηδέν ἐστιν εἶναι. Complete nihilism is nonsense, and no one follows it.

6.4 ἀπὸ τῆς: 'from this', the second wrong road from which the goddess holds the κοῦρος back (<εἴργω> in 1.3 being supplied by Diels for the MS lacuna from fr. 7.2). In contrast with that of the previous line, this road is popular and crowded.

6.5 πλάττονται: a unique form from πλάζω.

δίκρανοι: 'two-headed', in that they face opposite directions simultaneously.

6.5 -6 ἀμηχανίη . . . νόον: 'helplessness keeps in a straight line (along the wrong path) a mind astray'. (πλακτός is a variant of πλαγκτός.)

6.7 τεθηπότες: from τέθηπα - epic perfect verb, usually in the participle - 'muddled', 'dazed'. The mental deafness and blindness here are similar to that of early man in Aesch. *Prom.* 447-48; cf. E. 2.21.

6.8 -9 'for whom "it is" and "it is not" are considered the same and not the same'. Ordinary uncritical people constantly accept both 'it is' and 'it is not'. For them generalisations are qualified along the lines of 'sometimes yes, sometimes no', 'in some places or ways yes, in others no'. They do not understand the basic contradictions involved in their assumptions.

6.9 παλίντροπος . . . κέλευθος: 'backward-turning route'. The travellers (πάντων is probably masc. rather than neut.) walk up and down the one road, accepting successively and / or simultaneously ἔστι and οὐκ ἔστι. The criticism is general, but some see a particular reference to Heraclitus; cf. H. 37.

Fragment 7: The deception of habit.

7. Plato *Sophist* 237a and Sextus *Adv. math.* 7.114

The κοῦρος is explicitly urged not to be misled by conventional attitudes, but to judge the argument only on the criterion of logic.

7.1 οὐ ... μήποτε ... δαμῇ: οὐ μή and the aor. subjunctive (from δάμνημι / δαμάζω) for an emphatic future negative - 'there will never be the force to bring it about that (i.e. it will never be proved that) what are not are'.

7.2 τῆσδ' ἀφ' ὁδοῦ: i.e. from the road taken by the crowds of fr. 6, who accept οὐκ ἔστι along with ἔστι.

7.3 ἔθος πολύπειρον: 'lifelong (*lit.* much-experienced) habit'.
βιάσθω: 3rd sing. pres. imperative of the deponent form of βίαω (epic for βιάζω) with active meaning.

7.4 νωμᾶν: 'wield', 'make use of'.
ἄσκοπον: (from σκοπέω) - 'not looking', or (from σκέπτομαι) - 'not looking carefully'.
ἠχήεσσαν: fem. pres. participle from ἠχέω - 'sounding', 'ringing'; cf. fr. 6.7.

7.5 γλῶσσαν: a reference not to the sense of taste but to the usual ways of talking. The goddess asks the κοῦρος to ignore his own 'non-seeing' eyes, his ears full of empty sounds and other people's opinions, but to judge by reason alone the hard-hitting argument she is going to give. (πολύδηριν - active in sense, rather than the passive 'much-contested' - the argument has not been heard, so can hardly yet be contested.) ἔλεγχος is specifically an argument that refutes accepted opinion.

7.6 ἐμέθεν: epic form of ἐμοῦ.

Fragment 8.1-49: Ἀληθεία - the Road of Truth in detail.

Simplicius *In Phys*. 145.1

8.1-6. The argument of the one true road is first summarised in a listing of the signs which mark its progress.

8.1 μόνος . . . μῦθος ὁδοῖο: 'only one account of a road', i.e. 'an account of only one road' (an example of 'transferred epithet').

8.2 ὡς ἔστιν: '(namely) that it is'; cf. frs. 1.29 and 2.3-4.
ἐπὶ . . . ἔασι: tmesis - 'are on'.

8.3 ὡς . . . ἐστιν: the first deduction, proved in (i) 8.6-21. ὡς explains σήματα, and the participle is causal - '(indicating) that, since it is, it is ungenerated and imperishable' (i.e. that it has no temporal beginning or end).

8.4 οὖλον μουνογενές: 'whole, the only one of its kind', pointing forward to (ii) 8.22-25. (An inferior reading, adopted by Diels/Kranz, is ἐστι γὰρ οὐλομελές.) ἀτρεμὲς - 'motionless', is deduced in (iii) 8.26-33.
ἠδ' ἀτέλεστον: 'and incomplete', but this is the opposite of the final deduction in (iv), beginning at 8.42. It would be better to read the affirmative ἠδὲ τελεῖον, cf. Owen *CQ* 10 (1960) 102.

8.5 οὐδέ . . . ξυνεχές: the denial of tenses marks the trans-
-6 ition between the summary and the detailed proof of the impossibility of generation and destruction.

8.6-21. (i) A long argument, with supplements, to show that once οὐκ ἔστι is (rightly) rejected, there can be no temporal start or finish.

8.6 διζήσεαι: for the form, cf. fr. 1.31.
γέννᾰν: here 'origin', 'source of generation'.
αὐτοῦ: refers back to the subject of ἔστι in lines 2 and 5, which in turn goes back to fr. 6.1 - 'the object of thought and discourse'.

8.8 φάσθαι: poetic middle for active. φάτον is the verbal adjective with ὅπως οὐκ ἔστι as the subject - 'that "it is not" is (logically) unsayable and unthinkable.

8.9 ὦρσεν: from ὄρνυμι, with ἄν for the potential indicative (cf. *G.* 1338) - 'what obligation would have stimulated it, starting from nothing, to be born?' (φῦν: an aorist infinitive form.) The reference for ἀρξάμενον is ambiguous between μιν (which in turn refers back to αὐτοῦ; cf. on line 6) and χρέος.
ὕστερον ἢ πρόσθεν: 'later or sooner', i.e. 'at any time'; or perhaps 'later rather than sooner', i.e. 'at one time rather than another', with the more interesting implication of what came to be known as 'the principle of sufficient reason'.

8.11 οὕτως: equivalent to 'that is why'.

8.12 οὐδέ . . . αὐτό: 'and the strength of conviction (πίστιος
-13 - Ionic genitive of πίστις) will never let anything apart from itself come to be from what is not', i.e. nothing produces nothing. (Reinhardt emended ἐκ μὴ ἐόντος to the positive ἐκ τοῦ ἐόντος.)

8.13 εἵνεκεν: epic/Ionic for ἕνεκα.

8.14 ἀνῆκε: ἀνίημι with infinitive translates 'allow'; the object of the verb, and of ἔχει in the following line, is implied from αὐτοῦ; cf. on lines 9 and 6.
χαλάσασα πέδῃσιν: 'after slackening (or undoing) it by means of (her) bonds', for the more natural 'slackening the bonds' or 'untying the ropes'. (Bergk accepted the MSS πέδησιν as the accusative of an otherwise unknown noun.) The 'bonds of Δίκη', like those of Μοῖρα in 1.37, is Parmenidean for 'logical necessity'.

8.17 τὴν μὲν . . . τὴν δ᾽: the Roads are once again contrasted -
-18 that of οὐκ ἔστι is unthinkable and unnameable and so to be abandoned, that of ἔστι (or, as here, πέλει) is true. The syntax seems to be: κέκριται - 'it has been decided' τὴν μὲν ἐᾶν - 'to abandon the one' . . .; τὴν δ᾽ - 'but the other', ὥστε πέλειν - 'that it is', (sc. κέκριται - 'it has been decided') εἶναι - 'is' καὶ ἐτήτυμον 'indeed true'. Less convincing alternatives are: (κέκριται) ὥστε . . . - '(there has been a judgment) that the

other is and is true'; or, with an infinitive understood - 'but (to take) the other, that it is and is true'.

8.19 πῶς . . . ἐόν: 'how then, since it is (ἐόν with a causal sense) could it perish?'. (Cf. E. 2.33.) This is Karsten's emendation for the MSS ἔπειτα πέλοι τὸ ἐόν. ἔπειτα is ambiguous between 'therefore' and 'thereafter'.

ἄν κε: the particles coupled have the same function as either one separately.

8.20 -21 εἰ γὰρ . . . ὄλεθρος: generation or coming-to-be in the past or the future implies οὐκ ἔστι, the logical impossibility that has been abandoned. For that reason (τὼς) generation has been extinguished (ἀπέσβεσται - perf. pass. from ἀποσβέννυμι) and, *mutatis mutandis*, destruction or ceasing-to-be is inadmissible (ἄπυστος negating the root πυνθάνομαι - 'not to be heard of', unlearnable').

8.20 ἔγεντ': for ἐγένετο, as in Hesiod and elsewhere, *metri causa*.

οὐδ': used because of the previous negative - 'if it came into being, it is not, and (it is not) if it is going to be in the future'.

8.22-25. (ii) Furthermore, there can be no division into a succession of separate entities, nor any internal differentiation.

8.22 ὁμοῖον: adverbial - 'since it all equally is'; so Owen, *loc. cit.* 96-97, and cf. line 5 above; more traditionally - 'since it is all the same'. If there cannot be any start or stop (the conclusion of the previous section) there cannot be a series of starts and stops, and indivisibility is the consequence.

8.23 -24 οὐδέ . . . χειρότερον: 'and not more at all or less at all which (τό as relative pronoun) would prevent its continuity'.

8.25 τῷ . . . πελάζει: 'therefore it is a continuous whole, for what-is comes right up against what-is'. πελάζει is metaphorical; literal motion is denied in the next section.

8.26-33. (iii) From temporal continuity are deduced immobility and completeness.

8.26 ἀκίνητον: i.e. without change or movement.

ἐν πείρασι: from πεῖραρ, epic/Ionic form of πέρας - 'in the limitations' of great bonds, as in line 14 - 'the bonds of Δίκη', which impose restrictions of logical possibility.

8.28 πίστις ἀληθής: 'true conviction', almost 'the force of logic'. Since there is no genesis or destruction it cannot happen that what is not the case will come to be so, or that what was true at one time will not be true at another; and so no change or movement is possible.

8.29 ταὐτόν . . . μένει: the emphatic assertion of change-
-30 lessness and immobility - 'staying the same and in the same place it lies by itself and in this way stays firmly as it is'. (Proclus has μίμνει in line 29 for τε μένον; cf. X. 8.1.)

8.31 πείρατος ἐν δεσμοῖσιν: 'in the bonds of limit which encompasses it', a variation on line 26; necessity here imposes the (logical) restraints.

8.32 οὕνεκεν: 'wherefore', 'that is why', introducing a new but related point. There is no change and, since there is no deficiency, no need for change. ἐστί is then understood with θέμις - 'it is not right for what-is to be incomplete'. ἀτελεύτητον is 'unfinished' in the sense of 'incomplete' rather than 'without end or boundary'.

8.33 μὴ ἐὸν: μή is often deleted, and a variant ἐπιδευές then adopted to give: 'if it were (lacking), it would lack everything', taking the participle as conditional and ἄν with the imperfect for the present unfulfilled apodosis. With μὴ ἐόν we have either 'if it were not (not lacking)', i.e. 'otherwise', or preferably 'if there were what-is-not it would be completely deficient'. (The last two syllables of ἐπιδεές scan as one long - synezesis; and μὴ is short before ἐὸν by epic correption.)

8.34-41. The main conclusions of the argument so far are here summarised, with a reference back to two preliminary points - frs. 2.7 and 3 on νοεῖν and εἶναι, and fr. 6.4-9 on the confusions of ordinary mortals.

8.34 ταὐτὸν . . . ἔμεναι: 'what can be thought is the same as
-38 on-account-of-which there is thought' (i.e. 'the same as what exists to be thought', a restatement of fr. 3, explained by the repeated γάρ): 'for without what-is, on which what is expressed depends, you will not find thinking, for nothing else either (<ἢ> *add.* Preller) is or will be except what-is, since Μοῖρα has bound *this* (τό γε referring back to τὸ ἐόν) so as to be (ἐμέναι = εἶναι, consecutive infin.) whole and immobile'. Less plausibly οὕνεκέν ἐστι νόημα has been taken as 'the thought that "it is"', which identifies thought and being, and ἐν ᾧ πεφατισμένον ἐστίν as 'in what has been expressed' or 'in which it has been expressed'.

8.38 τῷ: 'therefore' (cf. *LSJ* s.v. ὁ, VII.2) all things will be names only', and not correspond to reality; an alternative reading is ὀνόμασται.

8.40 εἶναί τε καὶ οὐχί: they go wrong in combining 'it is not' with 'it is'; cf. fr. 6.8.

8.41 διά . . . ἀμείβειν: the infin. is διαμείβειν, the adverb-preposition separated by tmesis (cf. fr. 1.2) - 'to alter bright colour'. Locomotion is given in τόπον ἀλλάσσειν and the second sense of κίνησις (alteration) is summed up in the most obvious visible change - that of colour.

8.42-49. (iv) The last deduction, for spatial continuity, picks up the argument from 8.33.

The logical order of the complex argument of lines 42-49, with ἐπεί twice and γάρ three times, is as follows:

there is no what-is-not or what-is-more-or-less (46-48)
∴ there is no bigger or smaller here or there (44-45 - the spatial application)
and it is 'non-plunderable'. (48)
∴ it is equal to itself from every direction (49)
∴ it is equally balanced (44)
∴ complete like a ball. (42-43)

8.42 αὐτὰρ . . . πύματον: 'since (there is) the utmost limitation', referring back to the constraints of necessity (line 31), which forbid change and deficiency.
8.43 πάντοθεν: it is complete 'from every direction' - the argument now turns to the spatial implications.
εὐκύκλου . . . ὄγκῳ: 'like the mass of a well-rounded ball'; what-is is compared to but not identified with a sphere.
8.44 μεσσόθεν ἰσοπαλὲς πάντῃ: 'from the centre in every direction evenly matched', a reference not to radius length but to general uniformity.
8.44-45 τὸ . . . ἢ τῇ: τὸ is pronominal - 'for it cannot be bigger at all or smaller at all in one place than another' (cf. lines 23-24 above, and 49 below).
8.46 τό: here the relative pronoun, with οὐκ ἐόν as the antecedent - 'which would prevent it reaching to its like'.
8.47-48 οὔτ' . . . ἧσσον: 'nor is there a way in which what-is is more in one place and less in another than what-is'.
8.48 ἄσυλον: 'inviolate' or, more exactly, 'cannot be plundered' (from συλάω); 'bits' of ἐόν cannot be taken away.
8.49 οἷ . . . κύρει: 'for, equal from every direction to itself (reading οἷ with Diels for the MS οἱ) it keeps within its limitations uniformly'.

Fragment 8.50-61: Δόξα - the Road of Human Opinion

Simplicius *In Phys*. 38.30 and 146.23

This road, of falsehood and deception, posits two entities,

fire and night, each with its own separate characteristics.

8.52 κόσμον . . . ἀπατηλὸν: 'deceitful ordering of my words'. Fulfilling the promise given in fr. 1.28-30, the goddess gives instruction in both truth and falsehood.

8.53 κατέθεντο: the subject must be 'men in general', supplied from the adjective βροτείας in line 51 (cf. βροτῶν γνώμη 61). The singular γνώμη would be expected here for 'they laid down a judgment' (and there is a MS variant γνώμαις); the effect, with the position of δύο, is ambiguous between 'they made a decision to name two forms' and 'they were in two minds about naming forms' (cf. Mourelatos, 228-30).

8.54 τῶν μίαν οὐ χρεών ἐστιν: 'of which not one should be (named)'. Other interpretations are 'one (but not the other) should not be named', taking μίαν as ἑτέρην, and 'one (without the other) should not be named'. Since the two forms are then described with characteristics that have been denied in the Road of Truth, and the goddess in the prologue, now, and at the end of the section, insists on the wrongness of the Road of Opinion, attempts to salvage some truth from the Δόξα are misguided.

8.55 τἀντία . . . δέμας: 'they judged them opposite in form', with δέμας as acc. of respect (cf. line 59 below and also X. 2.2).

8.57 μέγ' [ἀραιὸν] ἐλαφρόν: both adjectives are needed - ἀραιόν to contrast with πυκινόν and ἐλαφρόν with ἐμβριθές - but one must be deleted to save the metre; the choice is open.

8.57 -58 ἑωυτῷ . . . μὴ τωὐτόν: 'everywhere the same as itself but not the same as the other' - the first expression of the concept of an element.

8.58 -59 κἀκεῖνο . . . ἀδαῆ: 'but also that one, independent, oppositely (τἀντία here is adverbial) dark night' (or perhaps 'unknowing night', the ambiguity is probably deliberate). Night was still thought of positively as a 'body', thick and heavy. Empedocles, as far as we know, was the first to recognise it as merely the absence of sunlight; cf. 31B48

8.60 τὸν . . . φατίζω: 'I tell you the whole plausible arrangement'. The Δόξα contained a comprehensive Milesian-type cosmology.

8.61 ὡς . . . παρελάσσῃ: the reason for giving the deceptive argument - 'so that no judgment of mortals may drive past you', i.e. granted that it starts from a mistaken double premise, this cosmology surpasses others.

Fragment 9: The cosmology based on light and dark.

Simplicius *In Phys.* 180.9

From the minimum pairing and the universality of light and night, it is concluded that all things are composed of them, solely and exclusively.

9.1 φάος: 'light', described in 8.56 as 'fire of flame in the sky'.
9.2 τά: ὀνόματα is probably the noun implied. The appearance and functioning of any one thing, which distinguishes it from another and determines its name, depend on the proportions of the constituent light and night.
9.4 ἴσων ἀμφοτέρων: 'both equal'; cf. E. 2.27.
ἐπεὶ . . . μηδέν: 'since (there is) nothing with either', i.e. everything has one or both. If μέτα and the implied ἐστι are taken as one verb, the sense then is - 'since nothing is not a part of either'.

Fragments 10-11: The programme for the Road of Human Opinion.

10 Clement *Strom.* 5.138

A summary list of celestial phenomena to be discussed.

10.1 αἰθερίαν φύσιν: 'the nature of aither' - the bright sky above the rain and mists, which is bounded by the οὐρανός.
10.3 ἀίδηλα: ambiguous between passive and active ('unseen', 'unknown' as well as 'making unseen', 'destructive') and contrasting with the previous two adjectives to give: 'the unknown / destructive deeds of the bright sun's pure torch'; the sun's function is both life-bringing and life-destroying.
10.4 περίφοιτα: epithet transferred from the genitive noun - 'of the circular moon as it travels round'.
10.5 εἰδήσεις: εἰδήσω and εἴσομαι (cf. line 1) are used as futures for οἶδα.
ἀμφὶς ἔχοντα: 'surrounding'; the οὐρανός is the outer circumference of the cosmos, to which the fixed stars were thought to be attached.
10.6 ἔνθεν ἔφυ τε: Sylberg's reading for the MS ἔνθεν μὲν γὰρ ἔφυγε.
ἐπέδησεν: from πεδάω, and with a consecutive infinitive; cf. 8.37-38.
πείρατα ἄστρων: 'the limits set by the (fixed) stars'.

11 Simplicius *In Cael.* 559.22

The opening of a cosmogony. There is some overlap with fr. 10 in the programme of subjects.

11.2 γάλα . . . οὐράνιον: the Milky Way.

11.2 ὄλυμπος ἔσχατος: a variation for οὐρανός, the extreme limit
-3 of the sky.

11.3 ὠρμήθησαν: passive for intransitive middle. The hot force of stars rushing to be born is a rare poetic touch for Parmenides.

Fragments 12-15: Some lines on cosmology.

12 Simplicius *In Phys*. 39.14 and 31.13

An obscure fragment about rings of fire and night and a central guiding goddess.

12.1 πλῆντο: so Bergk; Fränkel suggests πλῆνται for the MSS
-2 πάηντο or πύηντο. ἀκρήτοιο is Stein's suggestion for ἀκρή- or ἀκρίτοις. From Aetius 2.7.1 (A37) the feminine plural subject is στέφαναι 'crowns' or 'bands'.

μετὰ . . . ἵεται: i.e. μεθίεται - 'goes through', 'permeates'. Rings of fire presumably account for daylight and the sun, and rings of night with some fire for the night sky and stars; the details are irretrievable.

12.3 ἐν δὲ μέσῳ τούτων: i.e. halfway between earth and the οὐρανός, a position from which the goddess could control both the heavenly bodies and human life (cf. κατὰ μέσον in Plato's Myth of Er. *Rep*. 616c). The centre of the whole was occupied by the spherical earth (cf. Aetius *loc. cit.*) and some identify the goddess with a central fire within the earth.

δαίμων: the divinity is feminine, as the relative ἥ shows, but nameless. Possibly she is Ἀνάγκη from fr. 10.6, standing here for the physical necessity of celestial movements and animal reproduction. In her sexual function and connection with Eros she is like Aphrodite, and so perhaps influenced Empedocles' Φιλία.

12.4 ἄρχει: with the genitive, both 'begins' and 'controls'; πάντα is adverbial - 'in all respects', 'entirely'.

12.5 μιγῆν: a unique form of the aorist passive infinitive of μ(ε)ίγνυμι (if Stein's emendation of the MSS is correct), used here as an infinitive of purpose.

12.6 ἄρσεν θηλυτέρῳ: ἄρσην and θῆλυς are the general biological terms for male and female; the comparative 'indicates opposition rather than comparison', *LSJ* s.v. θῆλυς.

13 Simplicius *In Phys*. 39.18

μητίσατο: Simplicius gives the subject as the goddess in the context of fr. 12; 'devised Eros' is a strange expression and perhaps the meaning is 'brought it about that Eros was the first of the gods' (cf. Hesiod *Theogony* 116).

14 Plutarch *Adv. Col.* 1116a

The moon moves round the earth and shines with borrowed light.

νυκτιφαὲς: 'night-shining' of the moon.
ἀλλότριον φῶς: the Homeric phrase 'a man from somewhere else' is used for 'a light from somewhere else', repeated by Empedocles, B 45.

15 Plutarch *De fac. lun.* 929b

παπταίνουσα: also of the moon - 'looking with a searching glance'.

Fragment 16: The physical basis of intelligence.

Aristotle *Metaph.* 1009b22

A difficult but important fragment with variant readings and interpretations. The main point is that the proportion of light and night in the physical structure determines the nature of the thinking. The spectrum ranges from total light, which gives complete knowledge, to all dark, the state of the unknowing corpse.

16.1 ἑκάστοτ': so the E^1J MSS of Aristotle and those of Theophrastus (ἕκαστος Aristotle E^2, Alexander; ἑκάστῳ Aristotle Ab). κρᾶσις is Calogero's change for κρᾶσιν - 'as on each and every occasion the mixture of the much-wandering limbs holds, so does thought happen (παρίσταται Aristotle; παρεστήκεν Theophrastus) for men'. (Reading ἕκαστος and κρᾶσιν we have 'as each man has the mixture . . .'.) The quality of one's thought about the outside world and the quantity of knowledge one can take in depend on the amount of light in proportion to dark in the thinking subject.

16.2-4 τὸ γὰρ . . . πάντι: 'for it is the same thing which thinks, (namely) the nature of the limbs, for all men, each and every one'. More peculiarly, if ὅπερ is taken as accusative, the sense is 'the nature of the limbs is the same as what it thinks'.

16.4 τὸ πλέον: 'what there is more of' is, or determines, the thought - limited if dark predominates, wide-ranging and superior if light does; cf. H. 71, E. 14-15.

Fragment 17: Conclusion.

17(19) Simplicius *In Cael.* 558.9

The fragment sums up the Road of Human Opinion.

17.2 μετέπειτ᾽ ἀπὸ τοῦδε: 'hereafter in the future'.
τραφέντα: intransitive aorist - 'they will mature and die out', 'have their beginning and end'.

17.3 τοῖς: refers back to τάδε - the contents of the world of experience, in which each object has been given a distinctive name but, (from 8.38) a name only, having no reference to reality.

ZENO

Fragments 1-4: Arguments on plurality.

1 Simplicius *In Phys.* 141.1, 139.11

Fragments 1-3 are quoted in a long commentary by Simplicius on Aristotle *Physics* 187a1, which includes an extensive paraphrase of material from Zeno. Following Zeno's characteristic method, the section draws sets of contradictory conclusions from the ordinary assumption that there are may things in existence. Dealing first (in frs. 1 and 2) with the *spatial extent* of the 'many things', Zeno sets out to show that, if they are assumed *either* (i) to have no size *or* (ii) to have some size, absurd conclusions follow. Fr. 1 demolishes (i), the concept of many things with no size. The argument is summarised in the first sentence and then presented in detail.

εἰ . . . εἴη: 'if what exists had no size, it would not exist'.
εἰ . . . προσγένοιτο: 'for if it (the subject - τὸ ὄν, taken as 'any existing thing which is assumed to have no size') were added to any other existing thing . . .'.
μεγέθους . . . ἐπιδοῦναι: the genitive absolutes are conditional - 'if it has no size and is added on, it is not able to contribute anything to (the other's) size'.
ἂν . . . εἴη: potential, with οὐδὲν as complement - 'what is now being added on would be nothing'.
ἀπογινομένου: the subject of the genitive absolute is again the existing thing that has no size - 'and if, while it is being subtracted, the other thing is no less . . .'. (Future indicative in this type of open condition is generally translated by the present; cf. *G.* 1405.)
δῆλον ὅτι . . .: 'it is obvious that what was added or subtracted was nothing'.

2(1) Simplicius *In Phys.* 141.2

This fragment tackles (ii), the other horn of the dilemma. If it is assumed that the many things have size, then they can be shown to be infinitely big.

εἰ δέ ἐστιν: the subject is πολλά.
καὶ ἀπέχειν . . . ἑτέρου: 'and for one part of it to be distinct from another'. To have size and thickness, i.e. to be three dimensional, requires at the least that one surface is distinct or separate from another.
περὶ τοῦ προύχοντος: i.e. 'about the forward part'; προέξει αὐτοῦ τι 'it will project a little from it'. Any 'edge'

will have size (since it is a part of a body), and so itself will have an 'edge'.

ὅμοιον . . . λέγειν: 'to say this once is to say it for ever' - Greek for 'and so *ad infinitum*'.

οὐδὲν γὰρ . . . οὐκ ἔσται: 'for no such (part) of it will be last, and there will not be another without a further by it'. (Gomperz makes the second clause a result of the first, with ὥστε for οὔτε.)

οὕτως . . . ἄπειρα εἶναι: the unacceptable conclusions are put together. If there are many things, then *either* (i) they are so small as to have no size (and are nothing, fr. 1) *or* (ii) they have some size, which makes them infinitely big (fr. 2). ἄπειρα - 'without limit' could be for the indefinitely as well as the infinitely large.

3 Simplicius *In Phys.* 140.29

Here Zeno draws contradictory conclusions about the *number* of the many things assumed.

ἀνάγκη . . . ἐστί: 'they must be just as many as they are'.

πεπερασμένα: from περαίνω and connected with πέρας; cf. P. 8.26, 31 and 43. It means 'limited' in the senses of both a definite / specific number (as contrasted with any other number greater or smaller than it) and a finite number (contrasted with an infinite one)- cf. Hussey 103.

ἄπειρα: 'unlimited', '(numerically) infinite', i.e. counting them off is an unending process.

ἀεί . . . ἕτερα μεταξύ: 'for there will always be other things between the existing things, and others again between those'. μεταξύ with the genitive - 'in the middle of', 'between' is primarily spatial (cf. Hussey *loc. cit.*). Two entities, if they are to be two and not one, require a third to separate them, and then two more μεταξύ to separate the middle from the extremes, and so on; an infinite series is generated in this way.

4 Diogenes Laertius 9.72

This is a summary of a general argument on motion. The gist of the argument can be put together in the following way: anything that moves moves *either* in the place in which it is (but there it is at rest; cf. on 5 (iii) below) *or* in the place in which it is not (but that is impossible), and so it does not move.

ἐν ᾧ ἐστι τόπῳ: 'in the place in which it is'. With this type of relative there is a neat attraction of the antecedent into the clause (cf. *G.* 1037-38).

Fragment 5 (A25-28)

Aristotle *Phys*. 239b9-240a1

The famous four puzzles or 'paradoxes' are given here in Aristotle's brief summary, since the original wording is no longer extant. In this chapter of the *Physics* the text is interspersed with Aristotle's own comments. The subsequent literature on these paradoxes reflects the fascination that they have had for logical minds over the centuries. The short notes here are no more than a brief guide to the presentation of them.

(i) the Dichotomy

The original problem was probably put in terms of an athlete unable to run the set length of the stadium track (about 200 metres); cf. Aristotle *Topics* 160b8. At half-way, 100 metres are left, half-way of that and 50 metres are left, half-way of that 25, and so on; the position cannot be reached when there is not still a half of the remaining distance to be covered. It is therefore impossible to complete a movement over a set distance.

διά . . . τὸ τέλος: an extended example of the accusative and infinitive with the article dependent on a preposition (cf. *G*. 1546) - 'on the grounds that anything moving along must arrive at the half-way (position) before the finish'.

(ii) the Achilles

The problem is basically the same as the Dichotomy, on a runner being unable to reach his goal; here the 'goal' is on the move as well. When Achilles gets to the tortoise's first position, T_1, the tortoise will be at T_2; when Achilles reaches T_2 the tortoise will be at T_3, and so on. The distances between the two will continually decrease, but the tortoise will always be one move ahead.

τὸ βραδύτατον . . . θέον: 'the slowest . . . as it runs'. Simplicius tells us that the slow contestant was the tortoise.

ἔμπροσθεν . . . φεῦγον: 'for the pursuer must first reach (the position) from where the one running away started'. It is assumed that the slower starts ahead of his pursuer, for otherwise there would be no chase; how far ahead is immaterial.

ὥστε . . . τὸ βραδύτερον 'so that the slower must always be a bit (τι) ahead'.

(iii) the Arrow

The arrow puzzle could be set out as follows

the arrow is moving at any time (*t*) during its flight;

at any time (t) the arrow is at rest, in its own length; if the moving arrow is at rest at any time (t) in its flight, it is motionless throughout.

(For a different version, which involves the complete integration of fr. 4 with the Arrow, cf. Vlastos, *Phronesis* (1966) 3-18.)

ῥηθείς: from ἐρῶ, used as a passive participle for εἶπον.
ἕστηκεν: perfect form with present sense - 'stays still', 'is stationary'. The explanatory sentence in brackets is taken from an earlier discussion, at *Phys*. 239b6. The text is frequently emended; here the only change is to delete ἢ κινεῖται after πᾶν.
ὅταν . . . ἴσον: 'whenever it is according to the equal', i.e. 'whenever it is (in a place or space) equal to its own length'.
ἔστιν . . . νῦν: 'and anything moving is always in the now', i.e. is moving at any particular time during its flight.

(iv) the Stadium

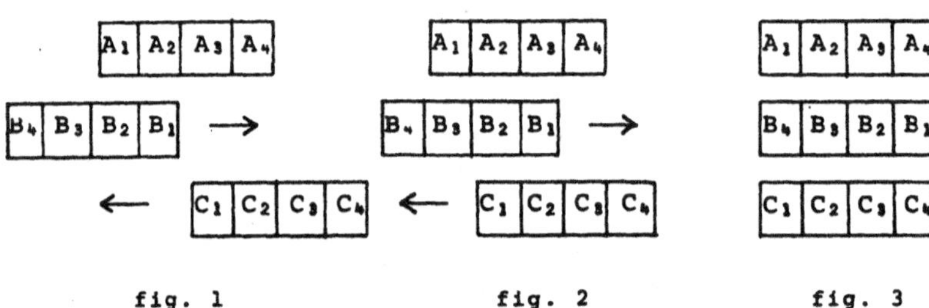

fig. 1 fig. 2 fig. 3

The B's and C's are the equal sets of contiguous blocks moving at equal speeds past each other and past the stationary set of A's. If it takes time t for one block to move past two blocks (B_1 past C_1 and C_2 in fig. 2), then it will take $\frac{1}{2}t$ to move past one (B_1 past A_3), but the two passings take the same time, therefore $\frac{1}{2}t = t$. Similarly, in fig. 3, it has taken $2t$ for B_1 to move past C_1 C_2 C_3 C_4, and t to move past A_3 and A_4, but it is the same time, and therefore $2t = t$.

The sentence translates as follows: 'the fourth (is) the one about equal blocks (ὄγκοι) moving past equal (blocks) from opposite directions in the stadium - one set from the end of the stadium and one from the middle - at the same speed, in which he thinks that half the time is equal to twice as much (i.e. that the given time is equal to twice itself)'. That there is a third set of stationary blocks emerges from the Aristotelian context; the 'middle' here is probably the half-way turning point at the other end of the course, rather than the middle of these stationary blocks.

MELISSUS

Fragments 1-6: Temporal and spatial infinity.

1 Simplicius *In Phys.* 162.24

Generation implies a previous state of non-existence, from which nothing can arise. From the summary at *In Phys.* 103.16 the following is sometimes taken as the first fragment of Melissus: εἰ μὲν μηδέν ἐστι, περὶ τούτου τί ἂν λέγοιτο ὡς ὄντος τινος; - 'if there is nothing, what could be said of it as if it were something?'.

εἰ γὰρ . . . ἐκ μηδενός: 'for if it came to be, necessarily there was a state of nothingness before its generation; so, if there was a state of nothingness, nothing at all would come from nothing'. Melissus uses μηδέν for Parmenides' more frequent (τὸ) μὴ ἐόν. Like Parmenides, he takes an initially indefinite subject and defines it in stages through the argument.

2 Simplicius *In Phys.* 29.22 and 109.20

Without generation there is no beginning or end, and so what-is is eternally.

ἄπειρον: 'temporally unlimited' in this context; cf. P. 8.22-25.

εἰ . . . εἶχεν: another mixed condition as in fr. 1 - 'if it had come to be it would have a beginning'.

ποτε γενόμενον: the participle implies a protasis for ἤρξατο ἂν and ἐτελεύτησε ἂν - 'having come / if it had come into being at some time, then it would have had a starting point (and a finish)'. Simplicius reads γινόμενον and understands it as completing the sense of the verbs - 'it would have begun coming into being'. Something like ὀλόμενον for the second instance would give an improved symmetry and argument (and the participle may have been corrupted by dittography); but after Parmenides there would be a ready assumption that generation implies destruction.

οὐ . . . ἐστι: 'for (it is) not possible (*lit.* achievable) for what does not exist as a whole to exist for ever'. πᾶν = 'a (temporally) continuous whole'; for ἀνυστόν, cf. P. 2.7.

3 Simplicius *In Phys.* 109.31

The spatial application of infinity.

τὸ μέγεθος: accusative of 'specification' with an adjective - 'unlimited as to / in extent'. The strict transference to space of the argument for the removal of temporal limits marks Melissus' significant development beyond Parmenides; cf. on P. 8.42-49 above.

4 Simplicius *In Phys.* 110.3

Beginning and end impose limits on existence.

οὐδὲν: a general negative subject - no thing that starts and stops is either temporally or spatially infinite.

5 Simplicius *In Phys.* 110.5

The compressed argument is filled out in fr. 6.

περανεῖ: contracted future in another mixed condition: 'if it were not one thing, it will impose a limit in relation to some other thing'.

6 Simplicius *In Cael.* 557.16

The lack of limitation implies uniqueness.

εἰ γὰρ . . . πρὸς ἄλληλα: 'if it were unlimited (which it is) it would be one, for if it were two (which it is not) one would limit the other'. <ἄπειρον> is Burnet's addition from the Simplicius context.

Fragment 7: Denials of change, pain, and emptiness.

7 Simplicius *In Phys.* 111.19

A long fragment in Parmenides' style, deducing a series of denials about what there is. Since (i), as has been shown, it is eternal, unlimited and one, it follows that (ii) there can be no change at all, (iii) no rearrangement, (iv)-(v) no pain, or (vi) distress. And (vii), since what is empty is nothing, it is not empty. So, being full, (viii) it does not admit of locomotion, or (ix)-(xi) of variation in density.

7(i) ὁμοῖον πᾶν: 'the same all over'; cf. P. 8.5, 22 and 48.

7(ii) καὶ . . . ἀνιᾶται: a programme of sections (ii)-(iv); cf. the σήματα in P. 8.2-6. The moods change from the optatives with ἄν - 'it could / will not perish' (the potential optative hardly differing from a future; cf. *G.* 1329) to the present indicative - 'and it does not feel pain nor is distressed'.

εἰ γὰρ . . . γίνεσθαι: 'if it alters, necessarily it is not homogeneous, but what was there before ceases to be, and what was not comes to be'. If something is 'the same all over all the time' it could not change, for change would have to begin at some time and in some spatially extended part; this would involve the destruction of that part as such and its replacement by what previously did not exist.

εἰ . . . χρόνῳ: a famous and enigmatic sentence. (ὄλοιτο is Mullach's change for ὀλεῖται. Simplicius (*In Cael.* 113.21) has γινόμενον, ὀλεῖται ἂν which Diels emends to γίνοιτο, ὀλεῖται πᾶν.) 'Moreover (τοίνυν), if the whole were to become different by (as much as) a single hair in ten thousand years, it would pass away in the whole of time.' θρίξ was proverbial for the perceptible minimum; cf. 'a hair's breadth'. The slightest change would initiate a process that would eventually end in total extinction; immutability is absolute.

7(iii)μετακοσμηθῆναι: of change, not by the loss of parts or the introduction of something new, but of internal rearrangement. For ἀνυστόν, cf. on fr. 2.7.

κόσμος: here for the internal arrangement, order or structure. Change of κόσμος involves destruction of the old arrangement and generation of a new one. Generation and destruction have been denied, and so then has the change of κόσμος.

πῶς . . . ᾖ: the text is Heidel's emendation for the MSS πῶς ἂν μετακοσμηθὲν (*add.* τῶν E) ἐόντων τι ᾗ. Diels keeps to this, with εἴη for τι ᾗ.

τι: adverbial - 'if it became different *in any way*, immediately (ἤδη) there would be a change of κόσμος.

7(iv): what is in pain cannot survive, and pain, being an addition or subtraction, is incompatible with homogeneity.

ἀλγέον: the participle is conditional - 'if it were in pain it could not be a (temporally consecutive) whole'.

χρῆμα ἀλγέον: the subject of δύναιτο - 'something in pain could not be for ever'. The next statement shows pain as a loss of δύναμις.

τευ: epic/Ionic for τινος, the subject of the genitive absolute. The sense is causal - 'it (the subject) would be in pain because something is being added or taken away'.

7(v): the argument in the first two sections of this fragment also ruled out pain, since pain involves change - from a healthy to a non-healthy state.

ἀπὸ . . . ὄλοιτο: = ἀπόλοιτο, a rare prose example of the separation of the preposition in a compound verb (tmesis; cf. *G.* 1222), common in Homer and the early poets. Pain involves the destruction of a present existing healthy state and the genesis of a new (previously non-existent) one.

7(vi) ὡυτός: = ὁ αὐτός. The same argument holds for 'distress' ἀνιάω in the passive tends to be used for mental grief or anguish, contrasting with the more physical ἀλγέω. The denials in (iv)-(vi) imply that the opposite condition, that of health and pleasant feeling, is to be attributed to the subject. On this, cf. X. 8 and 9, E. 4.

7(vii)-(xi): The remainder of the fragment is concerned with arguments about 'empty' and 'full'. Melissus and Empedocles recognise 'what is not' spatially as 'empty', but the technical term 'void', as a translation of κενόν, is not appropriate until the atomists.

7(vii) οὐδὲ . . . μηδέν: 'it is not empty at all (οὐδέν as emphatic negative adverb), for what is empty is nothing (the second οὐδέν is predicative), and then what is nothing (τὸ μηδέν - the standard Eleatic term) could not be'.

7(viii): for anything to move, empty place to move into is needed; but there is no empty place in the full to move into, and so no movement.

ἔχει: with an infinitive for capability - 'it cannot retreat in any direction'.

ἀλλὰ πλέων ἐστίν: since it has been shown not to be empty at all, obviously it is 'full', a *plenum*.

εἰ . . . τὸ κενόν: standard unreal conditions for the present, with imperfect indicative - 'if (part of) it were empty, (another part of) it would withdraw to the empty (part)'.

κενοῦ δὲ μὴ ἐόντος: 'if / since it is not empty'; the negative μή indicates how the genitive absolute is to be taken.

7(ix); the argument against its being dense or rare (cf. P. 8.23-24). The main proponent of variation in density had been Anaximenes.

τὸ γὰρ ἀραιὸν . . . πυκνῷ: 'it is not possible (ἀνυστόν - 'achievable', as at (iii) and in fr. 2) for what is rare to be full in the same way as the dense'. τὸ ἀραιόν γε - 'the rare *of course* is emptier than the dense'. The argument is obvious: to be 'rare' is to be more interspersed with what is empty; there is no empty, and so no variation of density.

7(x): a definition of 'full'.

ποιήσασθαι: middle voice - 'adapt', 'make for oneself'.

εἰ . . . χωρεῖ τι ἢ εἰσδέχεται: 'if it retreats (i.e. leaves a χώρα, 'an area') or takes in (anything)'.

7(xi): a restatement of the argument from plenitude to immobility.

Fragment 8

Simplicius *In Cael.* 558.21

A detailed and lively refutation of the pluralism and change accepted by the senses.

8(ii) εἰ γὰρ . . . ἓν εἶναι: 'if there were many things (the imperfect indicative for the unreal present) it is necessary for them to be such as I say the one is' Melissus refers particularly to the complex immutability of what there is, argued for in the previous fragment.

καὶ τὰ ἄλλα . . . ἀληθῆ: 'and all the other things which men say are true and real' (both senses are in ἀληθῆ).

τὸ πρῶτον: adverbial - 'as it seemed to us at first'.

ἀλλὰ ἀεὶ . . . πέρ ἐστιν: 'but (it is necessary) for each thing to be continually as it is'. Given the arguments of fr. 7 against any kind of change, and assuming we see and hear correctly, if follows that each thing must stay as it was first seen and heard.

8(iii): the section lists standard examples of perceptible changes.

φαμεν: 'we (i.e. men generally) say', 'it is a general assumption that', rather than the authoritative 'we' for 'I'. Melissus sets out to show that the ordinary assumption that the senses are reliable contradicts the very evidence of the senses. (Aristocles, who quotes 8(iii), takes φαμεν to refer to Melissus and criticises the argument as self-refuting scepticism; cf. DK 30A14, Barnes 1.300-301.)

συνιέναι: 'take notice', 'have awareness', to cover the senses generally.

δοκεῖ ἡμῖν: 'it seems / appears to us', rather than 'we decide' or 'we believe'.

τὸ ζῶον . . . ἐκ μὴ ζῶντος: τὸ ζῶν D (Simpl.); Kranz adds ζῶον after ζῶντος. The sense is not in doubt - 'what is living appears to us to die and (then) to be born from what is not living'. cf. H. 46 and 47. Plato's first argument for immortality draws on a similar list of opposites (cf. *Phaedo* 70-72).

καὶ. . . ἑτεροιοῦσθαι: 'and all these appear to us to be changes'.

ὁμουρέων: Ionic for ὁμορέων, and Bergk's suggestion for the Ms ὁμοῦ ῥέων. This perhaps means 'being in constant contact', but the sense of either reading is obscure.

ἐξ ὕδατός τε γῆ . . . γίνεσθαι: an example of a different kind, which perhaps looks back to Anaximenes' theory of 'compression'.

ὥστε . . . γινώσκειν: in Simplicius this is in the line above before ἐξ ὕδατος and is usually printed in this position. However, the language is anachronistic and the clause interrupts the argument; it is probably a marginal gloss (cf. Barnes, 1.340 n.3).

8(iv) φαμένοις: the participle is concessive - 'although we (i.e. people in general) say that there are many things, enduring, with (definite) shapes and having resilience . . .'. There is a contradiction between the evidence of change provided by the senses and the assumption of an abiding plurality.

ἐκ . . . ὁρωμένου: 'from what is seen at any one time'.

8(v) πολλά: subject - 'and that these many things actually exist (emphatic εἶναι) is an incorrect appearance'.

ἀληθῆ: 'real', 'really true'.

ἀλλ' ἦν: preceded by a comma rather than a colon, and ἂν taken with ἦν as well as with μετέπιπτεν - 'but each thing would actually be (all the time) such as it appeared (at any one time)'.

κρεῖσσον: 'more powerful' than what is real; cf. fr. 7 (iv) for the δύναμις required for continuous existence.

8(vi) ἢν = ἐάν; the mixed condition - 'if it changes, what there is has perished and what is not has come to be'.

οὕτως . . . τὸ ἕν: the final affirmation of 7 (ii) on the impossibility of change, together with the conclusion that was signposted at the beginning of 8 (i). Each entity in a plurality would have to be immutable and eternal.

Fragment 9

Simplicius *In Phys*. 110.1 and 87.6

The famous denial of σῶμα.

εἰ μὲν οὖν εἴη: Simplicius MS D has εἰ μὲν ὂν εἴη here, and all the MSS begin after the colon with ἓν δὲ ὂν δεῖ; but Melissus elsewhere uses ἐόν, the epic form of the participle. The subject of εἴη continues as indefinite - 'if then it (i.e. anything) exists, it must be one (only)'. Fr. 6 showed why, and gave the argument for unity that results from being ἄπειρον.

ἓν δ' ἐὸν: the participle is causal - 'since it is one (only), it must be the case that it has no σῶμα'. This denial is to be taken with (a) the following sentence - 'if it had πάχος ('thickness', 'bulk') it would have parts and no longer be one', (b) fr. 3 - 'it is unlimited in extent', and (c) 'it is not empty but full' at 7 (x). (And cf. Aristotle on the ἓν of Parmenides being κατὰ τὸν λόγον, and that of Melissus κατὰ τὴν ὕλην; *Metaph.* 986b18.) It is anachronistic to ask whether Melissus is arguing for incorporeality or not; here are first moves only in the direction of such a distinction. The thesis is perhaps as follows: 'what there is has no (tangible, visible, shaped) body, nor (concrete, feelable) bulk, nor even distinction of parts; nonetheless it is spatially and limitlessly extended, with no empty bits to mar its homogeneity'. Such a thesis puts a strain on the language then available, but it is not inherently absurd.

Fragment 10

Simplicius *In Phys*. 109.33

Divisibility into parts brings change, and change is irreconcilable with existence.

διῄρηται: perfect passive - 'if what there is has been divided, it moves and changes'. κινεῖται here covers all change, for change involves a division into parts which are added to, subtracted from or rearranged.

κινούμενον . . . εἴη: (MS D adds ἅμα after εἴη.) The participle is conditional rather than predicative - 'if it moves it would not be'.

EMPEDOCLES

Fragments 1-18 are a selection from over a hundred which may be attributed to the Περὶ φύσεως, and fragment 19-23 from a further thirty from the Καθαρμοί. The titles are unlikely to be Empedocles', however, and the allocation of fragments to one or the other of the poems is in many cases uncertain.

Fragment 1-3: The four 'roots', love and strife.

1(6) Aetius 1.3.20

Empedocles called his four elements of fire, air, earth and water 'roots', and in introducing them gives them enigmatic divine names.

ῥιζώματα: 'root clumps', literally of trees, but here more generally for both 'foundation' and 'source of growth'.

Ζεὺς . . . Ἀιδωνεύς: the correlation of the divine names with the roots was disputed even in antiquity. Aidoneus (i.e. Hades) is most obviously earth; φερέσβιος ('life-giving' can easily by understood of air as the breath of life; and 'bright Zeus', the partner of Hera, is the fire in the encircling heavens as well as its manifestations on earth (where it is also called 'Hephaistos').

ἣ . . . βρότειον: 'who makes to well up with her tears the mortal stream', i.e. her tears give the explanation for streams. Nestis obviously represents water, but otherwise she is unknown - perhaps a Sicilian water-nymph, or even a name for Persephone, from the streams which have underground sources.

2(17) Simplicius *In Phys.* 160.1

This, the longest and most important of Empedocles' fragments, gives the outline of his cosmic scheme. The four roots come together into one under the agency of love, and then separate as a result of strife. There are only these, but as they interchange positions and arrangements through the workings of the motive principles of attraction and repulsion, they take on the appearances of θνητά, the different temporary things familiar to us in the world.

2.1 -2 (=16-17) ηὐξήθη . . . εἶναι, διέφυ . . . εἶναι: the infinitives are consecutive (cf. Goodwin *Moods and Tenses* §775) - 'at one time it grew to be one only from many and at another again it divided to be many from one'. The subject may be undefined, as with the Eleatics, or be understood as an unexpressed πάντα (cf. line 4) or τὸ ὅλον.

2.3 ἀπόλειψις: the abstract noun is an unusual variant for ὄλεθρος (cf. P. 8.21). Its normal meaning is 'desertion' or, of rivers, 'failing'.

δοιή: 'double', 'twofold', in epic in the plural only, for δύο.

2.5 ἡ δὲ . . . διέπτη: the uniting of all things brings one (generation) to birth and destroys it, 'and the other is reared and scattered as they are again being divided'. The text and meaning of the line is much disputed. (The MSS have θρυφθεῖσα δρεπτή. Panzerbieter here emended the first word and Scaliger the second.) The two balancing pronouns (τὴν μὲν . . . ἡ δὲ) should probably each refer to both abstract nouns in line 3: there is a first generation and 'failing' when all things come into one, and a second when they divide. διαφύομαι is 'divide' here, elsewhere 'intervene', 'grow between'. πάντων is to be understood from line 4 as the subject of the genitive absolute. διέπτη is from διαπέτομαι - 'fly in different directions'.

2.6 ταῦτ': referring back to πάντα in line 4 and detailed in line 18 as fire, water, earth and air - 'these things never cease continually changing positions'.

2.8 φορεύμενα: Ionic form; the participle is dependent on λήγει in line 6 and, with συνερχόμενα, amplifies ἀλλάσσοντα - 'at one time all coming together into one through love, at another again being borne apart by strife's repulsion'.

2.9 The line is supplied from the quotation of B 26 by Aristotle and Simplicius, where it is followed by the repetition of lines 10-13 of this fragment. The subject is ἕν - 'so insofar as one is accustomed to arise from many'.

2.10 διαφύντος ἑνὸς: genitive with the verb rather than absolute - 'and many result from one as it is again being divided'.

2.11 ἔμπεδος αἰών: 'abiding life'. ἐστι is understood with the possessive dative.

2.13 ταύτῃ . . . κύκλον: 'so far they are for ever unaltered in the cycle'. ἀκίνητοι is 'unchanged', 'unaltered' in a mainly temporal sense (cf. P. 8.26). The 'exchange of positions' results in temporary compounds, but the succession of the exchanges from many to one and from one to many in cyclical time is without beginning or end.

2.14 ἀλλ' . . . κλῦθι: one of several monitions to Pausanias, to whom the poem as a whole is addressed, heralding a new or important topic, here the detailed explanation of the character of the four roots and love and strife. κλῦθι is the usual 2nd singular aorist imperative form of κλύω. μάθη γάρ τοι is Bergk's emendation of μάθησις γὰρ in Stobaeus' quotation of the line (Simplicius has μέθη γάρ τοι.).

2.15 πιφαύσκων πείρατα μυθῶν: 'declaring the range (*lit.* limits') of my discourse'.

2.18 ἠέρος . . . ὕψος: 'measureless height of air'. (Plutarch and Clement have αἰθέρος, and ἤπιον is another reading for ἄπλετον.)

2.19:'and pernicious strife apart from these, matched (to them) in every direction'. The point of ἀτάλαντον ἁπάντῃ is not that strife is as heavy as each or all of the roots, but that its power can extend uniformly over them (cf. P. 8.44).

2.20 ἴση . . . πλάτος τε: the accusatives are of 'specification' with the adjective (cf. *G.* 1058) - 'equal (to them) in length and breadth'. Love, like strife, can control the whole range of the roots.

2.21 τὴν . . . τεθηπώς: τὴν is pronominal, δέρκευ Ionic for δέρκου, ἧσο imperative from ἧμαι, and τεθηπὼς the participle of τέθηπα, epic perfect verb (cf. P. 6.7). The sense is 'contemplate her with the mind and do not sit dazed in your eyes (or staring dazed)'. There is a contrast between visual perception and intellectual recognition, as well as between the man of understanding and those in a stupor (cf. H. 1 and P. 6.7).

2.22 νομίζεται: with εἶναι understood - 'she is acknowledged to be inborn also in the limbs of men'.

2.23 τῇ: pronominal - 'because of her', 'by her agency'.

2.24 Γηθοσύνην . . . ἐπώνυμον: 'giving her the name "Joy"', personification of the (Homeric) word for delight or gladness. The name is in apposition to the internal accusative ἐπώνυμον (cf. *G.* 1052).

2.25 μετὰ τοῖσιν: the reference is to the roots, as in 1.20. (The phrase is Brandis' suggestion for the MSS unmetrical μετ' ὅσσοισιν.)

δεδάηκε: perfect of the defective verb δάω - 'has perceived (her)'; ἑλισσομένην - 'moving (or 'turning') swiftly'.

2.26 ἄκουε . . . ἀπατηλόν: an assertion of the truth of the account (contrast P. 8.52).

2.27 ταῦτα . . . ἔασι: 'all these (i.e. the four roots) are equal and of the same age' (ἥλικα neuter plural from ἧλιξ, and γένναν as specifying accusative).

2.28:'one has control of one prerogative and another of another, and to each is its ἦθος (here = 'particular character')'; cf. P. 8.57.

2.30 οὐδ' †ἄρ τι† ἐπιγίγνεται: to preserve the metre the iota of τι would have to be elided, which is generally considered unacceptable. There have been various attempts at emendation and οὐδ' ἄρ' ἐπιγίγνεται is easiest, with the sense that nothing else is generated as an addition to the four roots; cf. Barnes *CR* 32 (1982) 193.

2.31:regular counter-factual present condition with imperfects - 'for if they (i.e. the four roots) were continuously perishing, they would no longer exist'.

2.32 τοῦτο . . . κε: potential optative for the rhetorical question - 'and what would increase the whole?'.

2.33 πῇ δέ κε κήξαπόλοιτο: a similar construction to 2.32 - 'how would it be completely destroyed?'. (The last word is Diels' generally accepted emendation of the MSS καὶ κήρυξ ἀπόλοιτο.)

ἐπεὶ . . . ἐρῆμον: 'since nothing is empty of them', i.e. the roots occupy all the available space. Empedocles equates the Eleatic μὴ ὄν with κενόν, and then denies the existence of any empty place to interrrupt or alter the consistency of the roots (cf. P. 8.23-25 and 44-48).

2.34 αὔτ' ἔστιν ταῦτα: 'these are the only real things' or 'there are only these' (cf. *LSJ* s.v. αὐτός I.3 and 7; also Barnes *loc. cit.*).

2.35 ἠνεκὲς αἰὲν ὁμοῖα: '(are) throughout ever the same'. The roots preserve their individual character through the various exchanges of positions which account for the formation of θνητά.

3(8) Plutarch *Adv. Col.* 1111f. and Aetius 1.30.1.

There is no real genesis or destruction of mortal things but only arrangements and rearrangements of their component elements.

3.1 φύσις: there has been a dispute from ancient times over whether the word here means 'birth' or 'basic nature'. Although the latter meaning may be implied in Empedocles' other uses of the word at fr. 18.5 and B 63, the sense of γένεσις is needed here to contrast with θάνατος and this is how Plutarch understands it in his context. (There is a variant reading ἑκάστου for the last word of the line, but the sense is not affected.)

3.2 θανάτοιο τελευτή: a defining genitive - 'end that is death' rather than 'end of death or dying'. Paradoxically θνητά do not die because they are, strictly speaking, temporary compounds of immortal elements.

3.3 μίξις . . . μιγέντων: 'mixing, and separating of what has been mixed'. The mixing is not a chemical blending, but a mosaic-like arrangement, in which the pieces retain their character. Similarly in the 'painter' simile in B 23, pictures are built up from pigments of separate colours painted adjacent to each other.

3.4 φύσις . . . ἀνθρώποισιν: 'to these the name "birth" is given by men'. φύσις is not a common word for the average man to use, but Empedocles may be thinking more of the related verb - when a μίξις is formed, there occurs what is termed γενέσθαι or φύεσθαι.

Fragments 4-7: The move from one to many.

4(29/28) Hippolytus *Ref.* 7.29.13 and Stobaeus 1.15.2

After his outline of the basic moves on the cosmic scale of many to one and one to many, the nature of the eternal four roots and the control of love and strife over them, Empedocles went on to describe briefly the roots in separation and their coming together into one whole under the complete dominance of love. The sphere at this stage is described in terms of a divine being (cf. fr. 17).

4.1: 'two branches do not shoot up from his back'. ἀίσσονται is ambiguous between 'shoot up' of a tree and 'move about rapidly' and shows how Empedocles saw a similarity of parts in animals and plants (cf. B 82); for the denial of human form to the divine, cf. X. 2-4.

4.3: 'but in every direction he is equal to himself (<ἑοῖ> is supplied by Maas), without beginning and end'. The sphere is 'completely without limit' because it has no particular (spatial) start or finish and the mixture is so complete that no internal boundaries separate one element from another (cf. P. 8.49 and 57).

4.4 σφαῖρος: a masculine form of σφαῖρα, coined by Empedocles. μονίῃ . . . γαίων: 'rejoicing in circular stillness'. There is some dispute as to whether μονίη means 'rest' (from μένω) or 'solitude' (from μόνος). The former is more likely as a characteristic of Greek divinity (cf. X. 8) but the word was probably deliberately chosen for its ambiguity.

5(30) Aristotle *Metaph.* 1000b14

These lines give the time of the end of the perfect state under love and the emergence of strife.

5.1 αὐτὰρ ἐπεὶ: Simplicius' reading; the Aristotle MSS have ἀλλ' ὅτε δή. ἐθρέφθη: 'had grown', 'had increased in size', with μέγα attributive - 'so as to be great'. (Simplicius has ἐρέφθη.)

5.2 ἀνόρουσε: poetic verb, used only in the unaugmented aorist in Homer as here - 'leapt up (to claim its honours)'. τελειομένοιο χρόνοιο: genitive absolute with present participle - 'as the time was being completed'.

5.3 ὅς . . . ὅρκου: 'which, being (a time of) a mutual exchange for them, has been defined by a broad oath'. ἀμοιβαῖος describes time as 'giving like for like' - the period given to love to dominate comes to an end and one for strife follows.

ἐλήλαται: from ἐλαύνω. The time has been 'defined' for them by an oath, as a wall or trench is marked out. The 'broad oath' is a poetic device to add solemnity and certainty to the exchanges of times of power.

6(31) Simplicius *In Phys*. 1184.4

Strife's attack on the sphere destroys its unity and rest.

ἑξείης: 'in turn', 'one after the other'.
πελεμίζετο: unaugmented imperfect - 'began to tremble'.

7(22) Simplicius *In Phys*. 160.28

These lines show that earth, air, fire and water have the same character in the parts of themselves that make up mortal things as in their discernible world masses. The last six lines of the fragment (omitted here) are full of difficulties of text and interpretation but their general point is that love and strife also attract and repel in the same way in their cosmic functioning as they are known to do among men.

7.1: 'for all these (i.e. the four roots listed in the following line) are allied to the parts of themselves . . .'.
7.3: 'that have strayed and been cut off (the full sense of ἀποπλαχθέντα, from ἀποπλάζω) from them (the dative φιν is attached loosely to the clause) and born in mortal things'. The Doric form φιν for σφισιν was used quite widely, and need not be emended.

Fragment 8: The move from many to one.

8(35) Simplicius *In Cael*. 529.1 and *In Phys*. 32.13

Empedocles first outlined the cosmic moves given in fr. 2, then gave the main points of the genesis of this world, formed as all things move from one to many. He then in this fragment goes back to the prior movement of many to one, when the four roots were moving from a state of separation to the ideal unity of the sphere, and compounds were formed in the interchange. Aristotle complains that there was no detailed account of this period (*De Caelo* 301a15), and so it is likely that there was little more than the general description given here, and the particulars in the following three fragments.

8.1 παλίνορσος: adjective - 'backwards'.
8.2 ἐξοχετεύων: 'drawing off' of water into channels, the metaphor for the digression from the main topic of the explanation of the present world - 'I shall turn back to the channel of song which I recited before, drawing off

from (one) account this one'.

8.3 ἐπεὶ . . . γένηται: 'when strife had reached the lowest
-4 depths of the whirl, and love arises in the centre of
the eddy'. The δίνη and στροφάλιγξ both refer to the
cosmic rotation started at the separation of the four
masses. Then, love strikes at the centre from her position at the circumference (cf. line 10), and gradually consolidates her hold from there, compelling strife to make a gradual retreat.

8.6 ἀλλὰ . . . ἄλλα: 'but coming together variously from different directions at will'. (ἐ)θελημά - 'willing'; 'as volunteers', different parts join with the advance of love. The lines are written in the metaphor of a military compaign.

8.7 χεῖτ': unaugmented imperfect - 'countless types of mortal things kept pouring forth'.

8.8 πολλὰ . . . μετάρσιον: 'but many, which strife still re-
-9 strained from above (μετάρσιον) stayed unmixed, alternating with those which were combining'. ἕστηκε as an imperfect of στήκω - 'stand' or 'stay' could perhaps be accepted; with a rough breathing here the last consonant of the preceding word would need to be aspirated.

8.9 οὐ . . . κύκλου: 'for it had not yet perfectly (ἀμεμφέως)
-10 wholly taken up its position at the furthest limits of
the circle'. Strife eventually retreats to the circumference as love gradually dominates the whole.

8.11 μελέων: with ἐξεβεβήκει - 'part had gone out of the limbs', i.e. had moved out of the cosmic structure.

8.12: 'and, in proportion as it continually ran on ahead, a mild,
-13 immortal onrush of perfect love was continually pursuing
(it)'. ἠπιόφρων, 'gentle-thinking', 'mild' (perhaps Empedocles' coinage), and ἄμβροτος are epithets transferred from Φιλότης.

8.14 τὰ: relative, and μάθον unaugmented - 'which were formerly accustomed to be immortal'. The immortal roots, earlier unmixed, take on a variety of temporary forms as they mix with each other under the increasing power of love.

8.15 ζωρά τε πρὶν κέκρητο: 'and unmixed things (ζωρά) formerly were in a mixed state' (κέκρητο is pluperfect passive of κεράννυμι). Aristotle's quotation of the phrase (as an example of ambiguous punctuation) has κέκριτο, and other sources ἄκριτα or ἄκρητα. For a justification of the text and sense given here, cf. *CR* 12 (1962) 1-3.

8.17: 'fitted with all kinds of forms, a wonder to see'. ἀρηρότα is the Ionic form of the perfect participle of ἀραρίσκω. The limiting infinitive ἰδέσθαι (cf. *G.* 1528-9) is probably middle, used occasionally in poetry for the active.

Fragments 9-11: Compounds formed in the move from many to one.

9(96) Simplicius *In Phys.* 300.21

The fragment shows that it is not just an arrangement of roots which gives a compound its character but their relative proportions. In this notion Aristotle saw an antecedent for his 'formal cause' (cf. *De anima* 410a4).

9.1 ἐπίηρος: 'kindly', 'welcome', used here as a two termination adjective.
εὐστέρνοις: an alternative reading is εὐτύκτοις - 'well-made', which is inappropriate for holes in the earth. εὔστερνος is literally 'broad-chested', but the epithet does not transfer happily from earth to its hollows; perhaps it means little more than 'broad'.

9.2 τὼ: the dual is Steinhart's suggestion for the MSS variants τῶν, τὰς and τὰ. The ratio for bone is 2 parts earth : 2 water : 4 fire. Such parts of elements come together in the general movements and, where the proportions are suitable, love makes an organic part. (An alternative reading for μερέων is μοιράων or μοιρῶν - 'portions'.)
Νήστιδος αἴγλης: 'of the brightness of Nestis', Empedoclean for 'of water'.

9.4: 'held together by the glueing of harmony in a marvellous way'. For ἀρηρότα, cf. fr. 2.17 above. ἁρμονίη is a name for love, the artisan of living forms and their parts. The 'glue' (κόλλαι) is not an additional ingredient but water is kneaded into the earth and fire hardens the compound. θεσπεσίηθεν implies both a marvel and the work of a god.

10(57) Simplicius *In Cael.* 586.12 and 587.1

Animal parts are here thought of as shooting up from the earth and then floating aimlessly, until some are brought together. Empedocles seems to have used the many to one phrase briefly to account for mythical hybrids, but removing them from the present era.

10.1 ᾗ: 'here', 'on the earth'; κόρσαι ἀναύχενες are heads (*lit.* 'temples') without necks.

10.2 γυμνοὶ . . . βραχίονες: the arms are bare because they are εὔνιδες ὤμων - 'bereft of shoulders'.

10.3: 'and eyes needing foreheads strayed alone'.

11(59) Simplicius *In Cael.* 587.18

Simplicius sets these lines in the context of the increasing dominance of love.

11.1 δαίμονι δαίμων: the gods are the roots, which, as immortals, have divine status (and are frequently given divine names).

κατὰ μεῖζον is 'more, 'even further'. ἐμίσγετο is imperfect middle of μίσγω, a present form of μ(ε)ίγνυμι.

11.2 ταῦτα: the subject is still the roots, which come together by chance; this disorder is gradually brought under love's control.

11.3: 'many others in addition to these continually arose'. In another fragment Empedocles gives as examples man-faced bulls, bull-faced men, two-headed creatures, and hermaphrodites.

Fragment 12: The genesis of the human race.

12(62) Simplicius *In Phys*. 381.31

After the digression Empedocles returns to the main line of his account, explaining the genesis of men and women during the further articulation from one to many.

12.1 ὅπως . . . πῦρ: 'how fire, as it was being separated,
-2 brought up by night the shoots of men and pitiable women'. The passive sense of πολυκλαύτος - 'much wept for', 'pitiable' is earlier and more appropriate then the active 'tearful'. ἐννυχίους - 'by night', sometimes used of the dead; the origin of human life, like the abode of the dead, is in darkness. ὄρπηκας - 'shoots' is used of saplings, and again Empedocles relates human to plant life. κρινόμενον πῦρ - 'fire being separated out', i.e. parts of fire being drawn out from earth towards the fire already at the circumference of the cosmos.

12.3 ἀπόσκοπος . . . ἀδαήμων: two rare adjectives, the first meaning 'looking away', 'irrelevant', the second 'ignorant', 'uninformed' (found elsewhere only with a genitive).

12.4 οὐλοφυεῖς . . . τύποι: 'whole-nature forms'; the adjective is a unique compound. These 'forms' seem to be primitive shapes of warm, moist earth that later develop into articulate human figures.
ἐξανέτελλον: with χθονὸς - 'kept arising from the earth'.

12.5 εἴδεος: 'of heat', a form of ἴδος, ἴδεος.

12.6 θέλον . . . ἱκέσθαι: 'wanting (i.e. 'as it tended') to reach its like'; parts of the same root are aware of their like parts elsewhere, and tend towards them when not used by love as ingredients in compounds.

12.7: 'not as yet showing the lovely shape of limbs at all, or
-8 voice or organ native to men'. ἐνοπὴν - 'sound' or 'voice'; the τύποι are mute. The text of the rest of the line is doubtful. The MSS give the last word as γύων, the Aldine γῆρυν, while Stein suggests γυῖον. γῆρυν 'speech' may be right, taken with ἐνοπὴν as the inability to speak a language or even make a sound.

Fragments 13-15: Perception and thought.

13(109) Aristotle *De anima* 404b13

These are widely quoted lines, explaining the working of perception on the principle of like by like. It is by means of the elements within us that the external world is perceived, as a result of the symmetry of pores and effluences, and the attraction of similars. Empedocles suggests a range of awareness from the simplest perception of one part of a root for another like itself (cf. 12.6 above) through compounds that can sense similar compounds to human sensation and thought. Not only does fire in the eye enable us to see external fire, but complex mixtures can be understood by reason of our own complex structures (a development of Parmenides fr. 16), and the uniting and separating agents at work in them perceived by means of their presence in ourselves.

13.1 ὀπώπαμεν: Ionic second perfect form of ὁράω.
13.2 δῖον: acting as a two-termination adjective; αἰθήρ is feminine in Empedocles as in Homer.
ἀίδηλον: ambiguous between 'destructive' and 'unseen' (cf. P. 10.3).
13.3 στοργῆν: 'love', 'affection', a variant for φιλία; cf. στέργω.

14(108) Aristotle *Metaph.* 1009b19

An internal change of structure produces different thoughts. (External conditions also affect the thought patterns; cf. B 107.)

14.1 ὅσσον . . . μετέφυν: 'insofar as they have changed in their nature', i.e. 'have become different'; μετέφυν is second aorist of μεταφύομαι.
14.2 τὸ φρονεῖν ἀλλοῖα: 'thinking different things', 'changed thought'; the phrase is the subject of παρίσταται.

15(105) Stobaeus 1.49.53

The four elements are in their best mixture in the blood around the heart and this explains its functions as the organ of thought (cf. Theophrastus *De Sensu* 10). The Homeric precedents and the close connection of perception, emotion and thought, together with this theory of optimum mixture, here outweigh the suggestion (then being raised in medical circles) that the head rather than the heart area was the centre of intelligence.

15.1:'nourished in seas of blood coursing to and fro'. The subject is probably ἡ κραδίη. τεθραμμένη (from τρέφω) is Grotius' emendations of the MSS τετραμμένα. ἀντιθορόντος (aorist participle from ἀντιθρώσκω) - 'leap up in turn', 'leap up and back'.

15.2: 'there above all is what men call thought'. κικλήσκεται is a reduplicated form of καλέω; κυκλίσκεται is sometimes adopted, but such a verb is not known and Empedocles did not suppose that blood circulated but oscillated (cf. B 100).

15.3 αἷμα . . . περικάρδιον: the blood around the heart is where thought functions for men, in contrast to divine thought, which, being superior, takes a different form; cf. on 17.3 below.

Fragments 16 and 17: Divine mind.

16(133) Clement *Strom.* 5.81

Knowledge of the divine cannot be acquired by the senses.

16.1 πελάσασθαι: transitive, the object, from the context, being τὸ θεῖον - 'it is not possible to bring (the divine) near, within reach of the eyes' (*lit.* - 'so as to be caught / reached in the eyes', the 'capability' sense of the verbal in -τος; cf. *G.* 776.2).

16.2 ᾗπερ: Karsten's emendation from ἥπερ, and referring back to both sight and touch - 'by (the use of) which the broadest path of persuasion for men leads to the mind'. The road to knowledge via the senses, in matters non-divine, is direct and sure.

17(134) Ammonius *In Interp.* 249.1

God, as 'holy thought', is characterised by intellectual activity and cosmic movements, as well as by lack of anthropomorphic features (cf. X. 2-4 and 6-9; also on E. 4 above). (The first line in fr. 4, with μὲν for γὰρ, is repeated after line 1 here by Ammonius and is in the margin of the Tzetzes MS. The lines are better balanced, and more grammatical, without it.)

17.1 κέκασται: perfect passive from καίνυμι in the sense of 'furnish', 'equip'.

17.2: εἰσί and a possessive dative αὐτῷ are to be understood with the nouns - '(there are for him) no feet . . .'. (An alternative reading is χέρες for πόδες and στήθεα for μήδεα, perhaps because of the description of Hephaistos at *Il.* 18.413-14.)

17.3: 'but he is (aorist ἔπλετο with present sense as often in
-4 Homer) mind alone, holy and inexpressible, darting through

the whole cosmos with swift thoughts'.

Fragment 18: Exhortation and encouragement.

18(110) Hippolytus *Ref.* 7.29.25

Empedocles urges Pausanias to take the words that have been spoken (on the philosophy of nature), put them deep in his heart and reflect on them. Otherwise the thoughts, expressed in words and regarded as physical entities, will break up and return in time to their like elements.

18.1:'if, having pushed them (i.e. what I have said) under your
-2 crowded thoughts (the unknown σφαδίνησιν is corrected to σφ' ἀδινῇσιν), you contemplate them favourably with unsullied and constant attention'. The vocabulary of the second line is in the idiom of a revelation at an initiation ceremony.

18.3:'all these things (ταῦτα has the same reference as σφε in line 1) assuredly (μάλα) will be with you through life' (αἰών here being the span of Pausanias' life).

18.4 τῶνδε κτήσεαι: for the corrupt τωνδεκτ(ή.η)ται. Other suggestions are τῶνδ' ἐκτήσεαι (Diels) and τῶνδε κτήσεται (Bollack). -σεαι is the normal 2nd singular future indicative middle form in epic.

18.4 αὔξει: probably transitive with ἕκαστον as object - 'for
-5 of themselves (αὐτὰ) these will cause each thing to grow into the character, according to the nature of each'. The ἦθος is that of the listener who comes closer to the state of the wise man as the true words are admitted, the thoughts fostered and the receptiveness to further understanding increased.

18.6:'but if you reach out for things of a different kind
-7 (ἐπορέξεαι is 2nd sing. fut. indic. middle of ἐπορέγω, with genitive), the countless trivialities which come among men and which blunt their meditations'. (The correction from the MS τἀλλ' οἰῶν ἐπιρέξεις . . . μυρία δῆλα is Schneidewin's.)

18.8 ἦ . . . ὦφαρ: the particle is assertive - 'indeed straightaway'.

περιπλομένοιο χρόνοιο: 'as the time comes round', i.e. the time of Pausanias' death.

18.9:'longing to come to their own familiar kind'. If Pausanias becomes inattentive the wise thoughts will leave, the ingredients will separate and each part be drawn to its own elemental mass (cf. 12.6 above).

18.10 νώματος αἶσαν: 'a share of thought', with νῶμα as an Ionic form of νόημα.

Fragments 19 and 20: The decree of Necessity.

19(115) Plutarch *De exil.* 607c and Hippolytus *Ref.* 7.29.14-23

This important fragment comes, probably, in the Καθαρμοί after an introductory address to the citizens of Acragas. The text given is made up from five lines quoted by Plutarch and thirteen from Hippolytus, in a different order and interspersed with commentary. Lines 13-14 were quoted frequently and there was general agreement that Empedocles was speaking περὶ ψυχῆς here.

19.1: 'there is a proclamation of necessity, a decree (ratified) long ago by gods'. (ἔστιν is from Simplicius' quotation at *In Phys.* 1184.9; the MSS gives the metrically inadmissible ἔστι τι.) χρῆμα here is a unique noun from χράω - 'proclaim', used of gods and their oracles. ψήφισμα is for a decree passed by votes in an assembly.

19.2 πλατέεσσι . . . ὅρκοις: 'sealed by broad oaths' (cf. fr. 5.3). Gods, called δαίμονες in line 5, are represented as voting in favour of necessity's proclamation, and swearing to abide by it. The content is given in the following lines.

19.3: the line is only in Plutarch, where the reading of the last four words is: φοβῳ φίλα γυῖα μιν. The emendation printed here, that of Xylander, gives the sense - 'whenever one in error, from fear, (defiles) his own limbs'. Stephanus, and all editors since, read φόνῳ for φόβῳ.

19.4: another difficult line, in Hippolytus but not Plutarch. ὅρκον ὅτις κ' ἐπίορκον is suggested for the beginning of the line, with the sense 'who, having erred, made false the oath sworn' (cf. Hesiod *Theog.* 793-806). Diels has νείκει θ' ὅς κ(ε) ἐπίορκον and takes ἁμαρτήσας as equivalent to ὁμαρτήσας; on this reading the δαίμων acts with or follows strife.

19.5 δαίμονες: in apposition to the indefinite τις in line 3; the change from singular to plural is unexceptional (especially since δαιμόνων does not scan). The δαίμονες have 'long-lasting life' but are not immortal; they, like other forms of life, are composed of the four elements in combination; cf. B 21.12 and 23.8.

19.6: '(to the effect that) he wanders from the blessed ones for three times countless years'; the main clause of the content of the decree is expressed by the accusative (μιν) and the infinitive (ἀλάλησθαι, perfect infinitive of ἀλάομαι with present sense). ὥρα, lit. 'hour', can also be taken as a year or a season (i.e. a third of a year); μύριοι is for an indefinitely large number as well as 10,000. It is unlikely that the time is definite, as the individual has some control over the length of the process according to his actions and intentions (cf. on fr. 18 above.

19.7 φυόμενον . . . εἴδεα: the singular participle (emended by Bergk from the plural) refers back to τις in line 3 and gives a particular description of what an individual δαίμων suffers; the accusative is internal (cf. *G.* 1051) and was written as ἴδεα - 'born throughout the time as all kinds of mortal forms'.

19.8: 'exchanging one hard way of life for another', as explained in the following lines. βίοτος is an epic form of βίος ('life') in the sense of 'manner of living'.

19.9: the δαίμων takes on different forms of life in one element
-12 after another as he is rejected by each in turn.

αἰθέριον μένος: 'the force of αἰθήρ', little more than a periphrasis for αἰθήρ, in Empedocles the element of air.

ἀπέπτυσε: a forceful verb and, like the unaugmented ἔμβαλε, 'gnomic' aorist with present sense (cf. *G.* 1292) - 'sea spits him out onto earth's surface, and earth into the rays of blazing sun, and he (i.e. sun, which also signifies the element of fire) casts him into the eddies of air'.

19.13: 'I too am now one of these, an exile from the gods and a wanderer'. The first half of the line is Hippolytus' text, with νῦν imported from Plutarch, who has τὴν καὶ ἐγὼ νῦν εἰμι. The version in Philoponus and Asclepius is ὡς καὶ ἐγὼ δεῦρ' εἰμί.

19.14: 'trusting in (i.e. because I trusted in) raging strife'.

20(117) Hippolytus *Ref.* 1.3.1

This fragment was quoted frequently in late antiquity. A remembrance of past lives is not necessarily implied by it. Empedocles looks back and recognises that the constituent parts which now make up the recognisable ἐγώ have been used for different kinds of lives in different elements.

20.1 κοῦρος τε κόρη τε: also κούρη τε κόρος τε - 'boy and girl', normal Homeric vocabulary. The point would be that these were unsettled or unfinished lives, cut off before their prime.

20.2 θάμνος: 'bush'; the word is used in the Περὶ Φύσεως to cover plant life formed from combinations of the elements (cf. B 9.2 and 20.6). The text of this line is sometimes manipulated to include θήρ as in these preceding lists, but exact correspondence is not necessary.

ἔξαλος ἔλλοπος ἰχθύς: 'a mute fish from the sea', ἔλλοπος being an alternative form of ἔλλοψ. The fish's inability to communicate by sounds would be a sign of inadequate λόγος, but the text is corrupt- variants include ἔμπορος, ἔμπυρος, ἄμφορος and φαίδιμος.

Fragments 21 and 22: The ranking of lives.

21(127) Aelian *De natura animalium* 12.7

The fragment gives the highest form of animal and plant life. The subject of the verb would presumably be something like θνητοί or perhaps δαίμονες, i.e. those who have lived and died as temporary combinations of elements.

21.1 ὀρειλεχέες: 'who make their lairs on the hills', also in the Περὶ φύσεως at B 20.7 in the list of different forms of lives but not found elsewhere.
χαμαιεῦναι: a variant plural of χαμευνής - 'bedding on the ground'.

21.2 δάφναι: predicate ' and among fair-leafed trees as laurels'; cf. B 82 for hair and leaves being analogous parts.

22(146) Clement *Strom*. 4.150

A list of the best types of human existence which lead to the life of the gods. Empedocles may well have supposed that all four were united in himself.

22.1 ὑμνόπολοι: 'song-composers', 'minstrels'. The nouns are predicative - 'in the end they are prophets . . .'.

22.2 ἀναβλαστοῦσι: a shortened form of ἀναβλαστάνω - 'from there they arise as gods, highest in honours'.

A N A X A G O R A S

Fragments 1-4: The original mixture.

1 Simplicius *In Phys*. 155.26

Anaxagoras' work opened with these abrupt and uncompromising lines on the pre-cosmic state of affairs, when there was a universal mixture of all things, the ingredients being so fused that nothing was perceptible except the prevailing air and αἰθήρ.

ὁμοῦ πάντα χρήματα ἦν: the most frequently quoted statement of Anaxagoras, sometimes with the second and third words reversed. χρήματα, given here at the beginning without explanation, turn out to be the elementary components of the cosmos; cf. on fr. 4 (iii) below.

καὶ πλῆθος καὶ σμικρότητα: the accusatives are of 'specification' or 'respect', giving the particular application of the adjective (cf. *G*. 1058). The χρήματα are unlimited in number and, as restated in the γάρ clause, of unlimited smallness. (The initial sigma of σμικρός is an Ionic variant of the adjective μικρός, found especially after a vowel.)

πάντων . . . ἐόντων: the genitive absolute is causal - 'since all (things) were together'.

ὑπὸ σμικρότητος: ὑπό with the genitive of the abstract noun (equivalent to τὸ σμικρόν above) gives the cause or explanation.

κατεῖχεν: 'contained and prevailed over'. The vastly extending air / αἰθήρ mixture swamped the unlimited number of infinitely small χρήματα and stretched beyond them in all directions.

ταῦτα . . . μεγέθει: probably Simplicius' gloss on the meaning of κατεῖχεν as both 'dominated because of the greater amount of air / αἰθήρ mixture', and 'contained' or 'covered' because of its greater size. Further, for the anachronistic συμπᾶσι and final datives, cf. Sider 48-49.

2 Simplicius *In Phys*. 155.31

Simplicius quotes this fragment as 'a little later' than the first. Its subject matter belongs with frs. 14, 15 and part of 10 on the separation of the elemental masses, as well as here with the initial explanation of the extension of mixture.

καὶ γάρ: probably confirmatory - 'and indeed', as in fr. 1 above.

ἀποκρίνονται: continuous present - 'are (still) separating from'; cf. fr. 10 (iv) below.
ἀπὸ . . . περιέχοντος: 'from the bulk of what surrounds', i.e. from the encircling mass. (One MS has πόλον for πολλοῦ 'from the surrounding sphere of the heavens'.
τὸ πλῆθος: again a 'specification' accusative with the adjective - 'unlimited in amount'.

3 Simplicius *In Phys*. 164.17

The complete fusion of the original mixture contains a range of χρήματα from the small that is infinitely divisible to the great that can always be added to.

οὔτε . . . ἀεί: 'there is no smallest of the small but always a smaller' - the denial of an absolute minimum.
τὸ . . . εἶναι: 'for it is not possible for what-is not to be'; the 'superfluous' negative οὐ after μή is with negative verbs of possibility (cf. *G*. 1616). (The construction reads more easily if, as with Schofield 80, the second τὸ were deleted.) The sentence explains unlimited smallness - there cannot be a reachable minimum beyond which there is nothing. Zeller first suggested τομῇ for τὸ μὴ and then a further μὴ was inserted; cf. Sider 56 and Theodorsen 72. τομῇ <μὴ> οὐκ εἶναι would mean something like 'what-is cannot not be as a result of cutting'.
ἴσον . . . πλῆθος: 'and (the big) is equal to the small in amount', a provocative contradiction complemented by the final sentence 'and in itself each is both big and small'. There is an attempt here to do away with basic distinctions of size. Whatever the original amount (in number or bulk), infinite processes of addition and division are possible.

4 Simplicius *In Phys*. 34.21 and 29, 156.2 and 157.9

This fragment is not given continuously in Simplicius, but is put together from sections with various overlaps and lacunae. The numbering here indicates the most appropriate divisions.

4(i) Even now compounds contain a variety of ingredients, including 'seeds of all things', with all kinds of appearances, colours and savours.

συγκρινομένοις: the tense of the participle shows that the mixture persists in the compounds now being formed.
σπέρματα πάντων χρημάτων: 'seeds of all things'. There is much controversy over what these 'seeds' are; the minimal sense is that the constituents of compounds are capable of developing in a variety of ways; cf. on fr. 6 below.

καὶ . . . ἡδονάς: ἔχοντα is to be taken with σπέρματα, and the repetitions of καὶ list the objects of the participle. ἰδέας - 'aspects' or 'appearances' here, and ἡδονάς - 'savours', a specialised Ionic use for taste or smell (cf. H. 51).

4(ii) Men and animals are formed from the original mixture and elsewhere there could be communities like ours. The reference might be to other parts of our world (a development of Anaximander's suggestion of antipodes) or, less plausibly, identical copies of this world. The construction of the last sentence indicates a hypothesis - suppose another part of the mixture rotated and separated out, the result would be a world like ours.

συμπαγῆναι: second aorist infinitive of συμπήγνυμι as passive - 'have been put together', with the implication that the compound 'sets' or 'solidifies'; cf. Empedocles B 15, 75, 86 and 107.
καὶ ἀνθρώπους . . . χρῶνται: these two sentences are collected in ταῦτα and summed up in the ὅτι clause. ἄν with the infinitives συμπαγῆναι, etc., would make their hypothetical nature clearer but Greek prose was still relatively unsophisticated. Anaxagoras may have expected the infinitives to be taken as potential - 'men would have been formed . . . and there would be . . .'; or, more emphatically, 'men have been formed (once there has been a rotation), and there are . . .'.
τοῖς . . . ἀνθρώποισιν: dative of the agent with the perfect passive participles (cf. *G.* 1186) rather than possessive dative - 'cities settled by men'. The suffix -ιν is Ionic.
ἔργα κατεσκευασμένα: 'fields cultivated' or 'articles manufactured'.
τὰ ἄλλα: i.e. (presumably) stars and planets; again possibly a reference to the μετέωρα of the antipodes or to any world that would develop like ours, given the same initial conditions.
τὰ ὀνήιστα: Ionic adjective - 'best', 'most useful'; cf. Heraclitus B 121.
συνενεγκάμενοι: from συμφέρω - 'having gathered'. The Ionic form, perhaps preferable here, is συνενεικάμενοι.
περὶ τῆς ἀποκρίσιος: 'concerning the process of separation'. The introduction and use of abstract nouns in -σις is characteristic of the Presocratic style.
ὅτι . . . ἀποκριθείη: the clause gives the content of the preceding ταῦτα and summary of the section, with the potential optative (cf. *G.* 1327) - '(namely) that there could be a separating off not only with us but elsewhere too (given another similar rotation in the original mixture)'.

4(iii) A return to the description of the original mixture, with a more detailed account of the ingredients.

πάντων ὁμοῦ ἐόντων: the genitive absolute is causal - 'since

all things were together'.
χροιή: 'colour', the most obvious perceptible quality, immediately accessible to vision. (Cleve, *The Giants of Pre-Sophistic Greek Philosophy* 35, and others adapt an early meaning - 'skin' or 'surface'.)
σύμμιξις: 'commingling'; the abstract noun is perhaps Anaxagoras' coinage.
τοῦ . . . ζοφεροῦ: three pairs of opposites expressed by the article and the neuter singular adjective, and ambiguous between an abstract and a concrete noun; e.g. for θερμόν, - 'heat' and 'the hot'. The qualities are still understood as substances with real existence (cf. D. 5), but inseparable from their complementary opposites. διερόν here 'wetness' / 'the wet'; ζοφερόν of what is gloomy or dark, used by Hesiod of Chaos. Fr. 10 adds ἀραιόν and πυκνόν to this list.
καὶ γῆς . . . σπερμάτων: the genitives can be taken as continuing the list dependent on σύμμιξις or as absolute (with a second participle understood with σπερμάτων). There is little difference in the resulting sense that earth and seeds are in the mixture in addition to the opposites.
πλῆθος: again a 'specification' accusative with the adjective - 'unlimited in amount'. (The MSS πλήθους was emended by Schorn.)
ἐοικότων: genitive plural of the Ionic form of the participle εἰκώς from ἔοικα. οὐδὲν is adverbial - 'being in no way like each other'.
οὐδὲ . . . ἑτέρῳ: 'for of the other things none (οὐδὲν here is subject) is alike, one to another', i.e. if any two are taken together (hence ἕτερος) there is no exact resemblance.

4(iv) The conclusion looks back to the beginning of fr. 4 and to fr. 1.

ἐν τῷ σύμπαντι: 'in the whole' (or perhaps 'in everything'; cf. Barnes 2.17).
ἐνεῖναι: since the present infinitive can sometimes cover the imperfect (cf. *G.* 1285), this has been taken to refer to the (past) original mixture. But Anaxagoras could be concluding, non-trivially, that there are all things now in the whole as there were in the beginning, although varying degrees of articulation have come about as the result of διάκρισις and σύγκρισις (cf. fr. 6).

Fragments 5-8: Developments from the original mixture.

5 Simplicius *In Phys.* 156.10

A denial of any addition to or subtraction from the sum total.

τούτων: Simplicius refers the pronoun to the ὁμοιομερῆ, the

Peripatetic term for the ingredients in the mixture.
διακεκριμένων: from διακρίνω, a technical verb for the Presocratics. The genitive here is probably temporal rather than causal - 'when things have been separated in this way'.
ἀνυστόν: Parmenides' word; cf. P. 2.7.
πάντα ἴσα ἀεί: an enigmatic conclusion, to be taken with the previous section and with the general denial of γένεσις and φθορά. The sum total of χρήματα is never more nor less than it was at the time of the original mixture.

6 Simplicius *In Phys.* 164.26

All things are in everything.

ὅτε: causal, both here and in line 3.
μοῖραι: 'shares' or 'portions', to be distinguished from the particulate μέρη.
πλῆθος: 'specification' accusative with ἴσαι - 'equal in amount', i.e. every portion has the same complex structure, no matter what the size.
καὶ οὕτως . . . πάντα: 'and so there would be all things in everything' (ἂν εἴη, the 'mild' potential optative; cf. *G.* 1329).
ἔστιν: 'is possible'.
πάντα . . . μετέχει: 'all things have a part (or 'portion' or 'share') of everything'. Another famous and enigmatic *dictum*, to be taken in the context of frs. 1-10. All things were together in the uniform 'wash' of the original fusion. Different parts became articulated in the processes of division and accretion, but all keep their original characteristic of being able to develop in unlimited ways.
τοὐλάχιστον: ≐ τὸ ἐλάχιστον, with ἔστιν for possibility and μή (as occasionally) for generality - 'since it is not possible for there to be the smallest', i.e. an absolute minimum.
οὐκ ἂν δύναιτο . . . γενέσθαι: impersonal - 'there could not be any (complete) separation or independent generation'. Other versions take τὸ ἐλάχιστον as subject, or understand an indefinite subject - 'nothing could be separated'.
ἀρχήν: accusative as adverb - 'at first', 'in the beginning'.
εἶναι: with χρή understood. (Sider 83 argues that the infinitive is for the present indicative, attracted to the preceding infinitives.)
καὶ τῶν ἀποκρινομένων: '(including many) even of the things that are being separated off'. (Some take the phrase with the datives at the end of the sentence.)
ἴσα . . . ἐλάσσοσι: 'equal in amount, in bigger things and smaller'; cf. fr. 3.2-3. The universal fusion of the original mixture is such that any part, of whatever size, contains a portion of all the constituent ingredients.

7(8) Simplicius *In Phys*. 175.12 and 176.29

It is impossible to find an example of a pure quality.

κεχώρισται . . . ἀποκέκοπται: perfect passives - 'have not been nor are now separated or cut off'.
ἐν τῷ ἑνὶ κόσμῳ: 'in the one world-order (of ours)'; for the sense of κόσμος, cf. H. 53.
πελέκει: 'with an axe'. The complementary opposites are inseparable from each other; it is impossible for there to be a 'bit of hot' chopped off by itself, without the co-presence of cold. The transition is being made here from regarding opposites as things in themselves to understanding them as qualities inseparable from the objects they qualify (cf. on 4(iii) above).

8(10) Scholium on Gregory of Nazianzus (36-911 Migne)

The famous rhetorical question. Doubts have been raised as to its genuineness (cf. Schofield 135-43 and Sider 89-90) but the point made suits Anaxagoras' position; the question appears too forceful to have been invented by a compiler, and such rhetorical flourishes are in the Presocratic tradition (cf. P. 8.7 and E. 2.32-33).

ἐκ μὴ τριχὸς: sc. ἐόντος here (as with ἐκ μὴ σαρκός) - 'how could hair have come from what is not hair?' The particular question points to a basic difficulty Anaxagoras sees in Empedocles' theory of elements. His answer is to find a portion, however small, of everything in every part of the original fusion, and to maintain that principle in the parts that have undergone a certain articulation. There cannot be 'pure hair' (as in fr. 7 there could not be 'pure hot') nor anything without a portion of hair.

Fragments 9 and 10: The nature of mind.

9(11) Simplicius *In Phys*. 164.23

Only νοῦς is the exception to the principle of 'everything in everything'.

ἐν παντὶ παντὸς μοῖρα ἔνεστι: the basic *dictum* of Anaxagoras, slightly reworded (cf. on fr. 6.2 above).
νοῦς: usually translated 'mind' or 'intelligence'. For Anaxagoras it is the universal force which initiates the primary rotation and continues to hold power over life (cf. X. 7 and 9). Both Socrates (in Plato *Phaedo* 98) and Aristotle (*Metaph*. 985a18) criticise Anaxagoras for his arbitrary use of this force, and his inability to follow the implications through.

οἷσι: perhaps referring to all forms of life which have a share of ψυχή (cf. fr. 4(ii) above).

10(12) Simplicius *In Phys.* 156.13 and 164.24

This, the longest fragment of Anaxagoras, is concerned with the nature and activity of νοῦς and, in particular, with its independence, knowledge and control of the cosmos.

10(i) Mind is unlimited and self-ruling, and mixed with no other thing. Since there is a portion of everything in everything, if it were so mixed, it would be inextricably involved in everything and this would inhibit its overall mastery.

ἄπειρον: neuter - 'a (spatially unlimited) thing', since it extends everywhere. There is no need to emend with Zeller to ἁπλόον or ἄμοιρον.
αὐτοκρατές: again neuter - 'self-ruling', 'independent'.
μόνος . . . ἐστιν: 'is alone, itself by itself', i.e. it exists absolutely. The vocabulary is similar to that used later by Plato for the non-contingent existence of his Forms. ἐπ' ἑωυτοῦ is Ionic for ἐφ' ἑαυτοῦ here, in the next sentence, and at the end of the section.
εἰ . . . χρημάτων: mixed condition - 'if it were not by itself (now), but had been mixed with some other thing, it would partake of all things'.
τεῳ: Ionic for the indefinite τινι.
καὶ ἂν ἐκώλυεν: a second apodosis with τὰ συμμεμειγμένα as subject - 'and the things mixed with it would (now) be a hindrance to it'.
ὡς . . . ἑαυτοῦ: 'as (it does) being really alone (καὶ emphatic) by itself'. The accusative subject αὐτόν is implicit.

10(ii) The fineness, purity, knowledge and power of mind are listed, as well as its control over life.

λεπτότατον: mind is a χρῆμα and spatially extended, but of the thinnest possible material.
καθαρώτατον: 'cleanest', 'purest', used of clear water. Because it does not contain any admixture, mind has no perceptible character. No religious associations need be implied.
γνώμην: cf. H. 4 and 25. Anaxagoras' νοῦς is similar to the divine in Heraclitus in its comprehensive and intelligent control of the cosmos.
ἴσχει . . . ἰσχύει: an obvious use of verbal similarity, hence the reduplicated ἴσχω for ἔχω, μέγιστον is adverbial - 'is powerful in the greatest degree', 'wields highest power'.
τὰ μείζω καὶ τὰ ἐλάσσω: i.e. larger and smaller ζῷα, which come under the control of mind and in fact have a share of it (cf. fr. 9), as is shown by their power of awareness and

control. There is no further evidence of the connection between νοῦς and ψυχή.

10(iii) Mind initiated the rotation in the primary mixture and this still continues as more and more of that mixture is involved.

περιχωρήσιος: Ionic genitive. The abstract noun in -σις for the rotation is a coinage in the Presocratic manner.
περιχωρῆσαι: the subject of the infinitive and of the following sentence is unclear, possibly indefinite or impersonal - 'so that there was a rotation in the beginning'. The abstract περιχώρησις could not function as a subject, and an implied πάντα or ὁ κόσμος is unsuitable, since in the beginning only the centre is stirred.
ἀπό του σμικροῦ: 'from something small', 'in a small way'-- so Diels in preference to the accented article with the sense 'from the small'.
ἐπὶ δὲ πλέον: again Diels for the MSS ἐπεὶ δὲ πλέον.

10(iv) Mind has knowledge of past, present and future and is responsible for the present world order.

τὰ . . . διακρινόμενα: the verbs act as technical terms for the cosmic processes of complete mingling, separating off (of large portions of mixture) and separating out (which results in the articulation of particular objects).
ἔγνω: 'knew', i.e. 'was aware of and understood'; cf. γνώμην ἴσχει 10(ii) above.
διεκόσμησε: 'put into a κόσμος', 'arranged', 'ordered'.
ἣν: internal or cognate accusative with the intransitive verb (cf. *G*. 1051); it is usually translated with a preposition, so here - 'as to which / in which now revolve . . .'.
οἱ ἀποκρινόμενοι: 'that are being separated off'; the more general verb is appropriate for the emergence of the masses of air and αἰθήρ and the large heavenly bodies.

10(v) The opposites continue to separate out in the present but the process cannot be completed (cf. on fr. 7 above, and on 10(vi) below).

τοῦ ἀραιοῦ τὸ πυκνόν: this pair (rare / loose-textured and dense / compact) is an addition to the sets of opposites listed in 4(iii) as constituents of the original mixture. The separating off of material with prevailing opposite characteristics as a result of the rotation accounts for the present arrangement of the physical world.

10(vi) Everything except mind is a mixture, and takes its character from the dominant components.

νοῦς . . . ὁ ἐλάσσων: 'but mind is all alike, the greater and the smaller', i.e. any part of mind-material, no matter what size, is completely free from admixture, and

is therefore homogeneous; cf. P. 8(ii) and (iv).
[ὀυδενί]: the deletion was suggested by Wasserstein, *CR* 10 (1960) 48, and supported by Barnes (2.296 n.22). The context is a contrast between the innate simplicity of mind-material and the complexity of everything else - ('nothing else is all alike') rather than a comparison between one complex thing and another.
ἀλλ' ὅτων . . . ἦν: 'but of things of which (there are) most within, these most clearly each one is and was'. ἓν ἕκαστον is probably subject, with ταῦτα predicative and the coordinate for ὅτων. (For the MSS ὅτω Preller emended to ὅτεων, Diels to ὅτων. ὅτῳ is almost impossible to accommodate.) The prevailing ingredients give the overall character; an unlimited number of other components are present, but imperceptible because of their smallness.

Fragments 11-17: Mind and cosmogony.

11(13) Simplicius *In Phys*. 300.31

Mind initiated the rotation which led to the separation and subsequent articulation.

ἤρξατο κινεῖν: transitive - 'started movement', as the colloquial 'got things going'.
κινουμένου: passive; also ἀπεκρίνετο impersonal imperfect passive - 'from the whole, as it was being moved, there was a separating off'. (Guthrie vol. II 274 n.2 and others take νοῦς as subject and translate - 'it began to withdraw from'.)
κινουμένων . . . διακρινομένων: probably genitive absolutes with a general subject implied - 'while (things) were being set in motion and articulated'.
πολλῷ . . . διακρίνεσθαι: 'was making them much more articulate', as individuation within the elemental masses increased.

12(14) Simplicius *In Phys*. 157.7

The continued dominating presence of νοῦς.

ὅσα . . . κάρτα: the text is corrupt. Some suggestions here are ὃς ἀεί ἐστι, τὸ κάρτα, 'which ever is, certainly' (Diels), ὃς ἀεὶ ἦν καὶ ἔσται κάρτα (Marcovich) and ὅσα ἐστί τ' ἐκράτησε (Sider).
ἵνα: = 'where'.
πολλῷ: so Diels for the MSS πολλά - 'in the vast surrounding (mass)'.
προσκριθεῖσι: Anaxagoras' original compound. The meaning

in the context is not immediately clear; 'what was assimilated' or 'joined' (contrasting προσκρίνομαι with ἀποκρίνομαι) sounds atomistic but, if there is a careful distinction in the tenses of the participles, the reference is perhaps to the first effects of the rotation, which brought the earth-ish portions together towards the centre (cf. the next fragment).

13(15) Simplicius *In Phys.* 179.3

The beginning of the rotation caused parts of the mixture dominated by particular sets of opposites to move towards the centre or outwards. The same four pairs of opposites were mentioned at 10(v) above. To be pedantically exact <καὶ τὸ λαμπρόν> should be added after νῦν but it is easily understood. Similarly the inclusion of the article with every neuter adjective need not be expected.

συνεχώρησεν . . . ἐξεχώρησεν: the (predominantly) thick, wet, cold and dark came together to this place and now form the earth, whereas their opposites moved outwards. (<ἡ γῆ>is the Aldine supplement.)
εἰς τὸ πρόσω τοῦ αἰθέρος: 'to the further (part) of the αἰθήρ', 'further into the αἰθήρ'. The layers become rarer, warmer and drier in the gradations from the damp misty air close to the earth to the bright upper heavens, and the expansion is continuing (cf. on 10(iii) above).

14(9) Simplicius *In Phys.* 35.14

The fragment deals with the speed of the initial rotation. Simplicius cites it after phrases from 4(ii) and 4(i) with μετ' ὀλίγον φησί. The three quotations appear to be a casual collection gathered in support of his own neo-Platonic interpretation of a double cosmos. Their proximity in such a context need not inhibit the removal of this fragment to a section dealing more explicitly with the rotation.

τούτων: presumably the list of predominating opposites given in fr. 13.
ὑπὸ βίης: 'as a result of force'. The force is produced by the speed, and gives the impetus to the ἀπόκρισις.
τὴν ταχυτῆτα: accusative of specification (cf. *G.* 1058) - 'their speed is like with respect to speed no thing of the things that are now among men'. The phrasing is clumsy and the text may well be corrupt.
πάντως . . . ἐστι: 'is in all respect many times as swift'. Anaxagoras seems to be suggesting that the initial rotation was incredibly fast (when the centre of the vortex was stirred rapidly by mind) and from then on the rotation gradually slows as it extends further.

15(16) Simplicius *In Phys.* 179.8 and 155.21

Generation from the process of separating out is in the sequence: clouds, water, earth, stones.

τουτέων: Ionic for τούτων, referring probably to the opposites (cf. fr. 14).
συμπήγνυνται: present, as the process is continuous; for the verb, cf. on 4(ii) above.
ὑπὸ τοῦ ψυχροῦ: 'as a result of the cold'.
οὗτοι . . . ὕδατος: the stars that retreat more than water would seem to be those that spin off into the αἰθήρ, cf. Plutarch *Lys.* 12 and Hippolytus *Ref.* 1.8 (DK 59 A12 and A42).

16(18) Plutarch *De fac. lun.* 929b

The moon derives its light from the sun (cf. on P. 14).

τὸ λαμπρόν: one of the standard (material) opposites, physically passed from the sun to the moon.

17(19) Scholium ad *Il.* 17.547

The explanation of the rainbow.

Ἶριν: should this be capitalised for the goddess rather than the physical phenomenon? For Anaxagoras there would have been no such distinction (cf. X. 14).
τὸ . . . ἀντιλάμπον τῷ ἡλίῳ: 'that which shines opposite to (or 'in the face of') the sun'. Possibly the rainbow is envisaged as the curve of the base of a cone of light, of which the apex is the sun (cf. Sider 125). The scholiast continues with an explanation of the accompanying rain, in what is a paraphrase, rather than an extension of the original quotation (cf. Solmsen, *Hermes* (1963) 251f.).

Fragments 18-20: On perception and truth

18(21) Sextus *Adv. math.* 7.90

The feebleness of the senses is illustrated in the context by the inability to distinguish the change in water when ink is poured in drop by drop.

ὑπ' ἀφαυρότητος αὐτῶν: 'because of their feebleness', αὐτῶν referring back in Sextus' context to αἰσθήσεις. This is the only instance of the abstract noun, although the adjective ἀφαυρός ('feeble', 'powerless') is common in the comparative and superlative.
κρίνειν: both 'pick out' or 'distinguish' *and* 'judge'.

19(17) Simplicius *In Phys*. 163.20

The Eleatic denial of real generation and destruction (cf. P. 8(i), M. 7(ii) and E. 3).

οὐκ ὀρθῶς νομίζουσιν: 'do not have the right thoughts about . . .'.
συμμίσγεταί τε καὶ διακρίνεται: probably impersonal - 'there is (only) mixing and separating from things already existing', rather than with χρῆμα, χρήματα or πάντα understood as subject.
ἂν . . . καλοῖεν: potential optative - 'and so they would be right to call . . .'.

20(21a) Sextus *Adv. math*. 7.140

These five words were also attributed to Democritus and Diocles and have an independent history as a proverb.

τὰ φαινόμενα: subject - 'things seen', i.e. commonplace objects and events in the world. However, as the context is not known, the words may have had a particular reference.
ὄψις τῶν ἀδήλων: predicate - 'a sight of things unseen', i.e. a careful examination of the visible leads to an understanding of the invisible, and for Anaxagoras this would be the complex structure of the very small.

L E U C I P P U S

Fragment 1(2):

Aetius 1.25.4

This is the only surviving sentence from Leucippus, quoted from a work Περὶ νοῦ. It posits a general theory of causality, reinforced by the introductory remark in Aetius which identifies necessity here with fate (εἱμαρμένη). A similar statement attributed to Democritus ('everything happens κατ᾽ ἀνάγκην', D.L. 9.45), has a particular reference, connecting necessity with the δίνη ('whirl' or vortex'), which is responsible for the initial atomic movements and so eventually for the 'generation of everything'.

χρῆμα: a general term which covers things, situations and events.
μάτην: 'in vain', 'without explanation'.
ἐκ λόγου: 'for a reason', and then, more specifically, ὑπ᾽ ἀνάγκης 'because of the workings of necessity' (which are manifest in the movements of atoms in void).

Fragment 2(A7):

Aristotle *De generatione et corruptione* 325a23

Leucippus was usually taken, even in the ancient world, in conjunction with Democritus. This is a rare example of an argument attributed to Leucippus independently. Aristotle recasts it in his own way but the drift of the original is clear.

2.1 -2 πρὸς . . . λέγοντες: i.e. 'in agreement with the senses'.
2.3 τὸ πλῆθος τῶν ὄντων: 'the plurality of existing things'.
2.4 τοῖς . . . κατασκευάζουσιν: 'to those (i.e. the Eleatics) who set up the one thing'.
2.5 -7 τό τε . . . παμπλῆρες ὄν: 'and he says that the empty (i.e. void) is what is not, and that nothing of what is *is* what is not; for what is in the strict sense is completely full all over (i.e. is a *plenum*)'.
2.7 τὸ τοιοῦτον: 'something like this', i.e. a *plenum*, of which there is not one only for Leucippus, but an unlimited number.
2.8 καὶ . . . ὄγκων: 'and imperceptible because of the small size of the particles'. ὄγκοι are units with some size and some bulk or mass.

2.9 κενὸν γὰρ εἶναι: Leucippus wishes to claim both that there is void (the 'empty') and that the void is identifiable with the Eleatic μὴ ὄν. The universe contains both the existing things (atoms) and the empty place around them; cf. further on D. 8 below.

2.9 συνιστάμενα . . . διαλυόμενα: middle participle - 'as they
-10 come together . . . as they break apart'; for the former verb, cf. P. 4.4 and E. 8.6.

There is an additional report by Aristotle on the atomism of Leucippus and Democritus at *Metaphysics* 985b3-19, reproduced and translated in the *Appendix*, 'Aristotle on the Presocratics' below. The basic assumptions and arguments agree with the above section and are generally taken to be Leucippus' pioneering work. The unusual vocabulary for the technical terms is also probably his: ῥυσμός ('contour') for shape, διαθιγή ('contact') for order or arrangement and τροπή ('inclination') for position.

DEMOCRITUS

Fragments 1-7: Scepticism.

1(6) Sextus *Adv. math.* 7.137

The fragment comes from Democritus' Περὶ ἰδεῶν in a list of quotations condemning the evidence of the senses.

ἄνθρωπον: subject of the infinitive with χρή.
τῷδε τῷ κανόνι: 'according to this rule'. κανών is literally a straight rod and then a standard or rule. Democritus wrote a treatise of this title in the plural (from which fr. 3 is taken) and it became a technical term in Epicurean epistemology.
ἐτεῆς: the feminine noun ἐτεή ('truth, 'reality'), from the adjective ἐτε(ός) -ά -όν, is a coinage frequently (and it would seem exclusively) used by Demoscritus, always in the genitive or dative singular.

2(7) Sextus *Adv. math.* 7.137

The fragment is quoted immediately after fr. 1 with καὶ πάλιν. The content of the λόγος mentioned is unknown.

οὐδὲν . . . περὶ οὐδενός: the negatives are cumulative - 'in reality we know nothing about anything'.
ἐπιρυσμίη: a unique form (-ρρυσμίη in *LSJ*). The stem -ρυσμ- is Ionic for -ρυθμ- and ῥυθμός has a wide range of meanings, as well as being the word for atomic shape. The general sense here is that one's opinion (δόξις is Democritean for δόξα) depends on one's physical constitution, which is a certain arrangement of atoms (cf. P. 16 and E. 15). Perhaps the word means 'accompanying disposition' (cf. on fr. 6 below).

3(11) Sextus *Adv. math.* 7.139

The legitimate and the bastard kinds of knowing.

γνώμης: a characteristic Presocratic word; cf. H. 4 and 25 and A. 10(ii)
σκοτίη: 'in the dark', 'secret' and hence 'illegitimate', opposed to 'belonging to the γένος', 'legitimate', 'genuine'.
ὄψις . . . ψαῦσις: abstract nouns for the five senses; this is the first full listing of them.
ἡ δὲ . . . ταύτης: genuine knowledge is in a permanent state of separation (hence the perfect passive participle) from the spurious one resulting from the evidence of the senses.

4(117) Diogenes Laertius 9.72

The hopelessness of our attempts at knowledge.

ἴδμεν: the older form of ἴσμεν, as ὄδμη for ὀσμή in the previous fragment.
ἐν βυθῷ: as of the fathomless depths of the sea and for any deep hole (cf. H. 65).

5(9) Sextus *Adv. math.* 7.135

The fragment is also quoted by Galen (cf. B 125). It was a succinct (and famous) contrast between convention and reality, similar to the νόμος / φύσις contrast in ethics.

νόμῳ χροιή: Sextus' text has νόμῳ θερμόν, νόμῳ ψυχρόν before this but it is not in Galen and may be a later expansion; 'colour by convention' is out of line in a list of opposites but cf. P. 8.41. νόμος covers the range from 'usage', 'customary behaviour' (the sense here, especially in the dative singular) to 'decree' and 'law'.
ἄτομα: the first appearance of the word as a technical term, the use perhaps starting with Leucippus. Originally a two-termination adjective meaning 'uncut', 'impossible to cut' (derived from τέμνω), it became standard, in the neuter plural, for 'atoms'. Aristotle and Epicurus also keep the adjectival form in ἄτομα σώματα.

6(9) Sextus *Adv. math.* 7.136

A development of fr. 3, on the limitations of understanding imposed by the atomic structure of subject and object. The quotation is from Τὰ Κρατυντήρια, i.e. 'supports', 'additional arguments'.

ἀτρεκὲς: 'accurately', 'precisely', with συνίεμεν ambiguous between its literal and metaphorical senses - 'collect together', 'perceive' and 'understand'.
μεταπῖπτον: participle of the impersonal verb used as an accusative absolute (cf. *G.* 1569) - 'there being a change'.
κατὰ . . . διαθήκην: 'according to the condition (or 'disposition') of the body'. Menzel's emendation, διαθιγὴν ('mutual touching' or 'contact') is sometimes accepted.
καὶ . . . ἀντιστηριζόντων: 'both of the things (i.e. the atoms) which enter in and of those which press against it'. Our ability to be aware of the outside world, dependent on our physical constitution, continually changes in the very moment of perception, when the new atoms penetrate inside or push upon the outside of the body. Accurate observation is therefore impossible (cf. Aristotle *De generatione et corruptione* 315b9ff.).

7(125) Galen *De medic. empir.* (1259.8 Schöne)

The senses, personified, defend themselves against the attack made on them by reason. Some editors reject the fragment but there is no reason to deny Democritus' awareness of this crucial objection and the vivid presentation of it.

παρ' . . . κατάβλημα: 'do you take your evidence from (your use of) us and then set about overthrowing us? Our overthrow is your ruin'. Reason has to use the evidence of the senses as the first move in working out the theory that explains what is perceived. How can it then disparage or reject its own starting point without the collapse of what follows from it? We do not know what, if any, reply the φρήν made.

Fragments 8-11: Atoms and the 'whirl'.

8(156) Plutarch *Adv. Col.* 1109a

'Thing' (the atom) *is* to the same extent as 'no-thing' (the void).

μὴ μᾶλλον: οὐ μᾶλλον - 'no more (this than that)' - became a catch-phrase with the sceptics. It could be taken positively, as with Protagoras (the wind that is no more hot than cold is both hot and cold according to its relative effects), or negatively ('no more this than that'), meaning 'neither this nor that'. Although Democritus took the negative sense when speaking of qualities (honey is no more sweet than bitter because - actually - it is neither- cf. A134), here this basic postulate should be taken positively - atoms and void, things and no-thing, are equally real.

τὸ δὲν: μηδέν is literally μή-δ-ἕν ('not-one-thing') with the delta inserted for euphony. Democritus took it as μή-δέν and created a new word δέν (or perhaps used an existing rare one) for 'thing', with μηδέν as its negation. (The form of the pun is as old as Odysseus' Οὖτις at *Od.* 9.368.)

9(A37) Simplicius *In Cael.* 295.1

This is Aristotle's summary of the basic tenets of Democritus' atomic theory from his lost work *On Democritus*, quoted by Simplicius. In the absence of any original account it seemed appropriate to include it here. Some of the terms are known to be Democritus' own and much of the phrasing is in the Presocratic idiom. The Aristotelian fragment continues with a description of the movements and contacts of atoms in void, and of the formations and dissolutions of their compounds. It shows how the different shapes of the atoms - scalene, hooked, concave and convex - make the aggregations possible.

9.1 πλῆθος . . . μεγέθει: i.e. the atoms are unlimited in number, void unlimited in extent.
9.4 τῷ τε κενῷ . . . τῷ ὄντι: various terms for atoms are
-5 τὸ ὄν, τὸ δέν (cf. fr. 8 above) and τὸ ναστόν (the 'close-pressed', the 'solid'), and for the void τὸ κενόν, τὸ οὐδέν and (adapting Anaximander) τὸ ἄπειρον.
9.8 κατὰ μέγεθος διαφοράς: 'differences in size'. According to this passage, and on Aristotle's authority, Democritean atoms are too small to be perceptible, and they become visible to the eye (ὀφθαλμοφανεῖς) only when an atom grouping is formed. Two late notices (in Aetius at 68A47 and Dionysius A43, with which cf. Diogenes 9.44 at A1) assume Democritus posited very large atoms, Aetius even one that could be as big as a cosmos, but this is probably due to a misunderstanding of an Epicurean criticism. For some of the evidence in the controversy cf. Guthrie vol. II 394-95, and for a compromise solution of the logical but not empirical possibility of large atoms, cf. Barnes 2.46.

10(167) Simplicius *In Phys.* 327.24

The first stage of a cosmogony is the occurrence of a δῖνος, a 'whirl' or 'vortex' in a group of atoms, similar to the περιχώρησις in Anaxagoras' scheme.

παντοίων ἰδεῶν: with δῖνον - 'a whirl of all kinds of (atomic) forms'. ἰδέαι ('shapes', 'types', 'forms') could be used both for Democritean atoms and Platonic archetypes.

11(164) Sextus *Adv. math.* 7.117

The motion of the δῖνος causes a reaction similar to that of a sieve or riddle. Through the mechanical attraction of like for like, atoms of similar shape and size come together. The analogies, as Sextus explains in introducing the quotation, cover both living creatures and inanimate objects.

11.1 συναγελάζεται: a rare verb, middle and intransitive, which does not appear again until Aristotle; it means 'herd' or, as here of birds, 'flock together'. περιστεραί are doves or pigeons, and γέρανοι cranes. Such creatures, being ἄλογοι, cannot help but act according to their nature.
11.4 ἐπί τε . . . σπερμάτων: 'in the case of seeds that are being riddled'. The idea is not that the smaller seeds fall through the holes in a sieve, but that a continuous circular movement on a level surface results in seeds of the same type coming together.
11.4 ἐπὶ . . . ψηφίδων: 'in the case of pebbles on beaches', *lit.*
-5 at the wave-breakers or places where waves break. ψηφίς is a diminutive of ψῆφος.
11.6 διακριτικῶς: 'separatively', as a result of the separating

movement.

11.6 φακοὶ . . . πυρῶν: the seeds mentioned are lentils, barley
-7 and wheat.

11.8 ἐπιμήκεις: 'oblong' (though more exactly 'elongated' - they
-9 would not of course be rectilinear). περιφερεῖς - 'round'.

11.10 ὡς ἂν . . . ὁμοιότητος: ὡς ἂν is used elliptically (cf. *G.*
-11 1313) with the genitive absolute as a conditional clause. The word-order in English would be slightly different - 'as (they would) if the (very) similarity of the objects acted as a (force) bringing them together'.

Fragments 12-14: On perception.

12(166) Sextus *Adv. math.* 9.19

The impact of tall 'images' in sleep, which can bring premonitions of good or evil, was one of the atomists' explanations for a general belief in gods. This extract, which is only partly direct quotation, shows a certain irony in Democritus' attitude.

εἴδωλα: 'images', 'films', here in particular of dream images; it was a technical term (cf. fr. 13 below).

εὐλόγχων: (connecting with λαγχάνω) - 'lucky'.

13(67A29) Alexander *In De sensu* 56.12

This is a paraphrase and not a direct quotation but it has been included to explain the word εἴδωλα, which Democritus did use. εἴδωλα ('films' or 'emanations') preserve in two dimensions the images of the objects from which they continually flow. These 'films' impinge on the eye and, because they are ὁμοιόμορφα, i.e. of the same appearance as the original, vision occurs. The theory is a development of that of the effluences (ἀπορροαί) from all things posited by Empedocles at B89.

ᾐτιῶντο: the subject is explained in the following τοιοῦτοι. The grammar of the verb - allege (x) as the cause of (y) - requires an accusative (εἴδωλά τινα) and a genitive (τοῦ ὁρᾶν).

14(A122) Aristotle *De an.* 419a15

The quotation is indirect but the immediate effect of Democritus' words is clear. Aristotle of course does not agree with him.

ὁρᾶσθαι: the subject is μύρμηξ, kept for the climax in the

second protasis - 'if the intervening (space) were to become void, then it would be seen clearly, if there were an ant in the sky'. The explanation is that the εἴδωλα of the ant would descend intact and immediately to the eye below.

Fragment 15: Conic sections.

15(155) Plutarch *De communibus notitiis* 1079e

The fragment sets out a dilemma in the manner of Zeno. If a cone is sliced horizontally to its base, are the facing surfaces equal or not? If equal, the cone is cylindrical; if unequal, it is stepped; either conclusion is unacceptable. Some suggest that Democritus would have accepted the 'stepped' alternative in accordance with a theory of indivisible least units, others that the dilemma was a defensive counter-attack. Given Democritus' readiness, like any good philosopher, to be his own devil's advocate (cf. fr. 7), he may well have published the puzzle for its own interest. (The puzzle, together with a related one about planes making up the angled surface of a sphere was one of the first contributions to the theories of exhaustion, which were among the major achievements of Greek mathematics; cf. B.155a.)

παρὰ . . . ἐπιπέδῳ: 'at a level parallel to the base', with τὰς τῶν τμητάτων ἐπιφανείας as 'the (facing) surfaces of the sections'.
ἄνισοι . . . οὖσαι . . . ἴσων οὐσῶν: the participles are conditional.
ἀνώμαλον . . . πολλὰς . . . τραχύτητας: 'uneven . . . acquiring a series of stepped indentations and a jagged edge'.
ἴσων . . . κύκλων: 'but if they are equal, (the surfaces of) the segments will be equal, and the cone will obviously have ended up as a cylinder, built up of equal and not unequal discs'.

Fragments 16-20: Miscellanea.

16(154) Plutarch *De sollertia animalium* 974a

Anthropology, including the origins of language and the acquisition of human τέχνη, was one of the interests of the fifth century intellectuals. It is known that Democritus wrote extensively on the subject but very little remains. This fragment is on men learning some basic skills from the animal world.

ἡμᾶς: accusative subject, for Plutarch gives the quotation in *oratio obliqua*; the infinitive is the 'periphrastic' perfect - the perfect participle with εἶναι understood.

ἐν . . . ἀκεστικῇ: ὑφαντική and ἀκεστική are feminine adjectives agreeing with τέχνη implied. The spider is obviously a master craftsman in weaving; ἡ ἀκεστική means 'healing' in the sense both of 'curing' and 'repairing'.

καὶ τῶν λιγυρῶν . . . μίμησιν: 'and of the clear-voiced birds, the swan and the nightingale, in song by imitation', i.e. by imitating their song.

17(247) Stobaeus 3.40.7

Cosmopolitanism was another idea that was being aired and which was to have a long history in Stoic ethical theory. This, if genuine, is one of its earliest expressions.

βατή: from βαίνω, 'walkable over', 'accessible'; the whole earth is the wise man's domain.

18(230) Stobaeus 3.16.22

Over two hundred fragments attributed to Democritus are ethical maxims, the majority of them collected in Stobaeus. They are commonplace and philosophically uninteresting in the main; three are given here as a sample. The genuineness of this whole *corpus* has been called in question, and it is hard to reconcile these rather trite utterances with the intellectual brilliance which Democritus shows elsewhere.

ἀνεόρταστος . . . ἀπανδόκευτος: negative two-termination adjectives - 'without a holiday / festival (ἑορτή) . . . without an inn'.

19(211) Stobaeus 3.5.27

τὰ τερπνά: 'delights', particular enjoyments that are productive of ἡδονή.

ἀέξει: present tense, a poetic form of αὔξει, 'increase (in quality)'.

20(171) Stobaeus 2.7.3

ἐν βοσκήμασιν: *lit.* 'in what is fed'; βοσκήματα is used of herds of cattle and flocks of sheep.

A P P E N D I X

ARISTOTLE ON THE PRESOCRATICS

(from *Metaphysics* Book A)

Chapter 3

The four kinds of explanations or 'causes'

983a24 ἐπεὶ δὲ φανερὸν ὅτι τῶν ἐξ ἀρχῆς αἰτίων δεῖ λαβεῖν ἐπιστήμην (τότε γὰρ εἰδέναι φαμὲν ἕκαστον, ὅταν τὴν πρώτην αἰτίαν οἰώμεθα γνωρίζειν), τὰ δ' αἴτια λέγεται τετραχῶς, ὧν μίαν μὲν αἰτίαν φαμὲν εἶναι τὴν οὐσίαν καὶ τὸ τί ἦν εἶναι (ἀνάγεται γὰρ τὸ διὰ τί εἰς τὸν λόγον ἔσχατον, αἴτιον δὲ καὶ ἀρχὴ τὸ διὰ τί πρῶτον), ἑτέραν δὲ τὴν ὕλην καὶ τὸ ὑποκείμενον, τρίτην δὲ ὅθεν ἡ ἀρχὴ τῆς κινήσεως, τετάρτην δὲ τὴν ἀντικειμένην αἰτίαν ταύτῃ, τὸ οὗ ἕνεκα καὶ τἀγαθόν (τέλος γὰρ γενέσεως καὶ κινήσεως πάσης τοῦτ' ἐστίν), τεθεώρηται μὲν οὖν ἱκανῶς περὶ αὐτῶν ἡμῖν ἐν τοῖς περὶ φύσεως, ὅμως δὲ παραλάβωμεν καὶ τοὺς πρότερον ἡμῶν εἰς ἐπίσκεψιν τῶν ὄντων ἐλθόντας καὶ φιλοσοφήσαντας περὶ τῆς ἀληθείας. δῆλον γὰρ ὅτι κἀκεῖνοι λέγουσιν ἀρχάς τινας καὶ αἰτίας. ἐπελθοῦσιν οὖν ἔσται τι προὔργου τῇ μεθόδῳ τῇ νῦν· ἢ γὰρ ἕτερόν τι γένος εὑρήσομεν αἰτίας ἢ ταῖς νῦν λεγομέναις μᾶλλον πιστεύσομεν.

Material 'causes'

983b6 τῶν δὴ πρώτων φιλοσοφησάντων οἱ πλεῖστοι τὰς ἐν ὕλης εἴδει μόνας ᾠήθησαν ἀρχὰς εἶναι πάντων· ἐξ οὗ γὰρ ἔστιν ἅπαντα τὰ ὄντα καὶ ἐξ οὗ γίγνεται πρώτου καὶ εἰς ὃ φθείρεται τελευταῖον, τῆς μὲν οὐσίας ὑπομενούσης τοῖς δὲ πάθεσι μεταβαλλούσης, τοῦτο στοιχεῖον καὶ ταύτην ἀρχήν φασιν εἶναι τῶν ὄντων, καὶ διὰ τοῦτο οὔτε γίγνεσθαι οὐθὲν οἴονται οὔτε ἀπόλλυσθαι, ὡς τῆς τοιαύτης φύσεως ἀεὶ σῳζομένης, ὥσπερ οὐδὲ τὸν Σωκράτην φαμὲν οὔτε γίγνεσθαι ἁπλῶς ὅταν γίγνηται καλὸς ἢ μουσικὸς οὔτε ἀπόλλυσθαι ὅταν ἀποβάλλῃ ταύτας τὰς ἕξεις, διὰ τὸ ὑπομένειν τὸ ὑποκείμενον, τὸν Σωκράτην αὐτόν, οὕτως οὐδὲ τῶν ἄλλων οὐδέν· δεῖ γὰρ εἶναί τινα φύσιν ἢ μίαν ἢ πλείους μιᾶς ἐξ ὧν γίγνεται τἆλλα σῳζομένης ἐκείνης.

983b18 τὸ μέντοι πλῆθος καὶ τὸ εἶδος τῆς τοιαύτης ἀρχῆς οὐ τὸ αὐτὸ πάντες λέγουσιν, ἀλλὰ Θαλῆς μὲν ὁ τῆς τοιαύτης ἀρχηγὸς φιλοσοφίας ὕδωρ φησὶν εἶναι (διὸ καὶ τὴν γῆν ἐφ' ὕδατος ἀπεφήνατο εἶναι), λαβὼν ἴσως τὴν ὑπόληψιν ταύτην ἐκ τοῦ πάντων ὁρᾶν τὴν τροφὴν ὑγρὰν οὖσαν καὶ αὐτὸ τὸ θερμὸν ἐκ τούτου γιγνόμενον καὶ τούτῳ ζῶν (τὸ δ' ἐξ οὗ γίγνεται, τοῦτ' ἐστὶν ἀρχὴ πάντων) -

Chapter 3

The four kinds of explanations or 'causes'

983a24 It is clear that we must have knowledge of basic explanations (for we claim to know a thing when we think we understand its primary explanation), and explanations (or 'causes') are of four kinds: (i) we say the essence and form give an explanation (for 'why' is pushed back to the final definition, and 'cause' and 'first principle' answer the primary 'why'), (ii) the material and substrate, (iii) the source of the principle of movement and change, and (iv) - the complementary explanation to (iii) - its purpose and good (for this is the aim of all generation and movement). We have considered this in detail in the *Physics* but let us also look at those predecessors of ours who undertook a study of what there is, and who were philosophers concerned with truth. Obviously they too speak of principles and causes of some sort; and so a review will help our present enquiry, for we shall either find a further type of explanation or have increased confidence in the four we now suggest.

Material 'causes'

983b6 Now the majority of the earliest philosophers thought that the only general principles were those of a material kind. They say that the material of which all things consist, and from which they first come and into which they eventually disintegrate - the substance persisting while its attributes change - is the element and principle of things, and because of this they think that there is no generation or destruction at all, since a natural substance of this kind endures throughout. We do not, for example, say of Socrates that he comes to be in an absolute sense when he comes to be handsome or cultured, or that he is destroyed when he loses these qualities, for the substrate, Socrates himself, persists. So it is with everything else; for there always has to be some natural substance, one or more than one, which endures while the rest are generated from it.

983b18 They do not however all agree on the number and character of such a principle. Thales, the founder of this type of philosophy, says that the first principle is water, and that is why he claimed that the earth rests on water. Perhaps he came to this conclusion from observing that nourishment is universally moist, and that even heat is generated from moisture and fuelled by it (and the source of generation is a general prin-

διά τε δὴ τοῦτο τὴν ὑπόληψιν λαβὼν ταύτην καὶ
διὰ τὸ πάντων τὰ σπέρματα τὴν φύσιν ὑγρὰν ἔχειν·
τὸ δ' ὕδωρ ἀρχὴ τῆς φύσεώς ἐστι τοῖς ὑγροῖς.

983b27 εἰσὶ δέ τινες οἳ καὶ τοὺς παμπαλαίους καὶ πολὺ πρὸ
τῆς νῦν γενέσεως καὶ πρώτους θεολογήσαντας οὕτως
οἴονται περὶ τῆς φύσεως ὑπολαβεῖν· Ὠκεανόν τε
γὰρ καὶ Τηθὺν ἐποίησαν τῆς γενέσεως πατέρας, καὶ τὸν
ὅρκον τῶν θεῶν ὕδωρ, τὴν καλουμένην ὑπ' αὐτῶν Στύγα
[τῶν ποιητῶν]· τιμιώτατον μὲν γὰρ τὸ πρεσβύτατον,
ὅρκος δὲ τὸ τιμιώτατόν ἐστιν. εἰ μὲν οὖν ἀρχαία
984a τις αὕτη καὶ παλαιὰ τετύχηκεν οὖσα περὶ τῆς φύσεως
ἡ δόξα, τάχ' ἂν ἄδηλον εἴη, Θαλῆς μέντοι λέγεται
οὕτως ἀποφήνασθαι περὶ τῆς πρώτης αἰτίας.

984a5 Ἀναξιμένης δὲ ἀέρα καὶ Διογένης πρότερον ὕδατος καὶ
μάλιστ' ἀρχὴν τιθέασι τῶν ἁπλῶν σωμάτων, Ἵππασος
δὲ πῦρ ὁ Μεταποντῖνος καὶ Ἡράκλειτος ὁ Ἐφέσιος,
Ἐμπεδοκλῆς δὲ τὰ τέτταρα, πρὸς τοῖς εἰρημένοις
γῆν προστιθεὶς τέταρτον (ταῦτα γὰρ ἀεὶ διαμένειν καὶ
οὐ γίγνεσθαι ἀλλ' ἢ πλήθει καὶ ὀλιγότητι, συγκρινό-
μενα καὶ διακρινόμενα εἰς ἕν τε καὶ ἐξ ἑνός)·
Ἀναξαγόρας δὲ ὁ Κλαζομένιος, τῇ μὲν ἡλικίᾳ πρότερος
ὢν τούτου τοῖς δ' ἔργοις ὕστερος, ἀπείρους εἶναί
φησι τὰς ἀρχάς· σχεδὸν γὰρ ἅπαντα τὰ ὁμοιομερῆ καθάπερ
ὕδωρ ἢ πῦρ οὕτω γίγνεσθαι καὶ ἀπόλλυσθαί φησι, συγκ-
ρίσει καὶ διακρίσει μόνον, ἄλλως δ' οὔτε γίγνεσθαι
οὔτ' ἀπόλλυσθαι ἀλλὰ διαμένειν ἀΐδια.

Causes of movement and change

984a16 ἐκ μὲν οὖν τούτων μόνην τις αἰτίαν νομίσειεν ἂν τὴν
ἐν ὕλης εἴδει λεγομένην· προϊόντων δ' οὕτως αὐτὸ
τὸ πρᾶγμα ὡδοποίησεν αὐτοῖς καὶ συνηνάγκασε ζητεῖν·
εἰ γὰρ ὅτι μάλιστα πᾶσα γένεσις καὶ φθορὰ ἔκ τινος
ἑνὸς ἢ καὶ πλειόνων ἐστίν, διὰ τί τοῦτο συμβαίνει
καὶ τί τὸ αἴτιον; οὐ γὰρ δὴ τό γε ὑποκείμενον αὐτὸ
ποιεῖ μεταβάλλειν ἑαυτό· λέγω δ' οἷον οὔτε τὸ ξύλον
οὔτε ὁ χαλκὸς αἴτιος τοῦ μεταβάλλειν ἑκάτερον αὐτῶν,
οὐδὲ ποιεῖ τὸ μὲν ξύλον κλίνην ὁ δὲ χαλκὸς ἀνδριάντα,
ἀλλ' ἕτερόν τι τῆς μεταβολῆς αἴτιον. τὸ δὲ τοῦτο
ζητεῖν ἐστὶ τὸ τὴν ἑτέραν ἀρχὴν ζητεῖν, ὡς ἂν ἡμεῖς
φαίημεν, ὅθεν ἡ ἀρχὴ τῆς κινήσεως.

ciple and starting point). That is why he reached his conclusion, and also because seed generally has a moist character, and water is the principle of the natural character of what is moist.

983b27 Furthermore, some think that even the men in the distant past, who, long before the present generation, were the first to reason about the gods, held this view of natural substance, for they made Oceanus and Tethys the parents of generation, and the oath of the gods by water, which they called Styx (for the most ancient is the most honoured, and an oath is by what
984a is most honoured). It is quite uncertain whether this was the original and ancient belief about natural substance, but Thales at any rate is said to have spoken of the primary cause in this way.

984a5 Anaximenes however and Diogenes say that air is more primary than water, and has the strongest claim, of all the elementary substances, to be the first principle; Hippasus of Metapontum and Heraclitus of Ephesus say fire, and Empedocles all four, adding earth as a fourth to those already mentioned (for these persist throughout and are not generated, except in becoming many as they separate from one and few as they come together into one). Anaxagoras of Clazomenae, earlier than him in years but later in publication, claims that the principles are unlimited; for he more or less says that all the like-part substances such as water and fire are generated and destroyed only in the sense of combining and separating, and that otherwise they do not have a beginning or end but remain for ever.

Causes of movement and change

984a16 As a result of these theories it might be thought that the only type of cause or explanation is the one that has been described as 'of the material kind', but, as further progress was made, the very nature of the task showed the way forward and demanded investigation. Granted that all generation and disintegration is from one or more substances, why does this happen and what is the cause? The substrate surely does not make itself change. I mean for example that wood or bronze is not the cause of its own change - the wood does not make a bed nor the bronze a statue - but something else effects the transformation. A search for this is a search for the second principle - the principle of movement, as we would call it.

984a27 οἱ μὲν οὖν πάμπαν ἐξ ἀρχῆς ἁψάμενοι τῆς μεθόδου
τῆς τοιαύτης καὶ ἓν φάσκοντες εἶναι τὸ ὑποκείμενον
οὐθὲν ἐδυσχέραναν ἑαυτοῖς, ἀλλ᾽ ἔνιοί γε τῶν ἓν
λεγόντων, ὥσπερ ἡττηθέντες ὑπὸ ταύτης τῆς ζητήσεως,
τὸ ἓν ἀκίνητόν φασιν εἶναι καὶ τὴν φύσιν ὅλην οὐ
μόνον κατὰ γένεσιν καὶ φθοράν (τοῦτο μὲν γὰρ ἀρχαῖόν
τε καὶ πάντες ὡμολόγησαν) ἀλλὰ καὶ κατὰ τὴν ἄλλην
984b μεταβολὴν πᾶσαν· καὶ τοῦτο αὐτῶν ἴδιόν ἐστιν. τῶν
μὲν οὖν ἓν φασκόντων εἶναι τὸ πᾶν οὐθενὶ συνέβη τὴν
τοιαύτην συνιδεῖν αἰτίαν πλὴν εἰ ἄρα Παρμενίδῃ, καὶ
τούτῳ κατὰ τοσοῦτον ὅσον οὐ μόνον ἓν ἀλλὰ καὶ δύο
πως τίθησιν αἰτίας εἶναι· τοῖς δὲ δὴ πλείω ποιοῦσι
μᾶλλον ἐνδέχεται λέγειν, οἷον τοῖς θερμὸν καὶ ψυχ-
ρὸν ἢ πῦρ καὶ γῆν· χρῶνται γὰρ ὡς κινητικὴν ἔχοντι
τῷ πυρὶ τὴν φύσιν, ὕδατι δὲ καὶ γῇ καὶ τοῖς τοιού-
τοις τοὐναντίον.

984b8 μετὰ δὲ τούτους καὶ τὰς τοιαύτας ἀρχάς, ὡς οὐχ
ἱκανῶν οὐσῶν γεννῆσαι τὴν τῶν ὄντων φύσιν, πάλιν
ὑπ᾽ αὐτῆς τῆς ἀληθείας, ὥσπερ εἴπομεν, ἀναγκαζόμενοι
τὴν ἐχομένην ἐζήτησαν ἀρχήν. τοῦ γὰρ εὖ καὶ καλῶς
τὰ μὲν ἔχειν τὰ δὲ γίγνεσθαι τῶν ὄντων ἴσως οὔτε πῦρ
οὔτε γῆν οὔτ᾽ ἄλλο τῶν τοιούτων οὐθὲν οὔτ᾽ εἰκὸς
αἴτιον εἶναι οὔτ᾽ ἐκείνους οἰηθῆναι· οὐδ᾽ αὖ τῷ
αὐτομάτῳ καὶ τῇ τύχῃ τοσοῦτον ἐπιτρέψαι πρᾶγμα καλῶς
εἶχεν. νοῦν δή τις εἰπὼν ἐνεῖναι, καθάπερ ἐν τοῖς
ζῴοις, καὶ ἐν τῇ φύσει τὸν αἴτιον τοῦ κόσμου καὶ
τῆς τάξεως πάσης, οἷον νήφων ἐφάνη παρ᾽ εἰκῇ λέγον-
τας τοὺς πρότερον. φανερῶς μὲν οὖν Ἀναξαγόραν ἴσμεν
ἁψάμενον τούτων τῶν λόγων, αἰτίαν δ᾽ ἔχει πρότερον
Ἑρμότιμος ὁ Κλαζομένιος εἰπεῖν. οἱ μὲν οὖν οὕτως
ὑπολαμβάνοντες ἅμα τοῦ καλῶς τὴν αἰτίαν ἀρχὴν εἶναι
τῶν ὄντων ἔθεσαν, καὶ τὴν τοιαύτην ὅθεν ἡ κίνησις
ὑπάρχει τοῖς οὖσιν.

Chapter 4

Love as a principle of good

984b23 ὑποπτεύσειε δ᾽ ἄν τις Ἡσίοδον πρῶτον ζητῆσαι τὸ τοι-
οῦτον, κἂν εἴ τις ἄλλος ἔρωτα ἢ ἐπιθυμίαν ἐν τοῖς
οὖσιν ἔθηκεν ὡς ἀρχήν, οἷον καὶ Παρμενίδης· καὶ
γὰρ οὗτος κατασκευάζων τὴν τοῦ παντὸς γένεσιν
"πρῶτον μέν" φησιν "ἔρωτα θεῶν μητίσατο πάντων",

984a27 The very first to tackle this line of enquiry, those who said that the substrate was one, saw no difficulty. Some however of those who took it to be one seemed to be defeated by the problem; they claim that this one thing - in fact the whole natural world - is immutable not only in respect of generation and destruction (for
984b that was an old belief and universally accepted), but in any sense of change at all, and this theory is peculiar to them. None then of those who say that everything is one thing had a glimpse of this type of explanation except perhaps Parmenides, and he only in so far as he posits not just one entity but two causes somehow as well. Those however who set up a plurality, hot and cold for example or fire and earth, can develop the topic more fully, for they treat fire as if it had a kinetic character, with water, earth and the like contrary to it.

984b8 After these men and their type of principle, which were inadequate to account for the generation of the natural world, men were compelled, as we said, by the facts of the case to investigate the next principle. It is unlikely that fire or earth or anything else of that kind explains why some things are well and suitably constituted and others come to be so, or that these philosophers were thought to have used such an explanation. And it would not be appropriate to entrust a matter of such importance to accident or chance. So when one man said that mind is present, and it is this which is the cause of order and of every regular arrangement in nature as a whole as in living organisms, he looked like a sober man compared to his rambling predecessors. We are certain that Anaxagoras adopted this theory, but Hermotimus of Clazomenae is alleged to have produced it earlier. So those who think along these lines asserted both that the cause of the right arrangement of things was a first principle, and that it was the type of principle which acts as a source of change and movement in the world.

Chapter 4

Love as a principle of good

984b23 It could be suggested that Hesiod started this inquiry, or anyone else who posited love or desire in the world as a principle. Parmenides, for example, in describing the genesis of the universe, says: 'as first of all gods she devised eros', and Hesiod: 'first of all chaos came to be, and then broad-breasted earth . . . and eros,

Ἡσίοδος δὲ "πάντων μὲν πρώτιστα χάος γένετ', αὐτὰρ ἔπειτα / γαῖ' εὐρύστερνος . . . / ἠδ' ἔρος, ὃς πάντεσσι μεταπρέπει ἀθανάτοισιν", ὡς δέον ἐν τοῖς οὖσιν ὑπάρχειν τιν' αἰτίαν ἥτις κινήσει καὶ συνάξει τὰ πράγματα.

984b32 ἐπεὶ δὲ καὶ τἀναντία τοῖς ἀγαθοῖς ἐνόντα ἐφαίνετο
985a ἐν τῇ φύσει, καὶ οὐ μόνον τάξις καὶ τὸ καλὸν ἀλλὰ καὶ ἀταξία καὶ τὸ αἰσχρόν, καὶ πλείω τὰ κακὰ τῶν ἀγαθῶν καὶ τὰ φαῦλα τῶν καλῶν, οὕτως ἄλλος τις φιλίαν εἰσήνεγκε καὶ νεῖκος, ἑκάτερον ἑκατέρων αἴτιον τούτων. εἰ γάρ τις ἀκολουθοίη καὶ λαμβάνοι πρὸς τὴν διάνοιαν καὶ μὴ πρὸς ἃ ψελλίζεται λέγων Ἐμπεδοκλῆς, εὑρήσει τὴν μὲν φιλίαν αἰτίαν οὖσαν τῶν ἀγαθῶν τὸ δὲ νεῖκος τῶν κακῶν· ὥστ' εἴ τις φαίη τρόπον τινὰ καὶ λέγειν καὶ πρῶτον λέγειν τὸ κακὸν καὶ τὸ ἀγαθὸν ἀρχὰς Ἐμπεδοκλέα, τάχ' ἂν λέγοι καλῶς, εἴπερ τὸ τῶν ἀγαθῶν ἁπάντων αἴτιον αὐτὸ τἀγαθόν ἐστι.

985a10 οὗτοι μὲν οὖν, ὥσπερ λέγομεν, καὶ μέχρι τούτου δυοῖν αἰτίαιν ὧν ἡμεῖς διωρίσαμεν ἐν τοῖς περὶ φύσεως ἡμμένοι φαίνονται, τῆς τε ὕλης καὶ τοῦ ὅθεν ἡ κίνησις, ἀμυδρῶς μέντοι καὶ οὐθὲν σαφῶς, ἀλλ' οἷον ἐν ταῖς μάχαις οἱ ἀγύμναστοι ποιοῦσιν· καὶ γὰρ ἐκεῖνοι περιφερόμενοι τύπτουσι πολλάκις καλὰς πληγάς, ἀλλ' οὔτε ἐκεῖνοι ἀπὸ ἐπιστήμης, οὔτε οὗτοι ἐοίκασιν εἰδόσιν ὅ τι λέγουσιν· σχεδὸν γὰρ οὐθὲν χρώμενοι φαίνονται τούτοις ἀλλ' ἢ κατὰ μικρόν.

Anaxagoras and Empedocles

985a18 Ἀναξαγόρας τε γὰρ μηχανῇ χρῆται τῷ νῷ πρὸς τὴν κοσμοποιίαν, καὶ ὅταν ἀπορήσῃ διὰ τίν' αἰτίαν ἐξ ἀνάγκης ἐστί, τότε παρέλκει αὐτόν, ἐν δὲ τοῖς ἄλλοις πάντα μᾶλλον αἰτιᾶται τῶν γιγνομένων ἢ νοῦν, καὶ Ἐμπεδοκλῆς ἐπὶ πλέον μὲν τούτου χρῆται τοῖς αἰτίοις, οὐ μὴν οὔθ' ἱκανῶς, οὔτ' ἐν τούτοις εὑρίσκει τὸ ὁμολογούμενον. πολλαχοῦ γοῦν αὐτῷ ἡ μὲν φιλία διακρίνει τὸ δὲ νεῖκος συγκρίνει. ὅταν μὲν γὰρ εἰς τὰ στοιχεῖα διίστηται τὸ πᾶν ὑπὸ τοῦ νείκους, τό τε πῦρ εἰς ἓν συγκρίνεται καὶ τῶν ἄλλων στοιχείων ἕκαστον· ὅταν δὲ πάλιν ὑπὸ τῆς φιλίας συνίωσιν εἰς τὸ ἕν, ἀναγκαῖον ἐξ ἑκάστου τὰ μόρια διακρίνεσθαι πάλιν. Ἐμπεδοκλῆς μὲν οὖν παρὰ τοὺς πρότερον πρῶτος ταύτην τὴν αἰτίαν διελὼν εἰσήνεγκεν, οὐ μίαν ποιήσας τὴν τῆς κινήσεως ἀρχὴν ἀλλ' ἑτέρας τε καὶ ἐναντίας, ἔτι δὲ τὰ ὡς ἐν ὕλης εἴδει λεγόμενα στοιχεῖα τέτταρα πρῶτος εἶπεν· οὐ μὴν χρῆταί γε τέτταρσιν ἀλλ' ὡς δυσὶν οὖσι μόνοις, πυρὶ μὲν καθ' αὑτὸ τοῖς δ' ἀντι-

distinguished among all the immortals'. It is implied that there must be in the world some cause to start movement and bring things together.

984b32 Since it was clear that the opposites of good things
985a are also in nature, ugliness and disorder as well as beauty and order, and further that the bad outnumber the good and the inferior the fair, someone else then introduced love and strife as the causes of the two opposed classes. If one were to follow Empedocles through and understand his meaning rather than his lisping expression it would be found that love is the cause of good and strife of evil. So if we were to claim that in a sense Empedocles said and was the first to say that evil and good were principles, we would probably be right, since the good itself *is* the cause of all good things.

985a10 These then, as we say, evidently grasped to this extent two of the four causes which are distinguished in the *Physics* - the material and the source of movement and change - but with some confusion and no clarity. They behave like new recruits in a fight, who often deal some good blows in the mêlée but without understanding the art; these men similarly do not seem to realise what they are saying, for apparently they make hardly any use of their principles, or only in a minor way.

Anaxagoras and Empedocles

985a18 Anaxagoras uses mind in his cosmogony like a 'deus ex machina'. Whenever he is at a loss to give a reason why something is necessarily the case, he drags it in, but in other instances he explains generation by anything and everything rather than mind. Empedocles makes more use of causes than he does, but still inadequately, and even then he does not manage to be consistent. At least he often has love separate and strife combine, for whenever the whole is resolved into the elements by strife, then fire comes together into one and each of the other elements similarly, but when again they move together in unity as a result of love, the parts of each element necessarily separate again. Empedocles therefore differed from his predecessors in being the first to introduce a division into the cause, by making the principle of movement and change not one but two - different from each other and contrary. Furthermore, he was the first to make the so-called material elements four, yet he did not treat them as four but as if they were only

985b κειμένοις ὡς μιᾷ φύσει, γῇ τε καὶ ἀέρι καὶ ὕδατι· λάβοι δ' ἄν τις αὐτὸ θεωρῶν ἐκ τῶν ἐπῶν. οὗτος μὲν οὖν, ὥσπερ λέγομεν, οὕτω τε καὶ τοσαύτας εἴρηκε τὰς ἀρχάς.

Leuippus and Democritus

985b3 Λεύκιππος δὲ καὶ ὁ ἑταῖρος αὐτοῦ Δημόκριτος στοιχεῖα μὲν τὸ πλῆρες καὶ τὸ κενὸν εἶναί φασι, λέγοντες τὸ μὲν ὂν τὸ δὲ μὴ ὄν, τούτων δὲ τὸ μὲν πλῆρες καὶ στερεὸν τὸ ὄν, τὸ δὲ κενὸν τὸ μὴ ὄν (διὸ καὶ οὐθὲν μᾶλλον τὸ ὂν τοῦ μὴ ὄντος εἶναί φασιν, ὅτι οὐδὲ τὸ κενὸν τοῦ σώματος), αἴτια δὲ τῶν ὄντων ταῦτα ὡς ὕλην. καὶ καθάπερ οἱ ἓν ποιοῦντες τὴν ὑποκειμένην οὐσίαν τἆλλα τοῖς πάθεσιν αὐτῆς γεννῶσι, τὸ μανὸν καὶ τὸ πυκνὸν ἀρχὰς τιθέμενοι τῶν παθημάτων, τὸν αὐτὸν τρόπον καὶ οὗτοι τὰς διαφορὰς αἰτίας τῶν ἄλλων εἶναί φασιν. ταύτας μέντοι τρεῖς εἶναι λέγουσι, σχῆμά τε καὶ τάξιν καὶ θέσιν· διαφέρειν γάρ φασι τὸ ὂν ῥυσμῷ καὶ διαθιγῇ καὶ τροπῇ μόνον· τούτων δὲ ὁ μὲν ῥυσμὸς σχῆμά ἐστιν ἡ δὲ διαθιγὴ τάξις ἡ δὲ τροπὴ θέσις· διαφέρει γὰρ τὸ μὲν Α τοῦ Ν σχήματι τὸ δὲ ΑΝ τοῦ ΝΑ τάξει τὸ δὲ Ζ τοῦ Ν θέσει. περὶ δὲ κινήσεως, ὅθεν ἢ πῶς ὑπάρξει τοῖς οὖσι, καὶ οὗτοι παραπλησίως τοῖς ἄλλοις ῥᾳθύμως ἀφεῖσαν. περὶ μὲν οὖν τῶν δύο αἰτιῶν, ὥσπερ λέγομεν, ἐπὶ τοσοῦτον ἔοικεν ἐζητῆσθαι παρὰ τῶν πρότερον.

Chapter 5

The Eleatics (The first part of the chapter deals with the Pythagoreans and Alcmaeon.)

986b10 εἰσὶ δέ τινες οἳ περὶ τοῦ παντὸς ὡς μιᾶς οὔσης φύσεως ἀπεφήναντο, τρόπον δὲ οὐ τὸν αὐτὸν πάντες οὔτε τοῦ καλῶς οὔτε τοῦ κατὰ τὴν φύσιν. εἰς μὲν οὖν τὴν νῦν σκέψιν τῶν αἰτίων οὐδαμῶς συναρμόττει περὶ αὐτῶν ὁ λόγος (οὐ γὰρ ὥσπερ ἔνιοι τῶν φυσιόλογων ἓν ὑποθέμενοι τὸ ὂν ὅμως γεννῶσιν ὡς ἐξ ὕλης τοῦ ἑνός, ἀλλ' ἕτερον τρόπον οὗτοι λέγουσιν· ἐκεῖνοι μὲν γὰρ προστιθέασι κίνησιν, γεννῶντές γε τὸ πᾶν, οὗτοι δὲ ἀκίνητον εἶναί φασιν)· οὐ μὴν ἀλλὰ τοσοῦτόν γε οἰκεῖόν ἐστι τῇ νῦν σκέψει. Παρμενίδης μὲν γὰρ ἔοικε τοῦ κατὰ τὸν λόγον ἑνὸς ἅπτεσθαι, Μέλισσος δὲ τοῦ κατὰ τὴν ὕλην (διὸ καὶ ὁ μὲν πεπερασμένον ὁ δ' ἄπειρόν φησιν εἶναι αὐτό)· Ξενοφάνης δὲ πρῶτος τούτων ἑνίσας (ὁ γὰρ Παρμενίδης τούτου λέγεται γενέσθαι μαθητής) οὐθὲν διεσαφήνισεν, οὐδὲ τῆς

985b two, fire by itself, and, set against it, earth, air and water, as though they were of the same nature as each other. This can be understood from a close study of his verses. He then, as we say, dealt with principles of this number and in this way.

Leucippus and Democritus

985b3 Leucippus and his associate Democritus spoke of 'the full' and 'the empty' as elements, calling the one - the full and solid - 'what is' and the other - the empty - 'what is not' (and that is why they say that what is *is* no more than what is not, and that 'empty' is as real as body); these are the material explanations of things. And just as those who make the underlying substance one generate the rest from modifications of it, setting up the rare and the dense as the principles of the modifications, these men in the same way maintain that the differences explain everything else. They say that these differences are three - shape, order and position. The only distinctions that they make in what there is are in 'contour', 'contact' and 'inclination', and of these 'contour' is shape, 'contact' order and 'inclination' position, for A differs from N in shape, AN from NA in order and Z from N in position. They were as lazy as the rest in disregarding the source and manner of movement and change in the world. So, as we say, the inquiry into the subject of the two causes seems to have been taken this far by our predecessors.

Chapter 5

The Eleatics

986b10 There are some who spoke about the whole as if it were one single entity, but they differed in respect of the competence of their exposition and its conformity with the natural world. It is not at all relevant to our present inquiry into causation to discuss them, for, unlike some of the philosophers of nature who posit what there is as one, but say that generation takes place from the one as from material, they mean something else. The others, in having a generation for the whole, obviously assume movement and change, but these say that the whole is immutable. Yet there is a point which does relate to the present inquiry. Parmenides seems to fasten on to what is one in a formal, Melissus in a material sense (and that is why Parmenides says it is limited and Melissus unlimited). Xenophanes, the first of them to posit a 'one' (for Parmenides is said to have been a student of his) was not clear on anything,

φύσεως τούτων οὐδετέρας ἔοικε θιγεῖν, ἀλλ', εἰς τὸν ὅλον οὐρανὸν ἀποβλέψας, τὸ ἓν εἶναί φησι τὸν θεόν. οὗτοι μὲν οὖν, καθάπερ εἴπομεν, ἀφετέοι πρὸς τὴν νῦν ζήτησιν, οἱ μὲν δύο καὶ πάμπαν ὡς ὄντες μικρὸν ἀγροικότεροι, Ξενοφάνης καὶ Μέλισσος· Παρμενίδης δὲ μᾶλλον βλέπων ἔοικέ που λέγειν· παρὰ γὰρ τὸ ὂν τὸ μὴ ὂν οὐθὲν ἀξιῶν εἶναι, ἐξ ἀνάγκης ἓν οἴεται εἶναι τὸ ὂν καὶ ἄλλο οὐθέν (περὶ οὗ σαφέστερον ἐν τοῖς περὶ φύσεως εἰρήκαμεν), ἀναγκαζόμενος δ' ἀκολουθεῖν τοῖς φαινομένοις, καὶ τὸ ἓν μὲν κατὰ τὸν λόγον πλείω δὲ κατὰ τὴν αἴσθησιν ὑπολαμβάνων εἶναι, δύο τὰς αἰτίας καὶ δύο τὰς ἀρχὰς πάλιν τίθησι, θερμὸν καὶ ψυχρόν, οἷον πῦρ καὶ γῆν λέγων· τούτων
987a δὲ κατὰ μὲν τὸ ὂν τὸ θερμὸν τάττει θάτερον δὲ κατὰ τὸ μὴ ὄν.

Conclusion

987a2 ἐκ μὲν οὖν τῶν εἰρημένων καὶ παρὰ τῶν συνηδρευκότων ἤδη τῷ λόγῳ σοφῶν ταῦτα παρειλήφαμεν, παρὰ μὲν τῶν πρώτων σωματικήν τε τὴν ἀρχήν (ὕδωρ γὰρ καὶ πῦρ καὶ τὰ τοιαῦτα σώματά ἐστιν), καὶ τῶν μὲν μίαν τῶν δὲ πλείους τὰς ἀρχὰς τὰς σωματικάς, ἀμφοτέρων μέντοι ταύτας ὡς ἐν ὕλης εἴδει τιθέντων, παρὰ δέ τινων ταύτην τε τὴν αἰτίαν τιθέντων καὶ πρὸς ταύτῃ τὴν ὅθεν ἡ κίνησις, καὶ ταύτην παρὰ τῶν μὲν μίαν παρὰ τῶν δὲ δύο.

Chapter 7

The causes summarised (chapter 6 is on Plato)

988a18 συντόμως μὲν οὖν καὶ κεφαλαιωδῶς ἐπεληλύθαμεν τίνες τε καὶ πῶς τυγχάνουσιν εἰρηκότες περί τε τῶν ἀρχῶν καὶ τῆς ἀληθείας· ὅμως δὲ τοσοῦτόν γ' ἔχομεν ἐξ αὐτῶν, ὅτι τῶν λεγόντων περὶ ἀρχῆς καὶ αἰτίας οὐθεὶς ἔξω τῶν ἐν τοῖς περὶ φύσεως ἡμῖν διωρισμένων εἴρηκεν, ἀλλὰ πάντες ἀμυδρῶς μὲν ἐκείνων δέ πως φαίνονται θιγγάνοντες.

988a23 οἱ μὲν γὰρ ὡς ὕλην τὴν ἀρχὴν λέγουσιν, ἄν τε μίαν ἄν τε πλείους ὑποθῶσι, καὶ ἐάν τε σῶμα ἐάν τε ἀσώματον τοῦτο τιθῶσιν, οἷον Πλάτων μὲν τὸ μέγα καὶ τὸ μικρὸν λέγων, οἱ δ' Ἰταλικοὶ τὸ ἄπειρον, Ἐμπεδοκλῆς δὲ πῦρ καὶ γῆν καὶ ὕδωρ καὶ ἀέρα, Ἀναξαγόρας δὲ τὴν τῶν ὁμοιομερῶν ἀπειρίαν· οὗτοί τε δὴ πάντες τῆς τοιαύτης αἰτίας ἡμμένοι εἰσί, καὶ ἔτι ὅσοι ἀέρα

nor does he seem to have touched on the nature of either of these causes, but, regarding the universe as a whole, he says that the one is god. These then, as we said, can be disregarded in the present inquiry - two of them, Xenophanes and Melissus, entirely as being rather outlandish, but Parmenides seems to speak more astutely, for on the assumption that, contrasted with what is, what is not is nothing, he thinks that necessarily what there is is but one thing and nothing else. (We have treated this subject in more detail in the *Physics*.) He is however forced to take the sensible world into account, and so he assumes that logically there is one, but according to our senses many things; consequently he reintroduces two causes and principles, hot and cold,
987a as if he meant fire and earth. With these he relates the hot to what is and the other to what is not.

Conclusion

987a2 Thus, as a result of what we have said, and taking into account the learned men who have already considered the subject, we have come to this conclusion: from the earliest philosophers we have a bodily principle (for water, fire and the like are bodies), single for some and plural for others, but with both groups treating them as principles of a material kind. And some of those who posit this cause give, in addition, the source of movement and change - a single source in the theory of one set and a double in another.

Chapter 7

The causes summarised

988a18 Briefly, and in outline, we have dealt with the thinkers who spoke about first principles and reality, and the manner in which they treated them. Still, we have gathered this much from them - that of all who have talked about a first principle and cause none has mentioned any that has not been listed in the *Physics*, but all, although groping, are trying to reach out towards ours.

988a23 Some speak of the principle as material, whether they posit it as single or plural, and whether they assume it to be corporeal or incorporeal. Plato, for example, speaks of the great and small, the Italians of the unlimited, Empedocles of fire, earth, water and air, and Anaxagoras of the infinity of like-part substances. They all grasped this kind of cause, as did those who

ἢ πῦρ ἢ ὕδωρ ἢ πυρὸς μὲν πυκνότερον ἀέρος δὲ λεπτότερον· καὶ γάρ τοιοῦτόν τινες εἰρήκασιν εἶναι τὸ πρῶτον στοιχεῖον.

988a32 οὗτοι μὲν οὖν ταύτης τῆς αἰτίας ἥψαντο μόνον, ἕτεροι δέ τινες ὅθεν ἡ ἀρχὴ τῆς κινήσεως, οἷον ὅσοι φιλίαν καὶ νεῖκος ἢ νοῦν ἢ ἔρωτα ποιοῦσιν ἀρχήν.

988a34 τὸ δὲ τί ἦν εἶναι καὶ τὴν οὐσίαν σαφῶς μὲν οὐθεὶς ἀποδέδωκε, μάλιστα δ' οἱ τὰ εἴδη τιθέντες λέγουσιν,
988b οὔτε γὰρ ὡς ὕλην τοῖς αἰσθητοῖς τὰ εἴδη καὶ τὸ ἓν τοῖς εἴδεσιν οὔθ' ὡς ἐντεῦθεν τὴν ἀρχὴν τῆς κινήσεως γιγνομένην ὑπολαμβάνουσιν - ἀκινησίας γὰρ αἴτια μᾶλλον καὶ τοῦ ἐν ἠρεμίᾳ εἶναί φασιν - ἀλλὰ τὸ τί ἦν εἶναι ἑκάστῳ τῶν ἄλλων τὰ εἴδη παρέχονται, τοῖς δ' εἴδεσι τὸ ἕν.

988b6 τὸ δ' οὗ ἕνεκα αἱ πράξεις καὶ αἱ μεταβολαὶ καὶ αἱ κινήσεις τρόπον μέν τινα λέγουσιν αἴτιον, οὕτω δὲ οὐ λέγουσιν οὐδ' ὅνπερ πέφυκεν. οἱ μὲν γὰρ νοῦν λέγοντες ἢ φιλίαν ὡς ἀγαθὸν μὲν ταύτας τὰς αἰτίας τιθέασιν, οὐ μὴν ὡς ἕνεκά γε τούτων ἢ ὂν ἢ γιγνόμενόν τι τῶν ὄντων ἀλλ' ὡς ἀπὸ τούτων τὰς κινήσεις οὔσας λέγουσιν· . . .

Criticisms

988b20 πῶς δὲ τούτων ἕκαστος εἴρηκε καὶ πῶς ἔχει περὶ τῶν ἀρχῶν, τὰς ἐνδεχομένας ἀπορίας μετὰ τοῦτο διέλθωμεν περὶ αὐτῶν.

Chapter 8

Monists

ὅσοι μὲν οὖν ἕν τε τὸ πᾶν καὶ μίαν τινὰ φύσιν ὡς ὕλην τιθέασι, καὶ ταύτην σωματικὴν καὶ μέγεθος ἔχουσαν, δῆλον ὅτι πολλαχῶς ἁμαρτάνουσιν. τῶν γὰρ σωμάτων τὰ στοιχεῖα τιθέασι μόνον, τῶν δ' ἀσωμάτων οὔ [ὄντων καὶ ἀσωμάτων]. καὶ περὶ γενέσεως καὶ φθορᾶς ἐπιχειροῦντες τὰς αἰτίας λέγειν, καὶ περὶ πάντων φυσιολογοῦντες, τὸ τῆς κινήσεως αἴτιον ἀναιροῦσιν. ἔτι δὲ τῷ τὴν οὐσίαν μηθενὸς αἰτίαν τιθέναι

make a principle out of air or fire or water or something denser than fire but finer than air, for some have said that the prime element is this sort of thing.

988a32 These men then only understood this cause, but there were some who brought in the source of the beginning of movement and change, making love and strife, for example, a principle, or mind or eros.

988a34 No one has explicitly given the form or essence, but those who set up the Ideas are closest, for they do
988b not assume that the Ideas act as the material of the perceived world or the one as their material, not do they suppose that the principle of movement and change is derived from them - rather these are said to explain immutability and the state of rest; it is the form that the Ideas supply to everything else, and the one to the Ideas.

988b6 They speak in a way of purpose as an explanation for actions, changes and movements, but not in these terms, or according to its true nature. Those who talk about mind or love assume these causes to be a good, but they do not mean it in the sense that anything in the world is or arises for the sake of them, but that movements start from them . . .

Criticisms

988b20 Let us next go through some possible difficulties in what each has said and in their individual positions on the question of first principles.

Chapter 8

Monists

All those who suppose that the whole is one and who take one natural substance as its material, corporeal and spatially extended, are wrong on a number of counts. (i) They only posit elements of what is corporeal, not of the incorporeal [but the incorporeal exists as well]. (ii) Although they attempt to give reasons for generation and destruction, and to produce a comprehensive account of nature, they neglect any explanation of movement and change. (iii) They do not set out the essence

μηδὲ τὸ τί ἐστι, καὶ πρὸς τούτοις τῷ ῥᾳδίως τῶν ἁπλῶν σωμάτων λέγειν ἀρχὴν ὁτιοῦν πλὴν γῆς, οὐκ ἐπισκεψάμενοι τὴν ἐξ ἀλλήλων γένεσιν πῶς ποιοῦνται, λέγω δὲ πῦρ καὶ ὕδωρ καὶ γῆν καὶ ἀέρα. τὰ μὲν γὰρ συγκρίσει τὰ δὲ διακρίσει ἐξ ἀλλήλων γίγνεται, τοῦτο δὲ πρὸς τὸ πρότερον εἶναι καὶ ὕστερον διαφέρει πλεῖστον.

988b34 τῇ μὲν γὰρ ἂν δόξειε στοιχειωδέστατον εἶναι πάντων ἐξ
989a οὗ γίγνονται συγκρίσει πρώτου, τοιοῦτον δὲ τὸ μικ-
ρομερέστατον καὶ λεπτότατον ἂν εἴη τῶν σωμάτων, διό-
περ ὅσοι πῦρ ἀρχὴν τιθέασι, μάλιστα ὁμολογουμένως
ἂν τῷ λόγῳ τούτῳ λέγοιεν·. τοιοῦτον δὲ καὶ τῶν ἄλλων
ἕκαστος ὁμολογεῖ τὸ στοιχεῖον εἶναι τὸ τῶν σωμάτων·
οὐθεὶς γοῦν ἠξίωσε τῶν ἓν λεγόντων γῆν εἶναι στοιχ-
εῖον, δηλονότι διὰ τὴν μεγαλομέρειαν, τῶν δὲ τριῶν
ἕκαστον στοιχείων εἴληφέ τινα κριτήν, οἱ μὲν γὰρ πῦρ
οἱ δ' ὕδωρ οἱ δ' ἀέρα τοῦτ' εἶναί φασιν· καίτοι διὰ
τί ποτ' οὐ καὶ τὴν γῆν λέγουσιν, ὥσπερ οἱ πολλοὶ τῶν
ἀνθρώπων; πάντα γὰρ εἶναί φασι γῆν, φησὶ δὲ καὶ
'Ησίοδος τὴν γῆν πρώτην γενέσθαι τῶν σωμάτων· οὕτως
ἀρχαίαν καὶ δημοτικὴν συμβέβηκεν εἶναι τὴν ὑπόληψιν.

989a12 κατὰ μὲν οὖν τοῦτον τὸν λόγον οὔτ' εἴ τις τούτων τι λέγει πλὴν πυρός, οὔτ' εἴ τις ἀέρος μὲν πυκνότερον τοῦτο τίθησιν ὕδατος δὲ λεπτότερον, οὐκ ὀρθῶς ἂν λέγοι· εἰ δ' ἔστι τὸ τῇ γενέσει ὕστερον τῇ φύσει πρότερον, τὸ δὲ πεπεμμένον καὶ συγκεκριμένον ὕστερον τῇ γενέσει, τοὐναντίον ἂν εἴη τούτων, ὕδωρ μὲν ἀέρος πρότερον γῆ δὲ ὕδατος.

Pluralists

989a18 περὶ μὲν οὖν τῶν μίαν τιθεμένων αἰτίαν οἵαν εἴπομεν, ἔστω ταῦτ' εἰρημένα· τὸ δ' αὐτὸ κἂν εἴ τις ταῦτα πλείω τίθησιν, οἷον 'Εμπεδοκλῆς τέτταρά φησιν εἶναι σώματα τὴν ὕλην. καὶ γὰρ τούτῳ τὰ μὲν ταὐτὰ τὰ δ' ἴδια συμβαίνειν ἀνάγκη. γιγνόμενά τε γὰρ ἐξ ἀλλήλων ὁρῶμεν ὡς οὐκ ἀεὶ διαμένοντος πυρὸς καὶ γῆς τοῦ αὐτοῦ σώματος (εἴρηται δὲ ἐν τοῖς περὶ φύσεως περὶ αὐτῶν), καὶ περὶ τῆς τῶν κινουμένων αἰτίας, πότερον ἓν ἢ δύο θετέον, οὔτ' ὀρθῶς οὔτε εὐλόγως οἰητέον εἰρῆσθαι παντελῶς. ὅλως τε ἀλλοίωσιν ἀναιρεῖσθαι

or form to account for anything, and (iv) they unthinkingly call any one of the simple bodies except earth a principle, without considering how their generation from each other comes about. (I am speaking here of fire, water, earth and air.) Some are generated from each other by coming together and others by separating, and this is very important in deciding their relative priority.

988b34 In one way it might be thought that the most basic element is that from which everything is first gen-
989a erated by combination, and this would be the kind of
body that has the smallest parts and is the finest.
That is why the theory of those who take fire as the
first principle would be most in accord with this line
of argument, and even the others all agree that the ele-
ments of bodies must be like this. At least none of
those who assume one principle take the element to be
earth (obviously because of the great size of the parts),
but each of the other three has found an advocate,
some saying the element is fire, others water and others
air. Yet why is it that they do not speak of earth as
well, as most men do? For people in general say that
all things are earth, and Hesiod too that earth was the
first body to appear - of such antiquity and so widely
accepted has this belief turned out to be.

989a12 According to this argument then, if anyone names any of these except fire, or posits something denser than air and finer than water, he could not be right. And since what is later in generation is prior in nature, and compressions and aggregates are later in generation, there would be the opposite conclusion to the above - water prior to air and earth to water.

Pluralists

989a18 Enough has been said about those who set up one cause of the kind we described. The same criticism holds even if someone posits a plurality, like Empedocles saying that the material consists of four bodies, for the same consequences must follow for him, as well as his own problems. We see the four arising from each other, so that fire and earth do not always remain the same material substance (and this has been discussed in our works on natural science). And on the explanation for movement and change, whether a single or double cause is to be assumed, he cannot be thought to have spoken quite correctly or logically. Those who put forward this view must also deny all qualitative change,

ἀνάγκη τοῖς οὕτω λέγουσιν· οὐ γὰρ ἐκ θερμοῦ ψυχρὸν οὐδὲ ἐκ ψυχροῦ θερμὸν ἔσται. τί γὰρ αὐτὰ ἂν πάσχοι τἀναντία, καὶ τίς εἴη ἂν μία φύσις ἣ γιγνομένη πῦρ καὶ ὕδωρ, ὃ ἐκεῖνος οὔ φησιν.

989a30 'Ἀναξαγόραν δ' εἴ τις ὑπολάβοι δύο λέγειν στοιχεῖα,
μάλιστ' ἂν ὑπολάβοι κατὰ λόγον, ὃν ἐκεῖνος αὐτὸς
μὲν οὐ διήρθρωσεν, ἠκολούθησε μέντ' ἂν ἐξ ἀνάγκης
τοῖς ἐπάγουσιν αὐτόν. ἀτόπου γὰρ ὄντος καὶ ἄλλως
τοῦ φάσκειν μεμῖχθαι τὴν ἀρχὴν πάντα, καὶ διὰ τὸ
989b συμβαίνειν ἄμικτα δεῖν προϋπάρχειν καὶ διὰ τὸ μὴ
πεφυκέναι τῷ τυχόντι μίγνυσθαι τὸ τυχόν, πρὸς δὲ
τούτοις ὅτι τὰ πάθη καὶ τὰ συμβεβηκότα χωρίζοιτ'
ἂν τῶν οὐσιῶν (τῶν γὰρ αὐτῶν μῖξίς ἐστι καὶ χωρισμός),
ὅμως εἴ τις ἀκολουθήσειε συνδιαρθρῶν ἃ βούλεται λέγειν,
ἴσως ἂν φανείη καινοπρεπεστέρως λέγων.

989b6 ὅτε γὰρ οὐθὲν ἦν ἀποκεκριμένον, δῆλον ὡς οὐθὲν ἦν ἀληθὲς εἰπεῖν κατὰ τῆς οὐσίας ἐκείνης, λέγω δ' οἷον ὅτι οὔτε λευκὸν οὔτε μέλαν ἢ φαιὸν ἢ ἄλλο χρῶμα, ἀλλ' ἄχρων ἦν ἐξ ἀνάγκης· εἶχε γὰρ ἄν τι τούτων τῶν χρωμάτων· ὁμοίως δὲ καὶ ἄχυμον τῷ αὐτῷ λόγῳ τούτῳ, οὐδὲ ἄλλο τῶν ὁμοίων οὐθέν· οὔτε γὰρ ποιόν τι οἷόν τε αὐτὸ εἶναι οὔτε ποσὸν οὔτε τί. τῶν γὰρ ἐν μέρει τι λεγομένων εἰδῶν ὑπῆρχεν ἂν αὐτῷ, τοῦτο δὲ ἀδύνατον μεμιγμένων γε πάντων· ἤδη γὰρ ἂν ἀπεκέκριτο, φησὶ δ' εἶναι μεμιγμένα πάντα πλὴν τοῦ νοῦ, τοῦτον δὲ ἀμιγῆ μόνον καὶ καθαρόν.

989b17 ἐκ δὴ τούτων συμβαίνει λέγειν αὐτῷ τὰς ἀρχὰς τό τε ἕν (τοῦτο γὰρ ἁπλοῦν καὶ ἀμιγές) καὶ θάτερον (οἷον τίθεμεν τὸ ἀόριστον πρὶν ὁρισθῆναι καὶ μετασχεῖν εἴδους τινός), ὥστε λέγει μὲν οὔτ' ὀρθῶς οὔτε σαφῶς, βούλεται μέντοι τι παραπλήσιον τοῖς τε ὕστερον λέγουσι καὶ τοῖς νῦν φαινομένοις μᾶλλον.

Summary

989b21 ἀλλὰ γὰρ οὗτοι μὲν τοῖς περὶ γένεσιν λόγοις καὶ φθορὰν καὶ κίνησιν οἰκεῖοι τυγχάνουσι μόνον· σχεδὸν γὰρ περὶ τῆς τοιαύτης οὐσίας καὶ τὰς ἀρχὰς καὶ τὰς αἰτίας ζητοῦσι μόνης.

for there will be no cold from hot or hot from cold. That is because there must be something that suffers these contrary effects, and some one natural substance which becomes fire or water, and this Empedocles denies.

989a30 With Anaxagoras the most logical interpretation would
be to assume that he was speaking of two elements. He
did not make this clear himself, but he would have had
to follow a lead in that direction. It is absurd any-
way to say that all things were a mixture in the begin-
989b ning, and particularly because (i) they would have had
to have been in an unmixed state earlier, (ii) every-
thing is not naturally suited to mixing with any and
everything else, and (iii) qualities and contingent
attributes would become separated from these substances
(for the same things that mix also separate). Still,
if one were to work through his theory and present
clearly what he was trying to say, he might turn out
to be quite modern.

989b6 At the stage when nothing had been separated off, nothing, obviously, could be predicated of that original substance. I mean, for example, that it could not be called white or black or grey or any other colour, but it would have to be colourless, for otherwise it always would have one of these colours. Likewise, according to the same reasoning, it would not have any taste or similar attribute. It could not be of a certain quality or of a particular size or be an individual entity. When all things were mixed together it would have been impossible for any one of the particular forms to be realised in it, for it would have to have been already separated off, and he says that all things were mixed together except mind, and this alone was unmixed and pure.

989b17 It follows then from this that he means that his principles are the One (for that is single and unmixed) and the Other (as we call the indeterminate before it has been made articulate and has taken on a form). What he actually says is neither correct nor clear, but he is aiming at a theory close to those that came later, and to what is now more clearly seen to be the case.

Summary

989b21 These philosophers are concerned only with the study of generation, destruction and change, for their research overall concentrates on the principles and explanations of perceptible substance.

ARISTOTLE ON THE PRESOCRATICS : GLOSSARY

αἰτία	explanation/cause (ἐξ ἀρχῆς αἰτία/πρώτη αἰτία, basic/primary explanation)
αἴτιον	cause
ἀλήθεια	truth, fact, reality
ἀλλοίωσις	qualitative change
ἀρχή	beginning, (first) principle
διάκρισις	process of separation
ἕξις	quality, condition
κίνησις	movement/change (ἡ ἀρχὴ τῆς κινήσεως, the principle of movement and change)
λόγος	definition
	κατὰ τὸν λόγον - in a formal way, logically
μέγεθος	(spatial) extension
τὰ ὄντα	what there is/things/the world (ἅπαντα τὰ ὄντα/ἡ τῶν ὄντων φύσις, the natural world)
τὸ οὗ ἕνεκα	purpose
οὐσία	essence, substance
πάθημα/πάθος	attribute, modification
τὸ πᾶν	everything/the world/the whole
στοιχεῖον	element
σύγκρισις	process of combining (opp. of διάκρισις)
τὰ συμβεβηκότα	contingent attributes
σῶμα	body, material substance (ἁπλοῦν σῶμα, simple body, element)
τὸ τί ἦν εἶναι	form
ὕλη	material
ὑποκείμενον	substrate
φθορά	disintegration/destruction (opp. of γένεσις)
φύσις	nature, natural substance, (natural) character (ἡ φύσις ὅλη, the whole natural world; τὰ περὶ φύσεως, Aristotle's *Physics* (generally))

CONCORDANCE I

WRIGHT - DIELS/KRANZ

XENOPHANES

Wright	Diels/Kranz
X.1	21 B 11
X.2	21 B 14
X.3	21 B 15
X.4	21 B 16
X.5	21 B 18
X.6	21 B 23
X.7	21 B 24
X.8	21 B 26
X.9	21 B 25
X.10	21 B 29
X.11	21 B 27
X.12	21 B 28
X.13	21 B 30
X.14	21 B 32
X.15	21 B 35
X.16	21 B 34
X.17	21 B 38
X.18	21 B 7

HERACLITUS

Wright	Diels/Kranz
H.1	22 B 1
H.2	22 B 50
H.3	22 B 89
H.4	22 B 41
H.5	22 B 32
H.6	22 B 113
H.7	22 B 116
H.8	22 B 55
H.9	22 B 2
H.10	22 B 17
H.11	22 B 72
H.12	22 B 108
H.13	22 B 107
H.14	22 B 40
H.15	22 B 42
H.16	22 B 56
H.17	22 B 57
H.18	22 B 21
H.19	22 B 26
H.20	22 B 75
H.21	22 B 20
H.22	22 B 114
H.23	22 B 44
H.24	22 B 49
H.25	22 B 78
H.26	22 B 79
H.27	22 B 5
H.28	22 B 14
H.29	22 B 15
H.30	22 B 92
H.31	22 B 93
H.32	22 B 54
H.33	22 B 123
H.34	22 B 53
H.35	22 B 80
H.36	22 B 10
H.37	22 B 51
H.38	22 B 48
H.39	22 B 59
H.40	22 B 60
H.41	22 B 103
H.42	22 B 125
H.43	22 B 61
H.44	22 B 111
H.45	22 B 126
H.46	22 B 62
H.47	22 B 88
H.48	22 B 8
H.49	22 B 23
H.50	22 B 124
H.51	22 B 67
H.52	22 B 102
H.53	22 B 30
H.54	22 B 64
H.55	22 B 66
H.56	22 B 94
H.57	22 B 99
H.58	22 B 90
H.59	22 B 31
H.60	22 B 91
H.61	22 B 12
H.62	22 B 101
H.63	22 B 35
H.64	22 B 22
H.65	22 B 45
H.66	22 B 115
H.67	22 B 36
H.68	22 B 52
H.69	22 B 85
H.70	22 B 117
H.71	22 B 118
H.72	22 B 119

H.73	22 B 29
H.74	22 B 24
H.75	22 B 27
H.76	22 B 63

PARMENIDES

P.1	28 B 1
P.2	28 B 2
P.3	28 B 3
P.4	28 B 4
P.5	28 B 5
P.6	28 B 6
P.7	28 B 7
P.8	28 B 8
P.9	28 B 9
P.10	28 B 10
P.11	28 B 11
P.12	28 B 12
P.13	28 B 13
P.14	28 B 14
P.15	28 B 15
P.16	28 B 16
P.17	28 B 19

ZENO

Z.1	29 B 1,2
Z.2	29 B 1
Z.3	29 B 3
Z.4	29 B 4
Z.5	29 A 25-28

MELISSUS

M.1	30 B 1
M.2	30 B 2
M.3	30 B 3
M.4	30 B 4
M.5	30 B 5
M.6	30 B 6
M.7	30 B 7
M.8	30 B 8
M.9	30 B 9
M.10	30 B 10

EMPEDOCLES

E.1	31 B 6
E.2	31 B 17
E.3	31 B 8
E.4	31 B 29/28
E.5	31 B 30
E.6	31 B 31
E.7	31 B 22
E.8	31 B 35
E.9	31 B 96
E.10	31 B 57
E.11	31 B 59
E.12	31 B 62
E.13	31 B 109
E.14	31 B 108
E.15	31 B 105
E.16	31 B 133
E.17	31 B 134
E.18	31 B 110
E.19	31 B 115
E.20	31 B 117
E.21	31 B 127
E.22	31 B 146

ANAXAGORAS

A.1	59 B 1
A.2	59 B 2
A.3	59 B 3
A.4	59 B 4
A.5	59 B 5
A.6	59 B 6
A.7	59 B 8
A.8	59 B 10
A.9	59 B 11
A.10	59 B 12
A.11	59 B 13
A.12	59 B 14
A.13	59 B 15
A.14	59 B 9
A.15	59 B 16
A.16	59 B 18
A.17	59 B 19
A.18	59 B 21
A.19	59 B 17
A.20	59 B 21a

LEUCIPPUS

L.1	67 B 2
L.2	67 A 7

DEMOCRITUS

D.1	68 B 6
D.2	68 B 7
D.3	68 B 11
D.4	68 B 117
D.5	68 B 9
D.6	68 B 9
D.7	68 B 125
D.8	68 B 156
D.9	68 A 37
D.10	68 B 167
D.11	68 B 164
D.12	68 B 166
D.13	67 A 29
D.14	68 A 122
D.15	68 B 155
D.16	68 B 154
D.17	68 B 247
D.18	68 B 230
D.19	68 B 211
D.20	68 B 171

CONCORDANCE II

DIELS/KRANZ - WRIGHT

XENOPHANES

21 B 7	X.18
21 B 11	X.1
21 B 14	X.2
21 B 15	X.3
21 B 16	X.4
21 B 18	X.5
21 B 23	X.6
21 B 24	X.7
21 B 25	X.9
21 B 26	X.8
21 B 27	X.11
21 B 28	X.12
21 B 29	X.10
21 B 30	X.13
21 B 32	X.14
21 B 34	X.16
21 B 35	X.15
21 B 38	X.17

HERACLITUS

22 B 1	H.1
22 B 2	H.9
22 B 5	H.27
22 B 8	H.48
22 B 10	H.36
22 B 12	H.61
22 B 14	H.28
22 B 15	H.29
22 B 17	H.10
22 B 20	H.21
22 B 21	H.18
22 B 22	H.64
22 B 23	H.49
22 B 24	H.74
22 B 26	H.19
22 B 27	H.75
22 B 29	H.73
22 B 30	H.53
22 B 31	H.59
22 B 32	H.5
22 B 35	H.63
22 B 36	H.67
22 B 40	H.14
22 B 41	H.4
22 B 42	H.15
22 B 44	H.23
22 B 45	H.65
22 B 48	H.38
22 B 49	H.24
22 B 50	H.2
22 B 51	H.37
22 B 52	H.68
22 B 53	H.34
22 B 54	H.32
22 B 55	H.8
22 B 56	H.16
22 B 57	H.17
22 B 59	H.39
22 B 60	H.40
22 B 61	H.43
22 B 62	H.46
22 B 63	H.76
22 B 64	H.54
22 B 66	H.55
22 B 67	H.51
22 B 72	H.11
22 B 75	H.20
22 B 78	H.25
22 B 79	H.26
22 B 80	H.35
22 B 85	H.69
22 B 88	H.47
22 B 89	H.3
22 B 90	H.58
22 B 91	H.60
22 B 92	H.30
22 B 93	H.31
22 B 94	H.56
22 B 99	H.57
22 B 101	H.62
22 B 102	H.52
22 B 103	H.41
22 B 107	H.13
22 B 108	H.12
22 B 111	H.44
22 B 113	H.6
22 B 114	H.22
22 B 115	H.66
22 B 116	H.7
22 B 117	H.70

22 B 118	H.71
22 B 119	H.72
22 B 123	H.33
22 B 124	H.50
22 B 125	H.42
22 B 126	H.45

PARMENIDES

28 B 1	P.1
28 B 2	P.2
28 B 3	P.3
28 B 4	P.4
28 B 5	P.5
28 B 6	P.6
28 B 7	P.7
28 B 8	P.8
28 B 9	P.9
28 B 10	P.10
28 B 11	P.11
28 B 12	P.12
28 B 13	P.13
28 B 14	P.14
28 B 15	P.15
28 B 16	P.16
28 B 19	P.17

ZENO

29 A 25-28	Z.5
29 B 1,2	Z.1, 2
29 B 3	Z.3
29 B 4	Z.4

MELISSUS

30 B 1	M.1
30 B 2	M.2
30 B 3	M.3
30 B 4	M.4
30 B 5	M.5
30 B 6	M.6
30 B 7	M.7
30 B 8	M.8
30 B 9	M.9
30 B 10	M.10

EMPEDOCLES

31 B 6	E.1
31 B 8	E.3
31 B 17	E.2
31 B 22	E.7
31 B 28	E.4
31 B 29	E.4
31 B 30	E.5
31 B 31	E.6
31 B 35	E.8
31 B 57	E.10
31 B 59	E.11
31 B 62	E.12
31 B 96	E.9
31 B 105	E.15
31 B 108	E.14
31 B 109	E.13
31 B 110	E.18
31 B 115	E.19
31 B 117	E.20
31 B 127	E.21
31 B 133	E.16
31 B 134	E.17
31 B 146	E.22

ANAXAGORAS

59 B 1	A.1
59 B 2	A.2
59 B 3	A.3
59 B 4	A.4
59 B 5	A.5
59 B 6	A.6
59 B 8	A.7
59 B 9	A.14
59 B 10	A.8
59 B 11	A.9
59 B 12	A.10
59 B 13	A.11
59 B 14	A.12
59 B 15	A.13
59 B 16	A.15
59 B 17	A.19
59 B 18	A.16
59 B 19	A.17
59 B 21	A.18
59 B 21a	A.20

LEUCIPPUS

67 A 7	L.2
67 B 2	L.1

DEMOCRITUS

67 A 29	D.13
68 A 37	D.9
68 A 122	D.14
68 B 6	D.1
68 B 7	D.2
68 B 9	D.5, 6
68 B 11	D.3
68 B 117	D.4
68 B 125	D.7
68 B 154	D.16
68 B 155	D.15
68 B 156	D.8
68 B 164	D.11
68 B 166	D.12
68 B 167	D.10
68 B 171	D.20
68 B 211	D.19
68 B 230	D.18
68 B 247	D.17

www.ingramcontent.com/pod-product-compliance
Lightning Source LLC
Chambersburg PA
CBHW070535100726
47907CB00004B/1126
* 9 7 8 0 8 6 2 9 2 0 7 9 1 *